The MISCELLANY of Pitcairn's Island

Herbert Ford

Pacific Press Publishing Association
Mountain View, California
Omaha, Nebraska
Oshawa, Ontario

Acknowledgments

My thanks go to the following for special help in obtaining a complete file of *Pitcairn Miscellany* and for other kindnesses in connection with the preparation of this book:

Tom Christian; Georgia Kyracopoulos; Pacific Union College; members of the Pitcairn Islands Study Group; Eddie Pullen; and Ruth Stringer of Dove Creek, Colorado.

Cover design by Lauren Smith
Cover illustration by Tim Mitoma

Table of Contents

Pitcairn—A Brief Sketch of Its Geography and History

A small volcanic island in the South Pacific Ocean, Pitcairn is located some 3300 miles east-northeast from its present administrative headquarters in Auckland, New Zealand, and 4100 miles southwest from Panama. Three other islands are in the Pitcairn group—Oeno, 75 miles northwest of Pitcairn; Henderson, 105 miles east-northeast; and Ducie, 293 miles east. All three are uninhabited.

Pitcairn is irregular in shape—roughly two miles long by one mile wide—and comprising some 1120 acres of land, of which only about 88 acres are flat. Some 350 acres are rolling land; steeply sloping land accounts for 385 acres; and the cliffs, about 295 acres. According to *A Guide to Pitcairn*, "It is a rugged island of formidable cliffs of reddish-brown and black volcanic rock, nowhere giving easy access from the sea.

"From Hulianda Ridge just above the landing at Bounty Bay, rounding the southeast corner where St. Paul's Point rises lofty and bristling through Down Rope, with its tiny beach, past Gudgeon to Christian's Point at the western extremity, the cliffs are sheer and inhospitable, capped by volcanic ash and tuff. Many of the land slopes, too, on the western side are very steep, the highest point on Pawala Valley Ridge, only a few hundred yards from the coast, being 1,100 feet above sea level. In the north, from cliffs of over 200 feet, the land rises a little less precipitously to about 900 feet; and the slopes of Flatland, which nestles in the centre, run comparatively gently downwards to the northeast and the settlement of Adamstown.

"The original home of the *Bounty* mutineers, Adamstown, lies on a northerly slope, with the main path from the Edge, above the landing at Bounty Bay, running for about half a mile through the village. Numerous little lanes run from the main path to homes

5

which are scattered among bushes, ornamental shrubs and garden patches. Although there are some 70 houses in Adamstown, about 20 were in use in 1975, the others belonging to islanders now dead or living abroad, and [these structures are] in various stages of disrepair, soon to be claimed by the advance of the island's heavy bush.

"The Public Square is the heart of Pitcairn. Here, less than half a mile from the main path, are clustered the Court House, outside of which on a plinth stands one of the anchors of H.M.S. *Bounty;* the Seventh-day Adventist Church; and a building containing the dispensary, library and post office. In the Square is also located the bell which calls Pitcairners to both religious and secular occasions.

"Northwest of the Square, slightly more than half a mile along the path to Palau, are the Pitcairn Island School and teacher's residence. The island's radio station is located on Taro Ground to the south of Adamstown."

It was on April 28, 1789, while the ship was in the Tonga Islands of the Pacific Ocean, that Fletcher Christian, master's mate of His Majesty's armed vessel *Bounty,* and others mutinied. They cast adrift the commander, Lieutenant William Bligh, and 18 others in the ship's boat. Then the mutineers sailed the *Bounty* back to Tahiti, where they had earlier spent several months gathering young breadfruit trees for planting in the West Indies.

Some of the mutineers insisted on staying in Tahiti. Christian and nine others, feeling sure the long arm of British justice would find them on Tahiti, set sail in the *Bounty,* taking with them six Tahitian men and 12 women. The mutineers spent two months searching among the Cooks, Tonga, and the eastern islands of Fiji for a spot in which they could hide. When the search proved fruitless, Christian, remembering Captain Philip Carteret's account of discovering Pitcairn in 1767,* sailed eastward, arriving at Pitcairn on January 15, 1790. Finding the island suitable, the mutineers decided to make it their home. Not only was the island lonely and inaccessible, it was also fertile, warm, and uninhabited. Sometime after bringing supplies from the *Bounty* ashore, they burned the ship; its remains sank just off the tiny indentation later to become known as Bounty Bay.

Following a few years of relatively peaceful life, serious

*The title of this book retains the original name given to the island by Captain Carteret—the possessive form. Carteret wanted everyone to know that the island belonged to Major Pitcairn of the British marines, whose young son was a member of his crew. Thus Pitcairn's Island.

trouble started when one of the mutineers began brewing a potent drink from the roots of the ti plant which grew in abundance on the island. By 1800 only one of the mutineers, John Adams, formerly known as Alexander Smith, was still alive, the sole male survivor of the group that had come ashore 10 years earlier.

Adams realized that without a better moral order than had ruled on the island in the past the little colony could not survive the future. He decided to pattern the islanders' lives on principles found in the Bible and the Church of England's *Book of Common Prayer*. He set a personal example of virtue and piety that included family prayers and grace before and after every meal.

In 1808, Mayhew Folger, in command of the American sealing vessel *Topaz*, discovered the little colony. Six years later two British naval vessels, H.M.S. *Briton* and *Tagus*, stopped at the island. The British commanders, impressed by the simplicity and piety of the Pitcairners and their absolute reliance on Adams, decided not to take the old man back to England to stand trial for the *Bounty* mutiny. It would be "an act of great cruelty and inhumanity" to arrest him, the naval officers wrote.

As Adams grew older and more feeble, leadership of the island passed first to John Buffet, a shipwright from England; then to George H. Nobbs, who had arrived on Pitcairn in 1828. Adams died on March 5, 1829.

Before he died, Adams, fearful that the island could not support the rapidly growing population, requested of the British that the Pitcairners be relocated. In March 1831, all on Pitcairn were transported to Tahiti, where land had been offered. The emigration proved a disaster. The simple Pitcairners were appalled at what they considered the immoral habits of the Tahitians. Shortly after their arrival, an outbreak of disease killed several of their number. Finally, their six-month ordeal on Tahiti came to an end when they were returned to Pitcairn by Captain William Driver of the brig *Charles Dogget* out of Salem, Massachusetts.

Pitcairn's first constitution was drawn up by Captain Elliot of H.M.S. *Fly* in 1838. The islanders lived in tranquillity through the 1840s, but with the population nearing 160 in 1850, another request was made for emigrants from the island. In 1856 all 194 islanders boarded the naval transport *Morayshire* for relocation on Norfolk Island, a former penal colony which was well provided with houses, roads, and domestic animals.

Although Norfolk had many advantages, nostalgia for their

former home afflicted some of the Pitcairners. When the captain of the *Mary Ann*, en route to Tahiti, offered passage back to Pitcairn in late 1858, 16 of the islanders could not resist. In 1864, four additional families returned to Pitcairn, making a population of 43. Despite a visit in 1868 by some of the Norfolk Island settlers, during which they urged their relatives to rejoin the more prosperous community on Norfolk, the returned Pitcairners would not leave their home.

By 1882, the islanders, having had some bad experiences with "outsiders," prevailed on the commander of the visiting H.M.S. *Sappo* to enact a law forbidding strangers to settle on Pitcairn. Later the law was amended to allow those whose presence was considered a benefit to the island to settle.

From the early 1800s, when John Adams had recommended a life of piety and virtue, the Pitcairners had adhered to the beliefs of the Church of England. They were keen students of the Bible, and they considered the Scriptures to be absolute truth. It was natural, then, that there would be interest in a box of Christian literature from Seventh-day Adventists in the United States which arrived on Pitcairn in 1876. Ten years later a Seventh-day Adventist lay missionary, John I. Tay, visited the island from California and explained the beliefs of the Adventists in more detail.

As a result of Tay's visit, "The forms and prayers of the Church of England [were] laid aside. During the past week meetings were held to organize our church service on Sabbath [Saturday]," wrote Mary McCoy, one of the Pitcairners, in her diary. Saturday again became Pitcairn's day of rest, as it had been until 1814. Forgetting to correct the time when he had crossed the international dateline on his way from Tahiti to Pitcairn in 1790, Fletcher Christian had contributed to the islanders' thinking that they were resting on Sunday, when they were actually resting on Saturday.

A few years after Tay's visit, a Seventh-day Adventist missionary ship, the *Pitcairn*, called at the island, where ordained ministers of the church baptized those who wished to become members of the faith. Since 1890 most Pitcairners have been Seventh-day Adventists. The island's single house of worship is the Seventh-day Adventist church, located on the Public Square. The church pastor is assigned to a two-year pastorate on the island from the church's Australasian Division. The pastor's wife must be a registered nurse, since she serves as medical officer on the island.

In 1893 parliamentary government came to Pitcairn, when

Captain Rooke of H.M.S. *Champion*, at the islanders' request, set up a seven-member parliament with executive and judicial functions separated. The system of public work, which had been followed before the migration to Norfolk, was restored. The cumbersome parliamentary system lasted until 1904, when R. T. Simons, the British Counsel at Tahiti, reintroduced the post of Chief Magistrate and two committees to take charge of internal and external, or marine, affairs. All officials were made subject to election. In 1940, H. E. Maude, representing the British High Commissioner in Fiji, both consolidated and expanded Pitcairn's constitution and legal code.

The visits of British naval ships diminished in the twentieth century, but ocean liners, aided by the opening of the Panama Canal, began to call at Pitcairn. The hundreds of passengers helped the tiny island's economy when they bought mementos of their visit. With the advent of air travel, the ocean liners began to dwindle in number. Pitcairn's public economy was then sustained by the issuing of postage stamps, beginning in 1940—a move that has met with continuing approval by both philatelists of the world and Pitcairners alike. The dwindling number of visiting ships remains the chief economic problem of those on Pitcairn as we enter the 1980s.

Preface

Pitcairn!

What thoughts the name brings to mind: history's most celebrated sea adventure, involving a mere speck of land lost in the South Pacific—an adventure including exotic settings, sex, piracy, murder, and exile, and the finding of deep religious devotion.

"The history of your island will long, I may say always, be a wonder," wrote Robert Folger, son of the discoverer of the Pitcairn colony, Captain Mayhew Folger, to one of the Pitcairners. And a wonder the story still is, to young and old alike.

Through nearly 200 years the Pitcairn story has been told and retold. With the exception of a mere handful, however, the writers have never visited Pitcairn. Even that handful remained but a short time and so could see but a small part of life on the island. The only widely circulated book by a native of the island, *Mutiny of the Bounty and Story of Pitcairn from 1790 to 1894*, was written by Rosalind Amelia Young and published by the Pacific Press Publishing Company. It is perhaps appropriate then that *The Miscellany of Pitcairn's Island*, composed largely of accounts selected from the island's newssheet and written or suggested by the Pitcairners themselves, should, nearly 100 years later, be issued by the same firm, now known as the Pacific Press Publishing Association.

The reader will note that the publishers have retained the characteristic use of terms and the British spellings of words. Only minor changes in the quoted passages have been made from the way they originally appeared in the island's newssheet, which has been issued under various names since 1892 and has been known as *Pitcairn Miscellany* since 1959.

The first effort to publish a newspaper on Pitcairn Island began in November 1892, when Pastor E. H. Gates, who had come to the island on the Seventh-day Adventist missionary ship *Pitcairn*, started the *Monthly Pitcairnian*. A handwritten publication, the paper had its own staff of six reporters, who, according to Rosalind Young, "almost invariably failed to send in any news; nevertheless its pages were always full." A poem usually filled the front page, followed by an editorial by Gates, with the rest of the paper devoted to "Moral and Religious Topics, the Home Circle, News Items, Pleasantries, and All Sorts." The newspaper seemed an appropriate outlet for the 40-member literary society Pastor Gates had started on the island.

In February 1893 Miss Hattie Andre arrived on Pitcairn from California aboard the *Pitcairn* to organize and teach school on the island. By early April, students varying in age from 14 to 39 were enrolled in Miss Andre's school. Another 20 younger students were taught by one of the island women. Pastor Gates's literary society was merged into the school, and the *Monthly Pitcairnian* "passed into the hands of the students, who were expected to keep its columns well supplied, notwithstanding the lack of material to supply them with." Alas, with its passing into the hands of the students, the *Monthly Pitcairnian* also passed into extinction.

In July 1956 Pitcairn's second newspaper, *Pitcairn Pilhi*, edited by the education officer on the island, began a run of 18 months. A two-page mimeographed publication whose words sometimes ran off the page in the effort to get all the news out, *Pilhi* covered some important events of Pitcairn's history during its short run.

In Volume 2, Number 1 (January 1957), for example, the newspaper reported on the underwater explorations of National Geographic staffer Luis Marden, and the finding of the anchor of H.M.S. *Bounty* by Buzz Fawcett of Captain Irving Johnson's brigantine *Yankee:*

"When Buzz went over the side he looked down and saw a straight object. A diver *always* investigates a straight object, and thus it was that the *Bounty's* anchor was discovered, the date being Monday, 28th January, 1957."

The issue also reported that during his stay, Captain Johnson, one of the best friends the Pitcairn people had ever had, blasted dangerous rocks from the narrow channel leading into Bounty Bay to make it safer for longboats to enter and leave. "Water cascaded high in the air and rocks flew as high as the Edge, at times some 200 feet. Tons of rock were removed, leaving the channel deeper and safer," according to the paper.

In Volume 2, Number 6 (July 1957), *Pilhi* noted that a new set of Pitcairn postage stamps "did not meet with much approval on first view; but later, when placed on envelopes as a set, they showed up favourably. The Bounty Bay stamp is definitely disappointing, and much regret has been expressed that such a bad mistake has been made in the placing of the residence instead of the school on the school stamp." Considering the importance Pitcairn places on the integrity of its stamps, the story, though restrained in tone, was reporting something of a philatelic disaster.

Among other reports in *Pilhi's* July issue was a notice of the birth of a daughter to Fern and Wiles Warren, born at 2 a.m. on July 2, "the day which commemorates the sighting of Pitcairn (in 1767) by midshipman Pitcairn of H.M.S. *Swallow*."

In August 1957 *Pilhi* chronicled the first landing of helicopters on Pitcairn: "Word was released on Sunday, 28th July, that the *Warrior* [British naval vessel] was due on the following Wednesday.... During the next three days and nights the saws, rasps, knives, and sandpaper were going without stop [to prepare curios]. It was learned that the ship was an aircraft carrier with 900 men aboard. The [island] Council finalized arrangements for the Great Day; and, when Wednesday dawned, there were very few who were not ready to go up to the prepared landing ground at Oleander. Every vantage point was taken as the carrier came in to drop anchor.

"Soon two helicopters were hovering around; and, when the first landed, out stepped Commodore Hicks to greet Council members. A party including Parkin, Andrew, Vernon, Ivan, Pastor, and the Teacher were taken off to breakfast on the carrier. An hour later, the men [of the island] went aboard to trade. The day was beautifully fine, the sea moderately calm. Everyone was in a happy mood. . . . In the afternoon the sailors came ashore to roam around and fill shirts with oranges, mandarins, and whatever could be found while the women and children went out to the carrier to enjoy a party lunch of buns, cake, and ice cream. . . .

"On the flight deck Commodore Hicks presented the school children with a signed photograph of the *Warrior*. After their reply, Andrew read an address of Loyalty to the Queen and of thanks to the commodore, officers, and crew of the *Warrior*. With that came the time to leave the ship. Sailors were returning from the island by this time, and by five o'clock the invasion was over. From the shore a ship's Band could be heard. There was a feeling of contentment on the island. It had been a grand and memorable day, to which was added a lovely climax when a display of colourful rockets lit up the *Warrior* as she steamed away. Her lights blinked out—'Goodbye and thank you for a happy day.'

"The Pitcairn children were given signed Bibles by Commodore Hicks of the *Warrior* and the Padre [chaplain]."

When *Pilhi* ceased publication in December 1957, Pitcairn was without a newspaper for the next 13 months. Then in April 1959, *Pitcairn Miscellany* began publication. With only a few interruptions it has been published monthly since its first issue.

"It is planned that *Miscellany* should contain the highlights of overseas news, local news, ship news, entertainment news, church news and any other features that come to the notice of your editors and which are thought likely to interest you. Your news and views will always be welcome. Your contributions need not be original—even 'corny' jokes are sometimes worth printing," wrote Editor E. Schubert in Volume 1, Number 1 (April 16, 1959).

"Letters to the Editor will be more than welcome. If you have some praise to offer, a complaint to get off your chest, or an opinion to express, don't hesitate—send it along. Once in writing, it will be read many times and given much thought; and you may never know the end result."

Although started as a one-pager, back and front, *Miscellany* now usually consists of two $8^1/_2$- by 14-inch pages mimeographed on front and back. Page one is topped by a printed or mimeographed letterhead, depending on the availability of printed stock, which at various times has been supplied by Bill Rogers of Florida, and Don A. Roth and Gordon Engen, both officials of the Seventh-day Adventist Church. Four different printed letterheads have appeared, the first, beginning in 1964, being a large view of the island with *Pitcairn Miscellany* above the type, in bamboo characters. The line "Sponsored by the Pitcairn Island School, South Pacific Ocean" is reversed (appears white) in the picture of the water extending out from the island. Other printed letterheads have featured a picture of the Pitcairn school, a drawing of the island, and—the most recent—a view of the island, an anchor, a radio, and a Bible, arranged within a circle.

Funds for the paper and printing of the letterhead have come from many friends and benefits. In Volume 6, Number 9 (August 1964), the editor noted that "Finance for paper, etc., was obtained from a collection taken at a benefit programme in Takoma Park [Maryland, at which the world headquarters of the Seventh-day

Adventist Church is located] featuring Luis Marden of the *National Geographic* staff, well known to many, either personally through his visits to Pitcairn, or through the pages of the *National Geographic*, November 1957, in which appeared his article 'I Found the Bones of the Bounty.' Much of the printing was kindly donated by the Washington College Press at Columbia Union College [in Takoma Park]."

In Volume 19, Number 4, April 1977, *Miscellany's* editor reported: "Also aboard [the ship] *Yankee Trader* were 400 reams of *Miscellany* masthead and blank paper. This generous gift . . . (which will last) for at least the next 10 years, comes from Mr. Gordon Engen, assistant director of Public Affairs and Religious Liberty for the General Conference Organisation of Seventh-day Adventists, U.S.A., who, along with co-workers has obviously worked hard to acquire the paper and get it shipped to the Island."

Despite the convenience to the staff of the printed letterheads, many *Miscellany* readers in various parts of the world find the mimeographed drawings of such local scenes as Pitcairn's longboats struggling through heavy seas, the making of a local well, and the fire at the island's power shed most interesting. A host of local happenings have been depicted, nearly all of which show considerable artistic talent and skill with the stylus.

Distribution of *Miscellany* has always been free to Pitcairners, with costs varying for subscribers in other countries. In Volume 3, Number 12 (December 1961), locals were warned against attempting to profit from *Miscellany*: The paper "is issued free of charge to locals, with a penny per edition added for additional copies. Any persons, apart from the sponsors [The Island School], profiteering from this paper are likely to have their issues cancelled. The proceeds from the paper go to the school. P.S. Up to three copies are issued to locals free."

In December 1963 Editor S. A. Kinder reported (Volume 5, Number 12) that 300 copies of *Miscellany* were being printed monthly. "When one comes to realise that Pitcairn's population is under 90, the paper must have one of the highest ratios of copies to population of any similar publication in the world," wrote Kinder. By 1973 a total of 430 copies were sold to local people for posting overseas, with 75 complimentary copies being sent to a variety of people "who have semiofficial connections with Pitcairn." Volume 15, Number 3 (March 1973).

The editor, in Volume 19, Number 1 (January 1977), reported that "Monthly production of the Newsletter as of December 31, 1976, was 705 copies. As the local community has many friends overseas, 430 copies of *Miscellany* were distributed last month to them for posting overseas. The remaining 275 copies have been the responsibility of my patient wife, whom I must thank for being so patient in addressing the many envelopes frequently and for ensuring that the *Miscellany* is posted. I should point out that no back copies of past issues are available. The staples binding your *Miscellany* are more often than not the work of the four Senior school children who spend approximately two hours each month on this somewhat laborious task. As well, the children carefully count copies to ensure that the editor is doing his job properly."

"And where does *Miscellany* go? I am absolutely amazed, and I am sure that you will be too. How good is your geography? New Zealand, Australia, England, Wales, Scotland, Ireland, U.S.A., West Germany, Switzerland, Sweden, Norway, Netherlands, Canada, South Africa, France, Belgique, Japan, Norfolk Is., Tahiti, Fiji, Hawaii, Samoa, Malta, Israel, Puerto Rico, Barbados, Mexico, Bermuda, Reunion Is., New Guinea, Gilbert and Ellice Is., Magnetic Is., Mauritius—"

It is not unusual for *Miscellany* to miss an issue during the changeover from one education officer to another, due to delays in ship transportation from New Zealand. The island's education officer also serves as editor of *Miscellany*. Usually this kind of omission is corrected by issuing a combined issue the next month. In 1974 the editor explained: "First of all I would like to apologize for the fact that there have been no *Miscellanys* since March. There is, however, a most legitimate reason for this, and we hope that you have not despaired too much. The old duplicator gave up the ghost as I was preparing to do the April issue; so I sent it to New Zealand for repair or replacement. It turned out that the old machine was beyond repair; and, consequently a new one was ordered. As you may be aware, communications in the supply line are not the best on Pitcairn; and it was to be five months before the new duplicator eventually arrived. It is a beautiful machine and works both manually and electrically; so that tedious job of turning a handle nearly 3000 times for each issue will now be a thing of the past.

"Let me assure you that your subscriptions will all be adjusted accordingly; so you will be able to add a further six months onto the date when your subscription was due. With regard to paying for the subscriptions, could I ask those of you who pay by cheque to leave the date space blank for us to fill in, as a large number of cheques are out of date by the time they arrive here and can't be processed. This then involves a time-consuming job of returning the cheque to you and awaiting the return of a fresh one. American subscribers may find it more convenient to send postal money orders."

Scores, perhaps hundreds of publications have quoted from *Miscellany* during its history of more than two decades. The report of one such instance is noted in Volume 8, Number 1 (January 1966): "Roy Clark some time back handed us a little booklet entitled *The Latch String*, published in Alabama, in the back of which is an article based on a piece culled from *Miscellany*, 1st December, 1963. Readers with back numbers could check back to paragraph four and reread the words written by the previous editor in his last publication a few short weeks before the Commissioner and his wife arrived here on their first visit to Pitcairn Island. Briefly, it concerns speaking one's mind at public meetings, instead of keeping quiet and then criticising in small groups afterwards.

"*The Latch String* follows the quotation with this comment: 'Right there, to our way of thinking, is the nub of responsible citizenship, in the middle of the ocean, or in the middle of New York City.'

"*Miscellany* is sometimes quoted in other overseas publications, too, thus revealing the interest that this little island arouses—an interest arising largely from the romance of *Mutiny of the Bounty* and the effect from it on the present-day Pitcairn."

Throughout its history *Miscellany* has remained remarkably unchanged. Few concessions have been made to a changing world. The issues in the late 1970s continued to carry the eyeball-level stuff of Pitcairn living, handled with joshing good humor or sensitive concern, much as did the issues of the early 1960s. Ernest Schubert, first editor of *Miscellany*, in a letter to the editor printed in Volume 11, Number 8 (August 1969), spoke of world changes and life on the island as reported by the paper: "Today, 19th May, 1969, I received Volume 11, Number 3 of *Pitcairn Miscellany*. . . . When I finished reading [it], I went to my bookcase and took out Vol. 1, No. 1, dated 16th April, 1959, and reread it and a few later issues. What a difference those ten years have made. The world has staggered on from crisis to crisis. Vietnam has killed its thousands and troubled the consciences of millions more, while the Americans have travelled to the moon and back.

"While all this has gone on, what of Pitcairn? Reading *Miscellany*, I find some Pitcairners have travelled the world but have always been glad to return to Pitcairn shores. On the island changes have been thick, fast, and wide-ranging. Transport has gone from wheelbarrow to tractor and Mini-moke [small auto], or from walking to Honda-ing. The first retail co-operative store has greatly assisted the people in getting their imported foods in smaller, more manageable quantities. Individuals don't now have to order months ahead and outlay large sums of money at one time. A new post office and new dispensary have made for greater convenience, as have also the new Flying Fox [a telpher, or electrically driven car suspended from overhead cables, running from Pitcairn's landing upward to the top of the Edge] and a radio station. Now with a village power supply and graded roads Adamstown surely must be a vastly different place. How can we across the sea know all these things? By reading *Miscellany* of course. Yours sincerely, E. Schubert."

The issues of *Pitcairn Miscellany* are a faithful chronicle of life on one of the world's most interesting islands. In the newspaper's simple and straightforward reporting of island events the reader will recognize that, for all the changes that have come to our world, the Pitcairn people remain what they have always been—warm, good-hearted, devoted folk who can rightly lay claim to a history as rich as that found anywhere on earth.

2—M.P.I.

From the *Miscellany* of Pitcairn's Island

Airplanes

If the Pitcairners see fewer ships calling at their island these days because of changes in shipping lanes and transportation methods, they see even fewer airplanes. Almost any sighting of a plane from the island is news.

"July 2nd—On this quiet Sabbath morning several people heard booming sounds shortly after the French set off their bomb at Mururoa [in the Gambier Islands]. About 1:15 p.m. that same day we were all surprised to firstly hear, and then see, a large six-engine jet aeroplane, complete with the usual 'jet roar' and vapour trails, make a medium- to high-altitude sweep over the island, circle, and return, only to disappear in a westerly direction. To the best of our knowledge this is the first sighting of a jet plane in this area, although there have been possibilities earlier." Volume 8, Number 7, 1966.

"Aircraft have been seen or heard on at least four occasions this month, and we suppose they are testing upper atmosphere wind direction [in connection with atomic bomb tests]. Volume 10, Number 7 (July 1968).

Animals

"In response to overseas inquiries, a survey was made of domestic animals and vehicles [on Pitcairn]. For the records, there are: 14 dogs, 47 tame cats (approx.), 6 pet goats, 1 Muscovey duck, and 578 domestic fowl (approx.). Of the vehicles, 3 are Mini-moke cars, 38 motorcycles, and 20 Pitcairn wheelbarrows. Looking to the sea, there are 22 privately owned canoes." Volume 19, Number 1 (January 1977).

While he had no quarrel with the listing of animals in the article, reader Roy P. Clark did question the number of serviceable canoes in a letter to *Miscellany's* editor:

"Now to comment on the 22 canoes. I wonder, dear editor, if you have not given the impression that there are 22 serviceable sea-going canoes? Perhaps I am mistaken. On inquiry I found we have nine or 10 plank-made canoes with attached outboard motors. The other 12 listed must be the old canoes made from special trees found on the island in limited numbers. These old relics of a craftsmanship now nearly lost to the island, are cast aside in workshops or out-of-the-way places. . . . Roy P. Clark." Volume 19, Number 3 (March 1977).

Ants

The Pitcairn humor is a rare, sometimes rib-rattling thing, as seen in this example:

"ANTS. Seemed to be rather numerous recently. The other day I dropped a bit of bread as I was eating, and when I went to pick it up I found I could not, for the ants were pulling the other way. (Now an ant many be small, but at two million to one human being the odds are fairly even.) In any case, as I clutched at the piece of bread, I was dragged across the kitchen floor, through the wash house, and up the garden path, which is where I have been leading you." Volume 20, Number 5 (May 1978).

Arrowroot (and so on)

Arrowroot, along with sweet potatoes, yams, and taro, is one of the staple subsistence foods of Pitcairn. As a part of her schoolwork in 1966, Julie Christian described how arrowroot is prepared:

"After a hard day's work of digging arrowroot, we finally managed to start on the peeling. 'If you help me, I'll help you' was what they said when they were doing the peeling. When they were tired of peeling, they all tried to push the arrowroots under the husks. We call that rustling. The next morning when all the peeling was done, they started to make the flour. Firstly, it had to be washed, then put through a mill with someone feeding, grinding, and watering. Then, all of the muma had to be taken out and squeezed. (Muma is the name we give to the residue from the grinding.) It had to go through a tin with holes in it, and then into a bag for further straining. It has then to be left alone for a while to settle. They use the same water that is left over, to do the next lot of arrowroot. The children made the adults mad with them because they were throwing the muma, packed into tight balls, at each other. It was flying everywhere, and after a while it goes smelly. The arrowroot flour is used for making biscuits, starching clothes, etc." Volume 8, Number 8 (August 1966).

Bells

"From time to time I am sure you have read in *Miscellany* that a bell was rung. . . . There are three bells on Pitcairn—two are situated in The Square and one at Big Fence. Each set of rings has a definite meaning. One continuous ring means that some form of entertainment is due to take place, a series of two rings is the call to church, a series of three rings means that all men under the age of 65 must attend Public Works, a series of four rings means that there is to be a public 'share out' in the Square, and the one that gets the men moving the fastest is the series of five rings which herald the approach of a ship.

"As the populated area of Pitcairn is almost entirely centred around Adamstown, everyone is within hearing distance of the bells and can answer their call when necessary." Volume 17, Number 1 (January 1975).

Birthday Party

The birthday party or "feast" on Pitcairn is an institution all its own. Perhaps a third or more of the island's population—certainly all the close relatives—are invited to "tea," which is actually an elaborate meal including pillhai, a mixed vegetable dish; various meats; jellies; cold puddings; and cocoa. It is the job of the host to see that every "bally" is tight as a result of the feast, and that there is enough left over so those who wish may take home a parcel of bones or tidbits for the dogs. While the celebrations are usually held in various island homes, *Miscellany* reported in 1964 on one held at Bounty Bay:

"To celebrate Murray's birthday, Dobrey invited everyone to bring their 'tea' to the landing, where all enjoyed a really good time. Naturally, swimming took first priority as entertainment— children who entered in races across the bay were rewarded with sweets. All visitors were ducked with no special ceremony but they did ensure that they gave as good as they took. Nancy in particular appeared to suffer from generous pushoffs from the jetty. . . .

"To add to the fun of the occasion, four canoes went out beyond the breakers for time trials, on a course from a line with Bounty Bay around the rocks off Old Man's Fishing Place and back again." Volume 6, Number 3 (March 1964).

Boats

Nothing is more important to the Pitcairners than their launches, which usually measure about 36 feet in length, with a

20

nine-foot beam. The launches carry everybody and everything from Bounty Bay to passing ships. When a launch is damaged or destroyed, no Pitcairner rests easy until repairs are made or a new launch is built. The task of building may take several months, usually because the hard woods needed in construction are not available on the island. Often the various woods used in launch construction will come from several different countries.

In 1819, Captain Henry King of the *Elizabeth* visited Pitcairn. In return for the generosity of the islanders, King wrote in his journal, "I gave them a whaleboat, in return for their refreshments—" It is thought that the island's boats have been made to the pattern of this whaleboat ever since. Until recent time the "longboats" were powered by men at 14 oars, two at each thwart. Once on the open sea, sails were also used. As manpower on the island has declined, diesel engines have been installed in the boats.

The passage to and from Bounty Bay, a tiny indentation which can hardly be called a cove, has always been dangerous, its narrow channel and jagged rocks requiring some of the world's best seamanship. Recent improvements to the jetty and channel have helped, but the entry, even on a calm day, requires careful choosing of the right moment to enter the channel through the surf. When the cry of "Go ahead" is given, the boat picks up speed and shoots with the wave into the channel. Standing in the stern, the coxswain brings the boat in with a hard left-hand sweep of the rudder alongside the jetty out of the surf.

Many issues of *Miscellany* have told of happenings to the boats and their crews, and recounted the building of new launches:

"An experience many do not want again occurred in the early hours of the morning on April 19th, while going out to a calling ship. Just how it happened no one can recall very clearly, but the next moment men and all in the *Ho Ho* [the longboat] were tipped into the sea. Rescue work was undertaken by the crew of the other boat, which then returned to shore. A long ring at about 4 a.m. gave the alarm, and everyone rushed down to the Edge to give assistance. Albert, who suffered most, soon recovered from the incident; and the men, after changing into dry clothes, returned to the waiting ship, taking out the motorboat as well. After a pleasant stay on board, the search began for the mail and oars, which were all recovered. All mail was thoroughly saturated." Volume 3, Number 4 (April 1961).

"By D. H. Davies, Pastor. The wind had howled all night. Few had slept really well. Most were wondering what the sea would be like by 4 a.m., when the bell was expected to ring in preparation for the coming of the [ship] *Rangitata*. When the bell did ring and the menfolk and several women made their way up to the landing with torches to light the way, they soon discovered that the harbour was reasonably good, but the open sea rather boisterous.

"It was felt that three boats would be needed to care for the cargo and the people's orders from Duncan, Wallet & Co. Ltd. of London.

"The mood of the men at the launching of the boats conveyed the mood of the sea. They moved quietly around the boats. Above the soft murmur of voices could be heard the voice of the Chairman calling 'One, two, three, haul,' and his echo was drowned in the great waves as they pounded the rocky seashore. Silently three longboats slipped into the troubled waters of the harbour.

"It was not long before the boats were under control and faced out to sea, waiting for the opportune moment. The captains, with their faces strained and wet with perspiration and salt water stood up in the sterns of their respective boats, while their eager crews watched and waited for the words, 'Pull! Everyman!'

"The battle was on; the men against the sea.

"When all the boats were safely out of the harbour, the motorboat, like an old clucky hen with her chicks around her, was quickly attached to the other boats. We were on our way, and in about 35 minutes reached our rendezvous.

"The sky became overcast and the wind came in squalls; so the boats had to be kept on the move. The captain would nose the motorboat into the waves.

"This was a terrifying experience, for at the time the strong wind whipped tremendous waves which appeared to be about to engulf us. When we turned to cross them, our hearts seemed to come up in our throats, shutting off any words that might be uttered. The boat was turned in silence.

"Then came the hair-raising experience of surfing on the crest of the wave. Two boats behind would also be caught and come hurtling towards the motorboat. The silence was then broken, when several of the men began shouting instructions to the captain. He tried to calm our fears by saying all would be well.

"After nearly two hours of nerve-wracking rides in very heavy rain, Pervis, the motorboat captain, consulted with the other captains. Seeing that the ship had not come, and was now long overdue, the decision was made to return to land. I am sure that others, along with the writer, felt security in this decision—secu-

22

rity that was short-lived. To get our feet on terra firma was not to be our pleasure till 4.30 p.m. What had happened? Someone had called, 'Sail ho!' Out of the heavy squall the *Rangitata* appeared like a grizzly apparition.

"Once again the boats were turned round, and eventually we were aboard.

"During the next hour and a half, trading [of curios, stamps, etc.] was done and the extensive cargo unloaded from the ship into the longboats. The captain of the ship was reluctant to blow the whistle, being anxious for our safety; we were seven or eight miles out to sea and could not see the island for continuous heavy rain. He offered to tow us back nearer to land; but this was not successful, as the sea had become even rougher. Within a short time of taking up the tow it was realised that it was too dangerous with the heavy-laden boats; so we cut ourselves adrift, fearing fatal disaster. The motorboat, as it came to secure the two other boats, was caught in a big swell; and the current dragged it under the tow of the vessel. As the big black ship rose high above us and paused about to plunge toward the little boat, eyes bulged with fear—petrifying fear. We seemed only seconds from death, when a great wave suddenly shot the boat clear of the bow just as it plunged down where we had been a split second before. Some were unaware of what had happened, as they were busy bailing water or vomiting over the side of the boat. Providence alone averted a tragic disaster.

"We had been given our bearing and told that we were three miles from the island. . . . The *Rangitata* stood by, fearing to leave us in case further assistance was needed.

"After forty minutes of struggling under our own power, the ship came as close as possible and called to us over the megaphone that we had made no progress, and were still three miles from land. It was now felt by some of the crew that much of the cargo should go overboard. We were carrying heavy roofing iron, as well as the stores and a new water tank for the school; and the flywheel of the motor in the boat was now under water in spite of our continuous bailing. Realising we had no sails with us, we feared to think of our plight should the engine cut out. It certainly sounded sick, but somehow it kept going. The men were ordered to the oars, and this seemed to make the difference.

"By changing course and going east, working by compass alone, we attempted to reach land by coming up behind the island. We were now making slow but gradual progress; and the *Rangitata*, four hours delayed to stand by us, steamed slowly away, and we were alone.

"I personally thought of Captain Bligh and his men and wondered if the 'iniquities of the fathers' were being 'visited upon the children unto the third and fourth generation.'

"On this occasion there were with me the two school teachers—Mr. Howse, about to depart, and Mr. Kinder, recently arrived. What a farewell and initiation! I can still picture their faces, Mr. Howse thinking his farewell had indeed come, and Mr. Kinder wishing his had.

"Visibility cleared, and we could see the island a mile and a half away. We came along past 'Down Rope' towards 'St. Paul's,' making slow progress. As we came round the front of the island, we were into the wind once again.

"Nearing the historical place where the *Bounty* was grounded and burned, the motor cut out. Panic now set in, through fear that we too were about to be dashed against the rocks without control.

"Quickly the oars were snatched and the ropes cut, leaving the two following boats to fend for themselves. Almost superhuman effort was made, with only four oars to get the heavy motorboat away from the rocks and out to sea again.

"The condition of the harbour was now really dangerous; and only the experienced skill of hardened seamen could have possibly got the two boats safely in to quickly unload and go back to rescue the motorboat, now drifting further and further from land.

Every available woman and child was waiting at the new jetty to chain-handle the unloading of the soaked, sodden goods. This too, was a task, as every carton was wet and fell to pieces; and the tin goods had to be handled individually. The 140-pound bags of dripping-wet flour and sugar some of the women hauled in with amazing agility. Only a part of one carton of spaghetti was dropped into the sea, and this the children later dived for.

"Fully manning one boat and taking extra oars, a boat's crew now faced the sea again to go to the aid of the motorboat. When these two joined company, a considerable portion of the cargo was passed over from the vessel in distress; and both were then rowed back to harbour.

"Normally the entire trip should have taken about three hours, but this day eleven tense hours had tried the nerves of those at sea and those waiting anxiously ashore.

" 'The worst experience in 35 years,' was the general opinion among the men who have wrestled with the sea all their lives.

"The Christian is never promised a smooth path free from trials, but we are promised that He will care for His own. God certainly is watching and caring for the people of Pitcairn Island. After experiences such as this one, who can doubt His providential care." Volume 4, Numbers 2 & 3 (February-March 1962).

"With the launch out of commission since the visit of *Rangitata* —for when we were all safely in harbour a huge wave swamped it completely—the sails have had quite a shake-out, and I think all who have been out to ships since have enjoyed the opportunity of running before the wind.

"Since that shocking day there has been a great deal of activity at the Landing, with the men working very hard at repairing the boats.

"The launch has been a very big job. Because the engine had been so badly affected by salt water it was necessary to strip it down to the last bolt. Wiles and Len, ably assisted by Tom, Oscar, and others, have done an excellent job in cleaning it up, reassembling it, and having it run even better than it did before.

"While this was going on, there has been quite a gang of men working on the hull of the launch. Timbers have been replaced, old paint blistered off, the hull recaulked, and all repainted. We now have a very smart and efficient launch.

"The other boats also had a considerable amount of work done to them.

"We now hope it will not be long before the task of completing the new launch is undertaken." Volume 4, Numbers 2 & 3 (February-March 1962).

"There is never a dull moment when living on Pitcairn Island, for there is always something happening somewhere round about. If it is not a ship due, it is repairing the boats or carrying out the hundred and one other tasks which are waiting to be done. The month of May has been no exception, as can be seen from the following report:

"On the day the *Ceramic* called, outward-bound for New Zealand, the weather was not particularly bright. A heavy surf was running at the landing, and this made the handling of the boats in the harbour a difficult one. The two longboats negotiated the rollers after a considerable amount of bucking and prancing. Then came the turn of the launch. Instead of going over the top of one of the rollers, it ploughed straight through and, when clear, was seen to have several very wet people up forward. The ship gave opportunity for sending fruit to relatives and friends in Wellington, and over two hundred cases were forwarded.

"The island's supply of diesel fuel oil, kerosene, and petrol arrived on 22nd May aboard the British Petroleum tanker *British Mallard*, commanded by Captain Sadler. In the early hours of the morning the ship was seen to be standing off the island, and when the men were going down to the boats at dawn, she was still to be seen. Yet once we were out in the boats, all signs of her had vanished. The launch left the two longboats to go in search and, after running for several miles without spotting the ship, returned, and we all came ashore. Thomas [Christian] set off for the radio station to try and contact the missing vessel but only got as far as 'White Rock,' when it was spotted moving in very closely towards the island. Although it was originally planned that our boats would be alongside the tanker just after daylight, it was not until shortly after 10 a.m. that we finally made contact. The reason for the odd behaviour of the ship was engine trouble. This prevented the *British Mallard* from coming any closer than two miles from the island, making it a long haul for the launch. The unloading of the 240 ten-gallon drums was accomplished in two and a half hours. This was very good time, considering that each drum was lowered into the boats on a heaving line." Volume 4, Number 5 (May 1962).

"Sunday, 28th October saw the results of four months' labour on the part of many of the men under Elwyn's leadership, for the new launch was taken out for its first run. All who had a share in the construction of this boat must feel proud; for they have built something which is, we hope, going to serve our community for a good many years to come. It was a day for all, but most of all for the children. Not being certain about the behaviour of the new launch, the old one, which has served us faithfully for the last nine years, was also slid down into the harbour. With a crowd of adults and children on board, *Old Faithful* went out through the surf to wait there for its new companion.

"Back in the harbour, however, the new launch, despite the heaving of the crew and the churning of the propeller, was stuck hard and fast on the shallow bottom. After a quarter of an hour of struggling it at last started to move; and then, floating clear, was soon headed out to sea.

"After a few trial runs back and forth across Bounty Bay, the two launches made a trip right round the island; and during this journey the new addition to our fleet showed that it is worthy of a place alongside the others which have served us so well in the past.

"As the old launch was being hauled up to its resting place after our return to the harbour, it was noticed that the stern-post had been broken. This means we are still with only one launch in operation and that the men are now faced with another big repair job. Such is life on Pitcairn." Volume 4, Number 10 (November 1962).

"It was such a fine morning on Friday, 17th May, that Wiles, Pervis, Oscar, Warren, Charles, Clinton and Reynolds decided to go out fishing in their canoes, but while they were round off Ginger Valley a very sudden change in the weather was brought on by a strong northeasterly wind. The men quickly made up their minds to hurry back to the Landing, but on coming round St. Paul's Point to where they met the full force of the wind, they realised they were in for a sticky time. Already the sea had been whipped up; and there was a nasty surf running, with the wind and sea steadily increasing.

"Ashore, the womenfolk were becoming very anxious, and quite a group of them gathered at the Edge, from where they could see the four small boats bobbing about on the storm-tossed ocean like tiny corks.

"Clinton and Reynolds decided to make a go at getting in through the surf, and in this they were successful. But the sea, by the time the next boat was ready to make the run, was so bad it was too late.

Realising the peril in which the men were, the alarm was sounded; and within a very short time a sufficient number had gathered at the Landing to launch the motorboat. Once in the water, no time was lost in turning it around and starting the engine.

"With Christie at the helm, the passage through the surf was safely accomplished. We were soon alongside the first of the canoes, the occupants of which had been extremely busy, either rowing to keep the head up into the water, or bailing to keep down the water in the boat.

"Despite the high wind and the rough sea, the two fishermen and their outboard motor were brought into the launch and their boat hauled up and lashed. The same happened with the second boat, but there was no hope of also picking up the third boat because of lack of space. There was nothing for the launch to do but return to the landing, unload, and then go out again.

"As Charles was to be left out there on his own, Bruce volunteered to join him; so he dived overboard and swam across the stormy sea to climb into the canoe.

"Despite the sea, which was running, the launch made harbour safely; but on the second run out we ran into real trouble. Just as the boat entered the surf, a huge wave loomed up ahead; and before anything could be done to avoid the danger a great volume of water crashed into it. A few moments later the engine gave a few sputters and died. Fortunately, we were by this time outside the breakers, but not without casualties. Len, who had been tending the engine, was badly gashed by flying glass when the quarter-inch plate glass in the front of the cabin was shattered by the force of the water. Others, too, were battered, bruised, and cut.

"The men quickly got out the oars and commenced rowing the waterlogged boat. Those who were not rowing were bailing as fast as they could.

"By this time the torrential rain was falling, and this was a mixed blessing. It certainly helped to flatten the sea, but it also put a lot more water into the boat.

"Gradually the launch was brought round until it was alongside Charles' canoe. However, as there would be no room for the oarsmen if the boat was brought aboard, the two men decided to try for the harbour. After passing the outboard motor into the launch, we stood off, anxiously watching as Charles and Bruce gradually worked their way in. Fortunately, the rain and a sudden change of wind to the south brought sufficient improvement in the condition of the sea to relieve the most serious danger and allow them to reach safety.

"Now it was the turn of the launch. Slowly we came in toward the surf, when, just at the crucial moment, the engine burst into life—the efforts of Wiles had been rewarded. Without further incident the boat came in through the breakers, and all danger was passed. Another exciting incident in the life of Pitcairn was over." Volume 5, Number 6 (June 1963).

"Saturday, 21st March—the N. Z. Shipping Company's training ship *Rakaia*, carrying a cargo of apples for the United Kingdom from Napier and Nelson, called about 9:30 in the evening. While the launches were being put into Bounty Bay, they broke loose and drifted for a while, beam-on to the waves, until they were brought alongside the landing. During this upset, John was thrown off balance, and in landing heavily, hurt his shoulder. Although the *Rakaia* did not stay long, the men were still able to do some trading." Volume 6, Number 4 (April 1964).

"THE BOATS OF PITCAIRN'S ISLAND. By Roy Clark. Shortly after the arrival of the H.M.S. *Bounty* on Pitcairn's Island, its mutinous crew burnt all their bridges behind them—the *Bounty* and even her lifeboats went up in smoke. It was not long after this event before a change, of necessity, was wrought among the little community.

"Unrest, dissastisfaction, and discontent grew intensely

violent among native men because of the unfairness and harsh treatment of the mutineers toward their Polynesian friends. As is well known, next followed bloodshed, murder, hatred, and revenge, until some of the women secretly made a raft, fully intending to leave Pitcairn's blood-soaked soil and return to their native land. This attempt failed, but it marked the beginning of the second event of maritime history of the mutineers, the first being their landing on the island two years before.

"The rebellious crew of the *Bounty* passed on (save one), and the offspring of their Tahitian women took over. In 1795 the first two canoes were hewn out of logs—the beginning of over 172 years of canoe and boat building. The longboats of the islanders have become one of their most dearly treasured possessions, and this is only natural when these boats have been the only communication between shore and ship. They have through the years provided a livelihood and a means of supplementing island food supplies from passing ships, as well as a means of visiting two of the other islands of the group—Henderson and Oeno. (Henderson, 108 miles to the northeast, is visited to supplement stocks of Miro wood for the island's much-sought-after carvings, while Oeno, 75 miles to the nor'-nor'west, is visited about once a year by men, women, and children for a week's holiday. Ed.)

"In the island's history (now out of print), by Rosalind Amelia Young, is found an account of a boat from the island going off from land to meet two whaleboats from a passing whaler. This in the year 1808—18 years after settlement. The three men in the island boat welcomed the visitors and invited them to come ashore and visit with Alexander Smith, sole survivor of the nine mutineers.

"Forty-seven years later, in 1855, a whaleboat was launched from the island to go on the sad errand of bringing home the dead body of an islander who fell from the rocks while fishing with his wife. From this date on to the present time whaleboats (longboats, as we call them) have been the heartthrob of island life.

"It may interest our readers to refer to some of the most important and talked-of island boats in the last half century or more—their names and what part they have played in the maritime life of the island.

"Queen Victoria made a present to the islanders of three boats. Two at one time, and a third some years later. The first of these boats was named the *Life-Boat*, because it had sealed tanks enclosed in its structure. The second, named the *Drew*, was ever

found to be a leaky boat; and in later years, and even to the
present time, has been synonymous with all other leaky boats,
which are referred to as being leaky as the *Drew*. This boat came
to its end when coming through the passage into the harbour. Not
making the turn to the beach at the proper time, it was carried
onto the rocks and broke into exactly two halves.

"From the United States (California) was brought a whaleboat,
which proved to be a model for all successive boats built on the
island. It was named after the Magistrate's (Russell McCoy's)
daughter, Ella May. This boat was also called the *Belluga*. As a
model, the *Ella May's* pattern for the first island-made boat
proved most successful. The *Surprise* for years was the leading
sailing boat, even among the many longboats built after it. It
was a real clipper craft and a surprise to the community.

"As would seem natural, seacraft are built as near to the sea as
possible, but not one of the island boats was built near the sea,
but in the village, some 200 feet above sea-level. The incongruity
of the building of the *Surprise* was that it was built further inland
than any other boat—past the centre of the village. More than
one boat was named after the first *Surprise*.

Other boat names through the years have been, *Winchester* (or
Barge), *Nuni*, *Ho-Ho*, *Helen Hare*, *George's Boat*, *Herbert's Boat*,
Parkin's Boat (*The Comfort*)—and of the launches, *Helen Hare*,
Joucelyn, *Ronald Garvey*, *Boxhead* and *Reid Cowell*—these last
two boats being currently in service.

"The *Winchester* served its time for many years and was
eventually pulled to pieces. The *Ho-Ho* was another sturdy boat
that performed wonderfully at the sea, but ultimately became
worn out and almost rotted in service. Probably one of the
most-loved boats was the *Nuni*, which will be remembered for
generations to come as a good, fighting seacraft. The *Rodney*
and *Parkin's Boat* were both abandoned at sea, the crews of each
being taken into other boats.

"The good old sailing days are over, and there is no more
'ashing it' with 14 oars pulling against wind and tide. The
launches have made seagoing life all too easy. Maritime life on
Pitcairn for the younger generation is one of ease compared to
the hardships encountered in the days of the oar and sail."
Volume 9, Numbers 8 and 9 (August-September 1967).

"ONE OF THE OTHERS. By Anonymous. As the longboats
reach out once again through the heavy surf in Bounty Bay, I
think—'Well, here we go again.' Another ship visit.

"Earlier, on the track down to the Landing, I would have
stopped at White Rock to survey the sea in the Bay—good or bad,

we'll be going out; but I always stop there and cast an apprehensive look down anyway.

"Ships coming from the direction of Panama can be seen from the Edge and the time for launching the boats accurately defined. Those coming from behind the island will have been seen by a lookout at Taro Ground, who wastes no time getting down the hill to the village to ring the bell and give his estimate of how far off the ship is. Experienced eyes gauge distances with reasonable accuracy, but judging the speed of the ship in relation to wind and sea is difficult. One can only guess how long it will be before funnel and masts are seen through the gap at Matt's Rock.

"The boats must be got into the water as soon as the men reach the Landing in case there is any holdup in the launching. Even up at the Edge one can hear Morris's 'One, Two, S'ree,' as he calls for the men to throw their weight into hauling and pushing the heavy boats down the treacherous slope of the slipway. Stern first, with two crew members heaving themselves onto the boat at the last moment, the boat thunders into the water, sparks spitting like firecrackers as the steel-shod keel scrapes against the concrete. Sometimes, of course, the boat travels halfway to the water, then sticks with mulelike obstinancy. Then it's bars, levers, shoulders, and a good deal of talk, until the deed is accomplished. As quickly as they can, the crew turns the boat in the Bay with lines and oars until it is snug against the jetty, bow pointed seawards. Now a repeat performance with the second boat (and sometimes a third) which is turned as before and lashed securely to the first. Baskets of fruit, curios, mail, empty drums etc. are quickly loaded, while everyone moves to his accustomed place in one or the other of the boats. No easy task, this, at times, because of the jerking, swaying, and tugging as the boats are straining against the warps by the breaking seas.

"This is where I have my first qualms—those first feelings of hollowness within me, and I try and put all thoughts of seasickness out of my mind as the rest of the folk unconcernedly, laughing and joking, climb aboard. But not me—No sir, I'm one of the others.

"How far off is the ship? What's the sea like outside the harbour? How long will we be waiting for the ship to round the point? Should I have taken a seasick pill? I can do without a pill if the boats move straight out to a ship, but if we've got to wait a mile or two out—engines stopped and at the mercy of the waves—that's when I'm sure I'm one of the others—one of the few on Pitcairn who will never get used to small boats no matter if I am at sea every day for the rest of my life.

"At last the boat captain gives the word to let go the warps; and, with two men stationed at the bows wielding long oars to fend off from the other boat and the rocks, the boat is carefully positioned, awaiting the 'good time' to break through the surf in the harbour mouth. 'Full Ahead Cairn,' calls the boat captain from his standing position in the stern. One arm flung up for balance, the other grips the long steering oar with strong fingers. The diesel roars as the throttle is pushed wide open; and the boat—slowly, then with gathering impetus—moves forward through the narrow opening into the surf. If the right time has been picked, the exit is easily made; but sometimes a rogue wave or swell causes the boat to leap high in the air, to land with a shuddering, wetting thump on the shoulder of the following wave. Past the line of breakers, the steering oar is quickly shipped and replaced by a conventional rudder and tiller, while I can relax my desperate grip on the hand-grip of the engine house and begin my assessment of 'how the sea will be.' All eyes watch until the second boat is safely through the surf, then it's slow-ahead out from the island to the place the boat captain considers the best position to wait for the ship.

"It is always my fervent hope that the ship will appear before we are far enough out to stop engines and wait, but usually we are early, and my 'mind over matter' battle begins. The hardened types enjoy this lolloping, jolting, rocking, undulating, swinging, swaying, teetering, sickening vacillatory motion and calmly (to my horror) proceed to eat oranges, bananas, pawpaw, etc., with obvious relish and enjoyment, while the smell of the fruit, diesel fumes, bilgewater etc., merely adds more tremors to my already quaking stomach.

"Sometime later (three hours once), the call, 'Sail Ho,' brings some measure of relief and the knowledge that soon we will be safely on the firmer decks of the ship—providing one has safely negotiated the ascent of a swinging, twisting, rope ladder from the launch to the deck.

"Boarding ships by rope ladder is for the hale and agile. Me—I'm one of the others. Being sometimes soaking wet, dizzy from seasickness, and none too agile at the best of times makes this a formidable task for me. Climbing the ladder is not too bad. Getting onto the thing would sometimes gain deserved applause in a high-flying circus act. The usual drill is:

"1. Stand back while the eager beavers clamber up, festooned with their baskets of fruit, souvenirs etc.

"2. When all is clear, balance yourself precariously in the

rising, shifting boat at the bottom of the ladder.

"3. Watch the rise and fall of the boat and clutch firmly at the ladder at the highest upswing.

"4. Get your feet moving quickly up the first few rungs, or else the boat may surge up a few more feet and crush your limbs against the ship's side.

"5. Climb the remaining 15 or 20 feet up the towering side of the ship and heave yourself over the rail at the top.

"6. Try to appear to the watching passengers and crew that 'this is kid stuff' to you.

"You have to go ashore again, of course. Then you have to rerun the complete gamut of these marine calisthenics in reverse. Most of the others enjoy every minute of this. (Even the sight of people on the ship peering sadistically over the ship's side waiting for one of us to slip.) But me—I'll never get used to it because—" Volume 9, Numbers 9 and 10 (September-October 1967).

"At age 15 years, and with permission of those concerned, boys are allowed to begin visiting ships. Brian's chance came for his first visit when *Amalric* called. And when he took his place in *Boxhead*, he was the envy of every other schoolboy on Pitcairn. He certainly enjoyed his visit to the ship and was very helpful in doing his share of the lifting and carrying of cargo. But his greatest experience was to come, as both launches, heavily laden, began to journey home from a mile east of the island into high winds and rough seas.

"Only the slowest speed was possible. Spray, like bullets, was being swept down the length of both boats by the wind, and the pumps were in action almost from the time we left the ship's side.

"The cargo, tightly packed under the double tarpaulins, was safe enough, but the men, clinging precariously to whatever handholds they could find on the engine house and atop the cargo, were completely exposed to the elements. To lift one's head from the protecting folds of one's coat was to be rewarded by a face full of stinging spray, and a glance at Brian when halfway home showed him sitting on the engine house, water streaming down his face, and obviously enjoying every second.

"The sea between Adam's Rock and the island was very rough indeed, and our first sight of the harbour showed us that the seas had come up considerably since we had left two hours before. Huge breakers were pounding into the Bay in quick succession, breaking well out from the harbour mouth. The ship and boats had drifted out of the sight of those ashore, and there was apparently no one, either at the Landing or the Edge, as *Reid*

33

Cowell approached the white water to attempt an entry.

"*Reid Cowell* was already well loaded down with cargo, men, and a small quantity of water driven aboard by the wind; and very little freeboard was visible from the engine-house on back. As the boat was being positioned for its run in, a breaker burst in over the stern, cascading water into the rear cockpit, the weight of which made the boat much lower in the water. Before we had stopped gasping and spluttering at this inundation, two more waves quickly followed the first, each one bigger than the last, until the boat seemed ready to swamp and go under at any second. At this time we were 20 yards from 'Flattie' and in dire straits. What saved the day for us was the fact that, after the first wave, the engine was pushed ahead to give some 'weigh' on the boat. This, with an extra surge of power at the moment we came level with the end of the jetty, was enough to take us out of harm's way; but the boat was still in danger of sinking from the water surging into the harbour.

"With no one at the Landing to take a line, it was necessary for Len to jump into the water and swim the few yards to the jetty to make fast. Then followed the quickest boat-lightening exercise for years. Boxes of butter, eggs, meat, Co-op stores, baskets, hardwood, flour, apples, etc. were all off-loaded in short order and quickly carried off to higher ground. Three men with buckets spent a considerable time bailing out the boat before it was hauled up into the shed. After the bung (a drain plug in the bottom of the boat) was removed, water flowed freely from it for two hours.

"Surprisingly, very little of the cargo was spoiled, everything having been double-wrapped in canvas tarpaulins. The Co-op goods were most affected, when water seeped into the biscuits and breakfast foods.

"*Boxhead*, besides being less heavily laden, profited by *Reid Cowell's* experience and began her run in from further out.

"Cold, wet-through, but happy, Brian took his place beside the men; and, when asked how he enjoyed his first trip to sea, replied, 'Good ship.' " Volume 10, Number 9 (September 1968).

"Having had good weather for most of the month, Mother Nature decided to change her tune; and by 24th November, when the *Port Brisbane* arrived from U.K. at 8:15 a.m., the sea had started to become rough. The men had a long and weary day unloading the cargo and mail and did not arrive ashore until about 2 p.m., very wet and tired. Cargo had then to be unloaded and transported to the homes and 17 bags of mail handed out.

"By the morning of the 25th, the sea was becoming rougher;

and it was decided that the boats would have to leave Bounty Bay before dark to be sure of a safe exit through the passage. Three boats left at 7 p.m. and sheltered in the lee of the Island at Tedside to await the arrival of the ship *Tasmania Star* at 11.45 p.m. The men had just started to unload the cargo, when the heavens decided to open up; and down came the heaviest rain we have seen here on Pitcairn for many a day. With rough seas, rain, and 10 tons of cargo to unload, the men had a long night's work before the ship departed at 3.30 a.m. The boats then sheltered again in the lee until the first light of day, when the first boat, *Boxhead,* struck out and made for Bounty Bay, arriving just after 5 a.m. However, *Boxhead* was so heavily laden with cargo that when it drew up beside the landing it seemed to 'give up the ghost' and just sank and rested on the bottom of the harbour. Fortunately, at the time it was low tide; and, despite the fact that a wave broke right over the boat at this stage, little damage was done to the cargo, which was well covered with tarpaulins.

"Having unloaded its cargo, *Boxhead* had then to return to Tedside, taking a spare rudder for another of the boats, *Reid Cowell,* which was in difficulty with rudder trouble. The new rudder was installed, half of the cargo off-loaded to *Boxhead*, and then these two boats set off for home. All went well, and *Reid Cowell* and *Boxhead* made the safety of the harbour. (The third boat had by this time safely arrived in Bounty Bay.)" Volume 12, Number 11 (November 1970).

"The *Westward* returned on the evening of the 17th in good weather, and two loads of wood were taken out in *Dumpy* and loaded aboard before nightfall. During the night strong winds developed, making the sea very rough and the loading of the remaining eight boatloads of wood onto the *Westward* a heavy and dangerous task. The wood has to be loaded into the rowboat whilst it is afloat, as once loaded with the wood on the shore, it would be too heavy to push into the water. This means that in rough seas a group of men have to stand in waist-deep water holding the boat against the swell, whilst the timber is loaded. The men then have to row the boat against the swell of the waves through the narrow passage. On this occasion, with the heavy seas, *Dumpy* was twice thrown crossways up onto the reef with a full load of timber and men. On one of these occasions Dr. Harold Rehder, Senior Zoologist in the Division of Mollusks of the Smithsonian Institution, was aboard; and it is thought that it was an experience he will find hard to forget. However, after a long and arduous day's work, the yacht eventually departed

Henderson for Pitcairn Island at 7 p.m. on the 18th, with *Dumpy* again in tow.

"All went well until about 2 a.m., when Dennis Hewitt, the engineer aboard *Westward*, and Steve Christian—both of whom where standing watch—noticed that the towline to *Dumpy* had broken away, pulling the thwarts with it from the boat. The alarm was immediately given, and men tumbled out on deck. A searchlight was brought into action to locate *Dumpy*, a compass bearing taken, and the yacht turned around to go to *Dumpy's* aid. The seas were quite high, and some difficulty was experienced locating the boat. Finally a member of the yacht's crew climbed the rigging, sighted the boat, and the yacht came alongside. Pervis Young, Jacob Warren, and Steve Christian climbed down into the boat and bailed it out. A hole was then cut through the bow and a towline tied through. About 8 a.m. further running repairs had to be carried out to *Dumpy*, which was apparently breaking up fast in the rough seas. However, soon afterward, *Dumpy* drifted in too close to the yacht; and, as the ship came down on the crest of a wave, *Dumpy* was fatally squashed and soon afterwards had to be abandoned. It is interesting to note that no member of the party of Pitcairn Islanders aboard the *Westward* had the heart to finally cut the towline between the yacht and the wreck of *Dumpy*. Finally, one of the members of the *Westward* crew, Dean Cannoy, performed the sad task. . . . And so poor old *Dumpy* came to a watery end.

"A weary shipload of men finally arrived home in rough seas on the evening of the 19th about 7.30 p.m. On the 20th and 21st all the wood from the expedition was safely brought ashore from the yacht; and at 6.30 p.m. on the 21st *Westward* departed, bound for Rapa." Volume 13, Number 1 (January 1971).

"19th February—*Cap Finisterre*, bound for Dunkirk, stopped in the early afternoon. Some of the ladies visited the captain's wife, whom they had met while travelling to New Zealand on a previous trip aboard the *Cap Ortegal*.

"When returning to Bounty Bay, the men retrieved a tin containing mail, which had been dropped from the *Louvre Lloyd* as she passed the previous day. A radio message had been received which indicated that she intended to drop the tin with mail for posting on Pitcairn as she passed at 2.30 a.m., but a search along the northern side of the Island after daylight proved fruitless. It was indeed a lucky coincidence to sight the tin so long after it was dropped." Volume 14, Number 2 (February 1972).

"There was a high wind and heavy seas as the three launches were prepared for the trip out to the *Port Montreal*, carrying 14 tons of cargo from New Zealand. *Reid Cowell* waited in the small basin behind the jetty, while Len surveyed the incoming waves in order to pick the opportune time to put to sea. The moment chosen, Len's launch inched its way forward; but before it could gather way a heavy sea struck the bow and threw the head of the boat to port. Succeeding seas forced the launch further to port until it struck the rocks. The first impact punched a hole through the underside of the boat just forward of the wheelhouse.

"Warren had no option but to call, 'Every man for himself.' All but three threw themselves into the boiling sea on the starboard side, and by great good fortune they reached the safety of the rocks after a strength-sapping struggle. Everyone suffered bumps, scratches, and cuts of varying degrees.

"Three men remained in the doomed launch. Tom Christian jumped for the rocks and suffered a fractured right tibia. Jim Collier was thrown to the landward side and attained some measure of safety between the rocks. Craig Reeves, who had been holidaying here and was to leave for England to take up a position there, was also thrown towards the rocks, where he was struck by the rolling launch. Jim's attempts to assist him from the water were fruitless. Steve, who had swum across from the jetty, and Noggie were able to reach Craig; and they took him through the water to the concrete slipway. He was lifted from the water and found to have a fractured right femur.

"The recovery of Tom was a difficult task, as the rocks between Black Bank (where the accident occurred) and the Landing were large and rugged. The stretcher part eventually brought both men to the dispensary in the Square. X rays were taken by Pastor. Tom's fracture was set and placed in a cast. Craig's injuries were much more serious, as he had also suffered considerable muscle damage and possible pelvic injuries.

"Our Medical Officer, Mrs. Webster, decided that outside help was necessary; and Anderson rushed to the Radio Station to put out a call for medical assistance from nearby shipping. And then we waited . . . and waited.

"The two remaining launches made the hazardous trip to the *Port Montreal* and brought back the supplies and mail.

"Late in the evening a message was received to say that the *E. V. Henry* would be at the island in the morning. As soon as there was sufficient light, the men took a launch out through the wild sea to rendezvous with the French ship. A doctor and five medical orderlies were landed at Tedside, where the seas were quieter, and from there they were brought to the dispensary by motorbike.

"Dr. Jean Pierre Leroy took over the care of the patient, and our own hard-working medical team gained a respite.

"Through the good offices of the French Military Services, Craig was taken aboard the *E. V. Henry* the next morning in fine weather, and two hundred miles north of Pitcairn he was lifted by helicopter for a fast trip to the Gambier Islands. An aircraft flew him to a hospital in Tahiti. Eleven days after the accident, he was back in his hometown of Dunedin in New Zealand's South Island. A cable from his father has been received saying, 'Craig's condition satisfactory after operation. Prognosis for favourable recovery after lengthy hospitalisation. Please repeat our sincere thanks to Pitcairn People.'

"A dramatic rescue with many people involved. So many people to thank for the part they played. Of particular note was the outstanding work of Pastor and Mrs. Webster and Royal, our medical team, and Irma and Anderson of our radio staff. And without the French—" Volume 14, Number 6 (June 1972).

"The Public Work bell rang on the 20th September to call the men out to begin the search for trees which would provide the timber needed for the ribs, stem, and stern-post of a launch to be built to replace *Reid Cowell*. Three days of work followed, and the culmination of all the effort saw a healthy pile of timber assembled at Ethel's. As the month ended, the building site was cleared and the main keel was in position.

"During the time of construction which lies ahead there will be many calls on the men's time, but everyone will have to realise the need for sacrifices to enable a new launch to be in use as soon as possible. We only have to remember the cargo left aboard the *Majestic* to realise how essential the third boat is to the island." Volume 14, Number 9 (September 1972).

" 'NEW LAUNCH COMPLETED.' By Carol Christian. On the 11th of December I think many women were anxious to know just what was keeping their menfolk out working on the new launch until almost 6 p.m. instead of the usual 4 p.m. All knew that the boat was nearing completion and weren't surprised to learn that they were working overtime. With this final flurry of work the men completed caulking and puttying the seams and applied a first coat of paint so that it could dry overnight, ready for the launch's removal to Bounty Bay next morning.

"Shortly after 9 a.m. the following day, a long ring was put through on the telephone to let everybody know that the launch would be moving within a few minutes.

"It's not often that we see a 'passing parade' on the main road of the island, and almost everyone turned out to accompany the

39-foot, two-ton launch on her quarter-mile journey down the hill to the bay.

"She was towed down the steep, winding road by the tractor in record time until the final sharp corner by the boat-shed was reached. The turn proved too sharp for the tractor to take her round safely. However, with the help of the boat winch and the men's brawn, the boat was soon down the last lap of the road and at the water's edge.

"With all watching closely, the boys gave a mighty heave; and she was sent plunging into the waters of Bounty Bay. As she proudly rode on the waves, there were few who offered criticism, and on the whole I think the men were pleased with the good work they had done. I know the rest of us who watched share this pride." Volume 14, Number 12 (December 1972).

"August 12 the longboats were put to sea at 8:30 p.m. to make contact with *Megantic,* which was scheduled to arrive at 9:30 p.m. but arrived at 11 p.m. It rained prior to the longboats' leaving the Bay. Once out to sea, the crews waited. Suddenly there was a break in the overcast sky on the horizon—a light—it must be the *Megantic.* Away went a longboat in pursuit of the vessel. Further and further away from the island it went, but—something funny was happening—the light wasn't getting closer, and for some unknown reason the light source seemed to be getting bigger.

"Then—all of a sudden—'Harris, it's the moon!' yelled Jay.

"Ah well . . . just another Pitcairn experience." Volume 18, Number 8 (August 1976).

"Owing to unsuitable weather conditions for anchorage off Bounty Bay, the brigantine *Eye of the Wind* motored around to the lee of West Harbour and dropped its anchor. With the three motor launches from the Island being out of commission, the *Avon Rescue* boat, along with some of the local's canoes, had to be used to ferry our visitors ashore. . . .

"When the brigantine *Eye of the Wind* arrived from Easter Island on the 11th, history was relived; this was the first time since 1814—I'll repeat that—1814, that fishing canoes had to be used to visit ships. According to one of the Pitcairn's elder statesmen, Andrew Young, '. . . in 1814 George Young and Thursday October Christian visited *H.M.S. Briton* aboard their canoes.' " Volume 19, Number 5 (May 1977).

Bomb Tests

Early in the 1960s the French government decided to detonate a series of atomic devices in the atmosphere above the Gambier

Islands a few hundred miles from Pitcairn. Suddenly the outside world, from which many Pitcairners thought they were quite isolated, seemed to be moving too close to the island. First mention of the decisions of the French regarding the tests came in a *Miscellany* editorial by Editor S. A. Kinder:

"Up to the present time Pitcairn has seemed far away from the great problems which have kept the world in a state of uncertainty and unrest for so many years. Although by means of radio we are able to follow world events from day to day, because we are so isolated, these happenings are little more than words to us.

"Now, however, even this small island of only two square miles, halfway between New Zealand and Panama, is suddenly confronted with the threat of a nuclear and guided missile testing ground being established by the French Government in the Gambier Group of islands, only 300 miles from here and just 250 miles from Oeno Island, to which we make trips from time to time.

"Mangareva, the island on which it is believed the testing ground will be established, is one which has had close association with Pitciarn in the years gone by. All the other islanders here have very happy memories of the days when the trading schooner ran between Mangareva and Pitcairn, and of visits they made to the people there.

"Now the 600-odd people of Mangareva and the surrounding islands are being threatened with the possibility of being uprooted from their island home—their home for generations, to make way for what is called the progress of science, while here on Pitcairn fears for our safety are being expressed because of the small distance which separates us from this proposed testing ground.

"To the south of Mangareva lies nothing but water until the Antarctic continent is reached. To the north and west there exists a vast extent of ocean over which any nuclear fallout which may be created can be dispersed, but should there be some unexpected change in weather conditions Pitcairn Island could be in an extremely dangerous position.

"We have asked the South Pacific Office, our administrative headquarters in Fiji, to express to the appropriate authorities our grave concern at the prospects of finding ourselves next door to a nuclear and missile testing ground. Only time will tell as to how much effect our plea might have." Volume 4, Number 10 (1st November 1962).

Despite the concern of the Pitcairners, the French developed their testing site on Muroroa Atoll in the Gambiers. The British provided Royal Air Force monitors to constantly test the atmosphere over Pitcairn for fallout during the testing season. Ships of the British navy were also assigned to the area of Pitcairn during each testing period so the islanders could be evacuated quickly should the RAF monitors detect any unusual levels of radioactivity. By 1970 the ominous booms of the exploding nuclear devices were being heard on Pitcairn:

"Two more bombs have been exploded during the last five weeks. The first was on Saturday 30th and the last one on 24th June. On both occasions the noise was heard from here. It resembled someone having a good bang at a set of drums, or rather like distant thunder. The time the sound takes to reach here from the testing area (approx. 600 miles) seems to vary from one to one and a half hours. In both cases we have been assured we are in no danger; so all is still well on Pitcairn." Volume 12, Number 6 (June 1970).

Bounty Day

"Bounty Day," January 23, is, along with the Queen's Birthday, New Year's Day and Anzac Day, one of the public holidays on Pitcairn. It was on January 23, 1790, that the mutineers burned H.M.S. *Bounty* just off Bounty Bay. The holiday features the burning of a small replica of the *Bounty*, games, and, of course, plenty of food.

"The 188th anniversary of the burning of H.M.S. *Bounty* took place on Monday 23rd January. The surf was running well and surfing and swimming were the main pleasure. Slices and slices of delicious watermelon were always available and was certainly welcome in the heat. *Bounty I* (a replica) was launched at about 5.30 p.m., but disaster soon struck: the none-too-stable structure was lifted by a large swell and capsized before she could be lit. (After some head scratching *Bounty II* was built and launched, and this proved to be a far more stable structure.) Soon she was blazing end to end and slowly sinking. The day ended with a dinner party at the jetty—the host being Dobrey, who, along with Andrew Cox, had the foresight to be born on Bounty Day. A grand feast brought another Bounty Day to a close." Volume 20, Number 1 (January 1978).

"Bounty" Relics

Although she was stripped of most of her supplies before she was burned on the southeastern bluff of Bounty Bay in 1790, hundreds of items went to the bottom when the *Bounty* sank.

Through the years divers had recovered axes, ballast bars, sheathing nails, and many other relics. In 1933 Parkin Christian recovered the *Bounty's* rudder from six fathoms of water. Unfortunately, most of the relics have been taken from the island, the main exceptions being the Bounty Bible, now in the Seventh-day Adventist Church; the ship's anchor, in the Public Square; and the ship's anvil. In 1973 a flurry of diving activity resulted in recovery of several important *Bounty* relics. *Miscellany* reported on the diving with two stories:

"The site of the remains of the *Bounty* is well known, and the skin-divers visit the locality from time to time. Occasionally they are rewarded by finding a few pieces of copper and a few nails. There has been heightened interest at the site recently, and a lot of energy has been expended. At least one well-preserved cannon ball was brought up early in the month, and then on the 25th the barrel of a small cannon was landed by Steve and his cronies. An immediate application of oil was made to prevent rusting. It was thrilling to see this cannon in such good condition after 183 years on the sea floor.

"As the month ended, Len had freed a still bigger cannon; and recovery of this cumbersome relic was almost complete. Next month we hope to record the story of the recovery of these two guns, their present appearance, and other relevant details." Volume 15, Number 6 (June 1973).

"Kay and Steve were diving over the resting place of the *Bounty* on 25th June, when they sighted a coral-encrusted shape they recognised as a cannon, lying among the many ballast blocks which litter the area of clear bottom. After an hour's chipping with the crowbar, the metal was exposed; and the cannon was levered from its position. Steve and Kay then took turns at diving down and carrying the cannon along the bottom until they were under their canoe. There a rope was tied around the relic; and, with Steve in the canoe and Kay in the water, the lifting was successfully accomplished.

"The cannon was brought ashore, and a coat of oil was applied to prevent rust. It is remarkably well-preserved after 183 years on the bottom. Five bands running round the muzzle can be clearly seen, as well as the Government arrow and the initials IH. The taper hole is clean, and there is almost no evidence of the effect of the long immersion in the sea.

"The cannon is 34 inches long and weighs an estimated 100 pounds. The muzzle is three and a half inches across; and the butt has a diameter of six and a half inches, while the diameter of the bore is one and three-quarter inches.

42

"A larger cannon was first sighted over 15 years ago at the time of Luis Marden's visit for National Geographic. On 28th June Len and Steve spent two hours chipping two to three inches of bottom growth from the top of the cannon, which was lying in a crack among the rocks in about 15 to 20 feet of water. The following day a rope was passed under the cannon by digging a small transverse trench, and a chain hoist was used to tie the rope end to two empty 44-gallon drums. The chain hoist was then tightened, but the cannon did not budge until after the crowbar was used for additional leverage. With first lift, Len, Steve, Noggie, Dave, and Kay freed the cannon; and at last it was suspended beneath the drums and held steady by an anchor on the seaward side. Unfortunately, the anchor pulled free; and the waves carried the drums into six feet of water. Four hours' work and the situation was worse.

"On July 1st a launch was taken out and anchored off the rocks. Steve, Donald, Len, Noggie, and Dave took turns in the water. Great care had to be exercised, because the cannon was now in the surf amidst rugged rocks. The drums were refastened, and a pulling rope was taken out to the launch. As the larger waves lifted the drums, the men in the launch heaved on the line; and slowly the cannon began to move into deeper water. The strain proved too much for the anchor ropes, and they parted. There was a scurry to get the engine started and thus keep the launch safe. With the anchors set, the process commenced again; and, in shifts of 12 to 15 inches, the cannon was edged along until it floated free.

"The cannon was pulled up to the launch and tied, suspended four feet under the launch, which listed considerably. Once alongside the jetty, the ropes were freed; and the cannon lay on the harbour bottom directly under the derrick. It was a relatively simple matter to lift the cannon with the derrick and place it on the tractor for the trip up to the village. Four hours were spent on this final recovery, and there had been no small danger in working the cannon free of the surf-swept rocks.

"This cannon weighs perhaps half a ton: it is 5 feet 11 inches in length, measures 8 inches at the muzzle and 12 inches at the butt, and has $3^1/_4$ inch bore. No small plaything." Volume 15, Number 7 (July 1973).

Canoes

"The seas were calm enough on about five occasions during the month for the men to go fishing in their canoes. These canoes are locally made from Island timber, are about 18 feet long, average about 30 inches wide, are very sturdily built, and are very heavy. They are housed in small boatsheds down at the Landing at Bounty Bay. These days, most, if not all, of the boats are equipped with outboard motors. Although the seas are generally very calm when they are in use, it is still possible to see some exciting sights when the canoes are returning to harbour at the end of a day's fishing. Occasionally they will be caught on a wave at the harbour's entrance and fairly fly into Bounty Bay; and, although sometimes they look as if they will end on the rocks at the shore's edge, generally the men manage to guide them in safely. Being built of very heavy timber, it is quite a job to haul the boats up onto the slipway and get them safely stowed away in the sheds. Generally it takes about eight men to accomplish this—one hauling a rope and the others heaving on the One, Two, Three, Heave Call. . . ." Volume 13, Number 3 (March 1971).

"The tally of canoes at the Landing has risen by two since the last issue of *Miscellany*, when reference was made to the fact that the new boats were under construction. The third canoe is not yet finished.

"Pitcairn depends on two types of vessels for providing access to the broad sea which provides so much for the inhabitants. Most important are the three diesel-powered, 38-foot launches which carry the men to visiting ships and, on occasion, as far away as Henderson and Oeno Islands. The other craft is the canoe used for fishing in the narrow belt of fishable waters surrounding the Island.

"As the reed canoes of Lake Titicaca and the Polynesian outrigger are unique to their localities, so the Pitcairn fishing canoe is unique in design and construction methods.

"The design of the fishing canoe is credited to Moses Young, grandson of Edward Young, who was one of the Island's original settlers. The techniques of construction have been passed on by succeeding generations, and the methods used today are probably little changed from those used by the original designer over 100 years ago.

"Present-day canoes are built under the guidance of Elwyn, who constructed his first canoe 45 years ago. The details for this article have been provided by him, and it is to Elwyn that most people turn when advice about boat construction is required.

"The commencement of canoe construction was heralded late last month by the buzz of power saws felling the chosen mango trees. When wood supplies were more plentiful, other varieties of trees were considered more suitable; but today the mango is one of the few trees of suitable size and longevity. The shape of the tree is of prime consideration in choosing which will be used, as the builder will have already decided on the length and width of canoe he wants.

"The logs are then hauled by tractor to a clearing beside the track, immediately above and behind the Square. Here the initial measuring up is done. These canoes were to be 18 feet long, with a beam of 30 inches and an overall depth of just over two feet.

"Each canoe was built in two halves running lengthwise, and the two logs to form the bottom of the canoe were shaped with the aid of a power saw. This was the first time the power saw had been used for this purpose; and there was unanimous agreement among the men that it was much faster and easier than shaping with axes, as has been done in the past. The two halves were then laid side by side, leveled, and held in position with blocks driven into the ground.

"After an experienced eye had decided on the best shape for the sides of the canoe, a start was made with the building up of the sides, bow, and stern. Suitably shaped pieces of wood about three or four inches through were sawn and patiently fitted to match the bottom log; then these were fastened in place with trunnels—carefully shaped wooden pegs about six inches long which fit into corresponding holes bored in the two planks. Piece by piece, the sides grew until even the most inexperienced eye could see the ultimate shape taking form.

"As the sides grew upward, they were shaped with a plane; and where the timber was too thick, the laborious task of 'dubbing' with an axe gradually whittled it down to the required thickness.

"When the sides, bow, and stern reached the predetermined height, the two halves were separated, cleaned up, and reassembled upside down. The bottom of the canoe was then shaped with an adze and the two halves screwed together with four-inch screws spaced four inches apart. The false keel and stem were then attached, and the canoe was fast moving toward completion.

"Tipped on its side, the canoe was then planed to smooth the sides before being placed in an upright position for the placing of the seats and other interior fittings.

"Finally, after caulking an puttying of all joints, the canoe was painted and made ready for its launching. A fine tribute to the skill and patience of her builders.

"Both of the new canoes handled well in the water. Jacob and

Jay rowed out of Bounty Bay, seated in the conventional method. Pervis, standing, and rowing with a single oar, went out to join them. After a short outing the new canoes were brought ashore, and the new owners expressed satisfaction with their new craft. Pervis had cause for double pleasure, as this is the first canoe of which he has been the sole owner." Volume 14, Number 5 (May 1972).

John Christian's Trip

Although a number of Pitcairners have made visits or gone off to live in New Zealand or Australia, few of the islanders have traveled to other parts of the world. Fewer still are those who have traveled extensively. In 1962 *Miscellany* reported on a trip taken by the island's Chief Magistrate:

"Our Chief Magistrate, John Christian, is back with us after his wonderful tour round the world as the guest of the Royal Rotterdam Lloyd Shipping Co., Ltd., in their liner *Willem Ruys*. As it lay off Pitcairn until 70 days later, when he returned to his Island home, John's time was full of great experiences. What tales he had to tell of the great generosity of his hosts, the many and varied sights he saw, the interesting people he met, and the keen interest in Pitcairn Island of all who met him.

"The shipping company had engaged as John's guide and agent, one of the servants, Anna Marie. From all we hear, Anna did an excellent job of looking after him; and he is most grateful for her very kind attention.

"Balboa, in the Panama Canal Zone, was the first stop; and here John realized what lay ahead of him. People eager to speak to him, press members anxious to interview him, and questions, questions, questions.

"A representative of the shipping company's agents took John on a tour of Balboa and Panama. He also called on the American Governor of the Panama Canal, with whom he had quite a long talk.

"Through the Panama Canal and on to Fort Lauderdale, Florida, where soon after arrival a party for John was held aboard *Willem Ruys*.

"To this were invited 80 guests, including press, broadcasting, and television personnel. Adults were not the only ones to be given the opportunity of meeting our Chief Magistrate, for a group of 48 school children were also entertained by the ship to enable them to meet our world tourist. I understand John nearly had writer's cramp though having to sign so many autograph books. Once again the ship's agent showed him around. On these car trips he was accompanied by Bill Rogers and the pastor of the local Seventh-day Adventist Church.

"From Fort Lauderdale it was only a few days before Bermuda was reached—and another round of exciting events, interviews, and tours.

"It was just as well for John that it was a week's run to England, as it gave him a chance to get back his breath.

"Because of trouble at the docks of Southampton, the ship was diverted to Plymouth. Here 17 members of the Dutch press, radio, and television joined *Willem Ruys* so they could travel with John to Rotterdam and thus have some good opportunities of talking with him.

"Finally on Saturday at 6 a.m., *Willem Ruys* berthed at Rotterdam. John attended services at the Seventh-day Adventist Church that day and was given a warm welcome.

"Sunday saw him at the zoo, then Monday brought with it more official engagements. He met Mr. Theo Ruys, manager of the Royal Rotterdam Shipping Co. Ltd., and then on to the Town Hall, where he was received by the Burgomaster. The following day he travelled by car to Amsterdam, where he was received by the Burgomaster of that city. A trip along some of the canals which run through the city was a fascinating experience. Wednesday was spent in sight-seeing round Rotterdam and included visits to a high observation tower, from which an excellent view of the rebuilt city is obtained. Then by car tunnel under the docks to view a lovely old windmill, and on to the shipyards, in which was built the ship in which he was travelling. Captain Howell, at one time a commander of *Willem Ruys*, entertained John on Thursday; and a day later Dr. Weisser, a former surgeon from the city, took him for a flight over Holland. Just from the way he said it, I am inclined to think John would like to have had one foot firmly on the ground.

"A week after arriving in Holland, our Pitcairn tourist was back at the Seventh-day Adventist Church, where he was given a very warm welcome. From the proceeds of a function held by the church members, he was presented with a lovely slide projector for himself and approximately 40 pounds in cash for the Pitcairn Island community.

"The next day, John, once more aboard *Willem Ruys*, sailed from Rotterdam on the long journey back to Pitcairn.

"Southampton was the first port of call. Here officials of the Colonial Office and the Seventh-day Adventist Church, and press, broadcast, and television representatives met John. He called on the mayor of the city, was taken to what had been the home of the Christian family in the days gone by, and to the famous ship H.M.S. *Victory*, in which Lord Horatio Nelson was killed at the Battle of Trafalgar in 1805.

"From now on it was much the same from port to port. Port Said, and Colombo, Panama each brought their press, broadcast, and television representatives aboard to interview our Chief Magistrate and tour round the sights.

"When the ship called at Melbourne, after the usual run of interviews, John had the new experience of flying over part of the city in a helicopter.

"Parkin's (Christian) son Richard was amongst the group which greeted the tourist in Sydney. John stayed the night with Richard; and I believe they hardly had time to stop for meals, there was so much to talk about. Calls were made on the Lord Mayor, the Adventist Mission Centre, and the British Petroleum Ltd's tanker *British Mallard*. Chips Rafferty, the Australian movie star who is taking a leading part in the newly produced film 'Mutiny on the Bounty,' was also met.

"Wellington, the last call before home, saw the Pitcairn Island community out in force. John stayed the night with his sister Elsa, and what a time all present must have had, for he is still trying to get his coloured slides back in order. There was the last round of interviews and official calls, and then he started on the last stage of his world tour.

"It was a blustery Saturday afternoon when *Willem Ruys* arrived off Pitcairn. What a change; no press, broadcast, or television representatives, no official receptions, but a warm welcome from his own people.

" 'What was it like, John?' 'What's it like to be home, John?' These and dozens of other questions have been asked of our tourist; and in reply he has said just as many times, 'Wonderful, but it's good to be home. The Royal Rotterdam Lloyd Shipping Company has given me a marvellous time, and I am most grateful for all it has done for me. Holland is a fine place, but for me Pitcairn is still the best.' " Volume 4, Number 7 (July 1962).

Christmas

In a world gone slightly mad in the commercialization of Christmas, Pitcairn is a stark exception. Generally there are no advance notices or announcements of the coming holiday, and Christmas trees are never put up in private homes. Even the island's Southern Hemisphere weather, which may reach into the 80s on Christmas Day, seems to cooperate in deemphasizing the occasion. If Christmas falls on a Saturday, the Pitcairners postpone it until the following day, since they will not mix a holiday with their religious day of rest. Christmas gifts may be simple in the extreme—a piece of lead to serve as a sinker on a fishing line, a carving of Miro wood, some of the delicious pineapples, grapefruit, or oranges from the island. Gifts from the outside world must be ordered many months in advance, perhaps as early as May or June. If a ship is unavoidably delayed, some Christmas gifts may not show up until early or mid January.

On Christmas eve the Pitcairn children hang pandanus baskets on the front porches of their homes, since none of the island houses have fireplaces. With baskets filled with cookies, pineapples or other fruits, candies, trinkets, and balloons, the older Pitcairners tiptoe up to the homes in the dark and deposit goodies in each basket. Christmas day finds the entire community publicly exchanging other gifts at a special ceremony held in the Public Square. In 1961 and again in 1965, *Miscellany* used two of many reports on Christmas on the island.

"Owing to the serious flu epidemic, which put most of the islanders in bed, Christmas Day was postponed until the 31st. This meant that Santa had to stay in hiding for a longer period, but when he did arrive at 5 p.m. on the 31st he looked none the worse for the inconvenience caused.

"6:30 (Christmas morning) saw the members of the Entertainment Committee armed with axes, struggling up Jack's Yam in search of trees. The first tree cut was too big to fit in the Square, and despite Pastor's protests it was left where it fell. By 1 p.m. all trees were in place and at 4 p.m. the bell went for the decorating and placing of presents. Santa arrived at 5 p.m. and distributed gifts and balloons to all the children. This was followed until about 7 p.m. with the giving out of the gifts by the 10 callers.

"Christmas 1961 passed in a blaze of glory, leaving only a vivid memory of the happy spirits which existed, and of the unqualified beauty of the trees as they drooped under the burden of thousands of gifts, fruits, sweets, balloons, and decorations." Volume 3, Number 12 (December 1961).

"Pitcairn Island celebrated Christmas in its own unique way on Sunday, 26th December, with community Christmas trees in the square. A few of the menfolk, assisted by many children, spent part of the morning finding and then placing in the square several jesse bushes, which are the traditional Christmas tree here. Around 4 p.m. a bell was rung as a signal for all to bring their presents and hang them up for distribution later. When

49

everyone was assembled, half a dozen Father Christmases began the enjoyable task of present distribution. By the time everything had been shared and thanks exchanged it was time to take home all that had so generously been given.

"A film show after the evening meal completed a pleasant day." Volume 7, Number 12 (December 1965).

The Church

When the 35-cent stamps of the fifth definitive Pitcairn Island stamp issue in 1977 depicted the island's Seventh-day Adventist Church, it gave occasion for *Miscellany* to provide a background article by the Church's pastor, Wallace R. Ferguson:

"Most people who have heard of Pitcairn Island know that the religion of the Island is Seventh-day Adventist but are not aware of how it became such and when. Firstly, members of the Adventist Church around the world and on Pitcairn Island are made up of adult people. To become a member of the Adventist church, one needs to be baptised; that is, immersed in water, and this is granted only to a person who can make the choice. In other words, infant baptism on Pitcairn is unheard of.

"The Services of the Church on Pitcairn comprise four main phases. There is Sabbath School (this is divided up into a children's division and an adult division); there is the Divine Service, and this follows the Sabbath School at 11:15 a.m. Saturday morning. In the afternoon of the Sabbath, the Missionary Volunteer programme is held. Then, of course, there is the Tuesday prayer meeting at 7 p.m.; a part of this midweek service is the usual Faith For Today half-hour 16mm movie. Both black and white and colour movies are shown at this time, and the programme is enjoyed immensely by the attendants.

"Generally speaking, Friday (preparation day) is occupied by the folk in cleaning and cooking. Most times the Sabbath (Saturday) programme goes on without interruption. However, now and again ships call in on this day; and the programme is altered to suit. There are not many ships these days, and for a ship to call on Sabbath means the forgoing of carving sales for most people on the Island. You see, the economy of the Island is dependent on two things—the sale of the colourful and much-desired Island stamps, and the carvings from the famed Miro and Tau wood.

"Seventh-day Adventists around the world are a very missionary-minded people; but on Pitcairn this phase of life can be missing altogether, though some work is done on passing ships.

50

"The Adventist Church on Pitcairn Island is cared for by the expatriate Pastor, who is appointed for two years. His immediate superior is located a little over 3000 miles away in Auckland, New Zealand, and is the President of the Central Pacific Union Mission, which cares for most of the Polynesian Islands. Pitcairn comes under his jurisdiction, though he does not visit lonely and faraway Pitcairn very often.

". . . From the time the Bounty came to Pitcairn in 1790 and up to 1886, the people of Pitcairn had been Church of England in religion; but in 1876 a box of religious literature was sent by the Seventh-day Adventists in America. Not much was done in the next few years; but in 1886, 12 years after J. I. Tay, a sailor, had accepted the Adventist Church teachings, this very missionary-minded sailor found his way to Pitcairn. Quickly he learned to know the people and began Bible studies in the homes and later in the church. On October 30, 1886, the Island people kept their first seventh-day Sabbath; the report which John I. Tay took back to America caused great rejoicing. Then in 1887 the General Conference of Seventh-day Adventists decided to send a minister called Elder Cudney to Pitcairn with John I. Tay to baptise the people and organise the church there.

"A schooner called the Poebe Chapman was bought and refitted, and with Elder Cudney in charge it set sail but was never heard from again. Then in 1890 the General Conference ordered a schooner to be built. It was called the Pitcairn, and most of the money needed to build this vessel was raised by Sabbath Schools. The company which built the vessel deducted quite a sum from costs, three publishing houses in the United States gave a large number of books for sale, and a 'full set of flags was donated to the ship.'

"The first of six cruises made by this little missionary ship took place in late 1890. The Pitcairn was captained by Mr. J. M. Marsh, and various others helped. The missionaries aboard were E. H. Gates, A. J. Read, J. I. Tay, and their wives. Pitcairn Island was reached on November 25, 1890. At the baptism which took place, 82 people were baptised; and the first Seventh-day Adventist Church on Pitcairn was organised.

"It was in Fiji that John I. Tay chose to labour. He died there on 8 January 1892, aged 60 years. The vision of his missionary endeavour had been realised. He had seen Pitcairn and had brought to it and other islands a knowledge of the faith he loved.

"After the visit of John I. Tay about 100 years ago, Pitcairn turned over another leaf in her romantic history. When the people of Pitcairn became Seventh-day Adventists, they wondered how the British people might react to their change in faith; and with a little trepidation they awaited the arrival of the next ship. But they need not have worried; for when the next ship called and the people on it learned of the new faith, there was no difference in attitude.

"In the early days of Adventism on this Island, camp meetings were held up at 'Flatland.' The folk built temporary quarters there and strengthened their attachment to God. One of the visitors in the 1920s was Pastor Robert Hare, who led the islanders in one of these camp meetings. To hear Pastor Hare spoken of with such Christian love brings back memories of 1942, when the same Pastor Hare, now an old minister and retired, was invited to Avondale College, Australia to lead out in spiritual matters. The writer had the privilege of his Bible teaching for three months, and has not forgotten it.

"But back to Pitcairn Island. Rosalind Young, a Pitcairner and the writer of a very informative book on Pitcairn, spent a number of years teaching the children on the island. The church took on this added responsibility of running a school, but during the last 28 years the education of the children has been in the hands of the Government, so every two years a teacher has been appointed by the New Zealand Administration. Likewise, the church pastor has been appointed every two years, and his wife has been the medical officer; this has been an agreement for some time." Volume 19, Numbers 9, 10, and 11 (September-November 1977).

"Church News. The studies given on the great personalities of the Bible in our Tuesday night meetings have proved very interesting indeed. We have had the privilege of hearing different ones (of the islanders) reveal the characters and experiences of their favourite Bible personality, and it has brought inspiration and encouragement to us.

"It is wonderful to know that our God can take men with all their weaknesses and sinful tendencies and by His divine grace and power transform them. Paul reminds us in Hebrews 11:39, 40, 'And these all . . . received not the promise: God having provided some better thing for us, that they without us should not be made perfect.'

"The sermon in shoes
Is the sermon to choose,
That's practised in life
every day

'Tis the message that men
Will give heed to, and then
Will follow, because it's
   the way."

Volume 1, Number 6 (June 1959).

"Church News. By Pastor W. G. Ferris—The church building on Pitcairn has had a little face-lift during the month, and I am sure that all the members appreciate the difference it makes. The seats were all revarnished and so were all the front fittings. I think the interior of the Church now looks very attractive. Mr. (Eric) Were (a visiting photographer-artist) has painted a beautiful picture of Pitcairn to hang behind the pulpit, and it has the text, 'The Lord is my Rock and my Fortress.' We appreciate this gift to the Church and also a lovely Sabbath School chart which he painted, showing a little ship taking help to the needy of old Palestine from the children of Pitcairn.

"All appreciate the stronger lights in the Church, and we thank Warren for allowing us to connect with his more powerful engine. So now we can show 'Faith For Today' films and film strips. Thanks too must be mentioned to the folk who have provided light so willingly in the past." Volume 5, Number 8 (August 1963).

"Church News. The day was perfect for a small but impressive baptism at the end of this month. Bounty Bay witnessed many scenes of interest, but this one held the greatest interest for the angels of heaven. Reynold Warren and Noggie Young indicated their intention to follow the Lord, come what may, by being baptised.

"I was discussing the weather with a few men on the verandah of the courthouse last evening before Council meeting, when Oscar suddenly said, 'It's going to rain next week.'

" 'Why, Oscar,' I said, 'I didn't know you were a prophet. How do you know?'

" 'Well,' he said, 'next week is Week of Prayer, and it always rains during Week of Prayer.'

"Week of Prayer is from the 8th to the 15th—we hope it doesn't rain too much. Pastor L. A. J. Webster." Volume 9, Number 4 (April 1967).

"This year Ben and Irma are having a well-earned rest from leadership in the Pathfinder Club (a Seventh-day Adventist youth organization similar to Boy or Girl Scouts), having led out in this activity for the past two years. Pastor and his wife, along with five willing counsellors, are endeavouring to keep 26 lively boys and girls interested in the aims and ideals of Pathfinder activities for the first six months of the year. . . .

"One even ot interest so far this year was the part the Pathfinders played aboard M.S. *Sagafjord*. Indeed, the Pathfinders, cheerful and attentive in their bright green uniforms, captured the attention of all. If the number of clicking cameras was any indication, they were the star performers of the day.

"Promptly at 3:30 p.m., they appeared on the verandah deck. Some 400 spectators ranged around, many looking from the promenade deck above. Then, to the beat of the drum, down the deck they marched singing lustily, 'For We Are the Pathfinders Strong.' Following were recitations, marching, and more songs; and everybody gave hearty applause to every item.

"If you were to look in today at one of the regular fortnightly meetings, you would find a group of boys and girls very much interested in their respective hobby work. The boys are so determined to finish their 'Acrobat Man and Solitaire Board' that it is hard to get them to stop when time is up for that section of the programme. . . .

"Over the last few months the following Missionary Volunteer honours have been gained: Intermediate Swimming, 3; Weather, 2; Dogs, 5; Bookkeeping, 2; Beginners Swimming, 18; Communications, 2; Trees, 1. We congratulate the various members who worked so hard to qualify for these tokens. . . ." Volume 9, Number 3 (March 1967).

"Pathfinder Concert: On the 30th the Pathfinders entertained members of the public with a concert held in the Courthouse. A wide variety of items were presented, but the major production of the evening was provided by a play in eight scenes based on the events in the life of Joseph Bates (an early Seventh-day Adventist leader).

"If there had been any TV talent scouts about, we feel sure that they would have offered Jimmy an audition after his portrayal of the mother of three errant teenage sons." Volume 14, Number 12 (December 1972).

"We don't know when Pitcairn last heard such serenading, but it was a joy to hear the singing following Young People's meeting on the 24th. A large group moved around the village, singing hymns outside the homes of those whose health would not allow them to attend church. This brought pleasure to the older folk, and the young people are to be commended for this thoughtful action." Volume 15, Number 11 (November 1973).

"As many readers of *Miscellany* will know, the Week of Prayer meetings are a central feature in Seventh-day Adventist Churches the whole world round each year.

"A booklet of special 'readings' for seniors and for young folks is prepared each year.

"On Pitcairn, the week began with a Family night in the church on Friday night the 18th of October. This was a date of special significance to Pitcairn, because it was exactly 88 years ago that in the early morning, the ship *Pelican* arrived off the Island. Erelong, two boats with a number of the Island men came alongside. The *Pelican* was a British warship bound from Tahiti to distant shores via Pitcairn. When the Captain told the Islanders that he had a passenger on board who wished to stay with them, he was told that there was a law that forbade strangers staying on shore. . . . However, Tay, the passenger, soon won the interest of some of the fathers of the community, when it was discovered that he represented the people who, ten years before, had sent Seventh-day Adventist literature with their old friend Captain Knowles.'

"It was an auspicious anniversary on which to begin the 1974 Week of Prayer. From Sunday till Friday, meetings were held in the Church each night . . . , and each morning, three meetings were held in various homes on the Island. What these lovely 'get-togethers' for prayer and Bible Study meant to one and all who took part in them, as most on the Island did!

"Not the least interesting was the morning when Christy Warren brought a silver jug with a golden apple in it. Your guess as to what he talked about that morning before all enjoyed a season of prayer? You're right, "A word fitly spoken is like apples of gold in pitchers of silver."

"Another anniversary also occurred during the week, and it was duly and specially noted. On October 22nd it was 130 years, Adventists truly believe, since Christ began His High Priestly ministry in the sanctuary of heaven. Pitcairners prayed that that wonderful ministry might soon end with the personal coming of Jesus to earth once again. They pray that in that day all Pitcairners, wherever they may be found, and all who love His appearing, will be ready for 'Sail-Ho' . . . and the last 'Five Bells.' John J. Dever, The Pastor." Volume 16, Number 4 (October 1974).

"Attendance at Tuesday evening prayer meetings has been very good. However, it was anticipated that following the power-plant catastrophe (fire destroyed the engine, power shed, and generation plant), night meetings with kerosene lamps wouldn't be the same. I cleaned the two lamp glasses and put the lamps in position ready for the evening meeting; but Mavis and

Jacob, with technical assistance from Oscar and Jay, made the using of the lamps unnecessary. Each Tuesday evening we have light and power supplied from Jacob's home lighting unit. A big thank you to all concerned.

"At a recent church business meeting it was decided to proceed with fund raising to build a new room at the rear of the church to provide accommodation for the children's division of the Sabbath School. At present the children meet in the public hall; and this is far from being ideal, both for children and teachers. Each week the room has to be set up, and then all aids have to be removed away and stored for another week. A ship's captain gave us a good donation to the fund, and this was much appreciated. I hope that before my term of service closes on Pitcairn, the new Sabbath School room will be a reality.

"When the longboats came back to Bounty Bay heavily laden with passengers from *Yankee Trader* after the initial contact on Tuesday 19 April, many mysterious boxes came ashore. I said to somebody, 'I wonder what's inside those boxes.' It was not long before the contents of the boxes were known; clothing, material, toys, and as well a hand Singer sewing machine—all gifts from (Seventh-day Adventist) Dorcas Societies in Michigan, U.S.A.

"It was not planned to have a 'Share Out' until later; but, on going up to the back room of the church Thursday morning 21 April, we saw so many cartons (and about four of them had got wet; fortunately nothing was spoiled) we decided that a 'Share Out' be made that day. While Dennis and I worked on the guttering of the Cooperative store, we saw many folk going to and fro with boxes of goods. When our job was finished, a little after 5 p.m., I decided to go into the Courthouse and see for myself. Well, there was only one word for what I saw. WOW! The womenfolk were opening boxes and sharing out as fairly as possible. Not one person on the Island was left out; even the newly born baby, Darlene, got her share.

"I guess the Dorcas Societies of Michigan have been quite busy getting ready for this gift; I have just been through the 21 letters found in these boxes—one was dated May 4, 1975. So no doubt the preparations have gone on for some time.

"Well, the 'Share Out' came as a surprise, a thrill to many folk. Thank you, brothers and sisters of Michigan. I am sure that if you could have seen the joy on the faces of the recipients you would have thought it well worthwhile. Apart from the literal gifts, the knowledge that there are people who care helped the Pitcairn mind. Might I say thank you for your kindness and thoughtfulness, Michigan. Yours sincerely in service of Christ,

56

Wallace R. Ferguson, Island Pastor." Volume 19, Number 4 (April 1977).

Coat of Arms

"By Pastor Ferris, ex-Pastor of Pitcairn Island—Here on Pitcairn Island we love the Union Jack and are very happy to be classed as one of the fortunate countries to come under the rulership of Her Gracious Majesty, Queen Elizabeth II. Pitcairn is a little colony, but it is one just the same! With apologies to Canada I use their flag poem:

> I'm proud of Pitcairn!
> Is Pitcairn proud of me?
> What she wants are citizens
> Loyal as can be.
> I love my island and Britain's Flag
> that waves from sea to sea.
> O, I am proud of Home and Motherland
> and I'll make them proud of me.

"Each country in the Commonwealth has a distinctive badge or Coat of Arms to represent it on its Flag or on official papers. This Coat of Arms is placed in the centre of either the blue or red portion of the flag. This badge is also used on official documents and is recognized as the mark of authority. A Coat of Arms has finally been prepared for the Colony of Pitcairn, and the Council has seen it and accepted it. When signed by our Governor and registered in London, it will be available for use by the Government and people of Pitcairn. It will then be placed on our own blue and red Ensigns and proudly flown. It is a very beautiful Coat of Arms and is decidedly Pitcairn in every way.

"It will not be possible for the Coat of Arms to be made available until the preparation of the Royal Warrant and Registration in London. We do appreciate what has been accomplished thus far, and we sincerely hope that many proud sons and daughters of Pitcairn will return to live here and enjoy the wonderful privileges that this badge really represents.

"(Note: In the last mail received from Suva [Fiji] we received a supply of colour prints of Pitcairn's Coat of Arms. It is very attractive and colourful and features the Bounty Bible, Bounty Anchor, Pitcairn wheelbarrow, and a slip of Miro leaves and flower—Editor.)" Volume 12, Number 5 (May 1970).

Cooperative Store

As the reliance of the Pitcairners on goods and supplies not found on the island increased in recent years, individuals found it ever more difficult to place orders and have supplies shipped from Auckland, London, or Panama in the limited quantity desired by a single person or family. And so the development of Pitcairn's Cooperative Store in the late 1960's met a special need. A decade after the store's founding, *Miscellany* gave a history and progress report:

"Is there a real need for a Cooperative on Pitcairn? What business can we expect to get from each member? Will we have difficulty in getting stocks for our store? Will we have enough capital?

"These were some of the questions which were being discussed on the Island ten years ago as F. E. M. Warner (then Assistant Commissioner to Pitcairn) placed before the community the advantages of having a Cooperative store on the Island.

"Reporting on this historical event, Mr. Bert Reeves (then Government Adviser to the Island) mentioned how initial response to this concept by the local people was not enthusiastic; but, after much dialogue subscriptions to get the Cooperative 'off the ground' flowed in freely.

"At its first meeting on Monday, April 24, the first Cooperative Society Committee, consisting of: Pastor L. Webster (chairman), the late Mrs. V. McCoy (Treasurer), Mr. A. A. Reeves (Secretary), and Mrs. T. Brown and Mr. C. Christian (committee), discussed ordering of stock and suitable sites for the Cooperative store. A piece of land was acquired from the late Mrs. Vi McCoy for the princely sum of one shilling. Owing to the unavailability of a building to commence business when stores eventually began to reach the Island, it was agreed to use the art room at Pulau school; and the doors for the first bit of shopping on Pitcairn were opened on July 9, 1967. It was reported that 90 percent of the community turned out for the big occasion; and in a space of two hours, $210 was taken; and, what is more, . . . 'the carefully prepared shelves were almost entirely depleted of stock. One more two-hour trading period the following Thursday soon sold off the remaining goods, and the executives met immediately to make out an order for replacement.'

"Then in October, 1967, the first blocks of the new building were laid; and it wasn't until 23 June 1969 that the store was officially opened for business, following a simple ceremony. Owing to expanding business, a storeroom was added to the existing store in April 1973.

"And what of the Cooperative store today? Irma Christian, as a hard-working officer of the Society, offers the following remarks:

58

"Spiraling prices, difficulty in acquiring goods, and uncertainty with shipping have been the biggest handicaps of our Cooperative store. We too are dragged along with the rest of the world as they battle with that mysterious fiend called inflation.

"Because of our isolation and local conditions, it is rather difficult to successfully run a Cooperative store in a manner which combines acceptable service and financial returns with a profit. Here we have no room for expansion or increase in financial returns apart from increasing prices. The latter part of 1976 has seen an upsurge in business because of the extra income derived from the recently completed Harbour project.

"Mr. Livingstone of the British Consulate-General in Auckland is an important link between our Society and suppliers, by way of placing orders for us and paying our accounts from our funds on deposit with the British Consulate-General. This has enabled us to maintain good financial relationships with our suppliers, and we are ever so grateful to Mr. Livingstone for his help." Volume 19, Number 4 (April 1977).

Cricket

In earlier days, before the population decline set in, cricket matches on Pitcairn were day-long affairs, played in a full-throttle manner that few but the British would understand. Now the matches are usually half-day affairs generally played on public holidays and sometimes interrupted by the five strokes of the bell announcing the arrival of a ship:

"Cricket. The teams were named on the notice board; the date for the match was set, October 17th; and the gauntlet had been thrown and accepted. The day before the match Noggie and Donald and some others took the tractor up to Outer Valley and dozed a wicket; they also used the wheeled tractor to knock down some of the cow-grass and lantana on the infield.

"On the day of the match . . . a ship turned up! However, it wasn't too bad, because it was only the *Townsville Star* dropping dunnage, and merely meant a slight delay in starting time. While the men went out to the ship, the women unrolled the coconut matting on the wicket and made a start with a game. Some good batting was seen and some terrible bowling! The game was rather spoiled by the early return of the men, who decided they needed to eat before they could start to play. Naturally, the women had to stop their game so the men could eat.

"About 18 slices of pumpkin pie later, the game proper began.

59

Both teams lost early wickets, and it was the middle and lower order batsmen who raised the score to some level of respectability. Reynold (26 runs) and Steve (20 runs) were top scorers. The Blue team, captained and coached by Len, made 86 runs in a cliffhanger finish. The fact that only 15 people batted for the Blue team, while the White team had 23 batsmen, may have had some influence on the final result; but to be fair to all it must be pointed out that eight of the White team did not score any runs. To one way of thinking that makes the sides even, doesn't it? Well, doesn't it?

"Let's have no more bloodletting. It was a very enjoyable game." Volume 15, Number 10 (October 1973).

Death

One writer has stated that on Pitcairn "The island-born today are far more interested in their heavenly future than in their *Bounty* past." There is considerable truth in the statement. That they are interested in their heavenly future, though, does not keep the Pitcairner from expressing a genuine sense of loss, however shortlived it might be, when a fellow islander dies. The services so readily available to the outside world, such as embalming, are not available on Pitcairn; so the delay between death and burial that might be expected elsewhere just does not happen on Pitcairn; burial usually takes place the same day, or almost certainly the day following death.

The *Miscellany* has carefully marked the fall of every Pitcairner. The paper's columns have recorded, among others, the deaths of Lila Young, Fred and Flora Christian, Melville Christian, Fred Brown, and Violet and Floyd McCoy. In 1963 the island newspaper spoke for the entire community in expressing sorrow at the death of President John F. Kennedy. And in 1965, *Miscellany* noted that "The flags at Pulau were immediately set to half mast, and a message of condolence cabled to Lady Churchill by the Island Magistrate on behalf of the Council and people," when the great British leader died. A Memorial Service for Sir Winston Churchill was also conducted by the island Pastor at the worship hour at 11:15 a.m., Saturday, January 30, 1965.

Miscellany sometimes used extended reports on better-known Pitcairners who had died:

"George Francis Christopher Warren died at 1 p.m. on September 2nd, 1959, at the age of 82 years. George Warren was born in 1877, the son of Samuel James Warren and Agnes Warren, on Pitcairn Island. His mother was the daughter of

Thursday October Christian and the granddaughter of Fletcher; and she married Samuel Warren, an American sailor from a whaling ship, while on Norfolk Island. They were among the second group of Pitcairners to return to their Island home from Norfolk on board the *St. Kilda* in 1864.

"George Warren attended school on Pitcairn and was taught by Simon and Rosalind Young and later by Hattie Andre, and although he was never fond of school, yet he did have a liking for arithmetic, and this was to stand him in good stead in his later study of navigation. He also attended some night classes by Elder Gates.

"In 1897 he married Lillian Butler, and the ceremony was held in the old Courthouse. Alfred Young, the Chief Magistrate, officiated.

"When Captain G. F. Jones brought the 38-foot sailing ship *Pitcairn* to the island, George Warren was chosen to study navigation and was the only successful student to pass and receive his papers from the British Consul in Tahiti. He was in charge of this ship for two and a half years; and during that time he made quite a few trips to Mangareva, taking produce from Pitcairn for trade. This ship was later sunk while in charge of others about eight and a half miles offshore.

"It was decided to build another ship on the island; so the *Messenger* was begun. This was a 45-foot-long boat made of Island timber and took one year to complete. George Warren was made the skipper; and he was responsible for the *Messenger* for two and a half years, during which time he sailed it to Tahiti to the Seventh-day Adventist mission headquarters to offer the vessel for mission service in the South Pacific. However, it was found not suitable for the purpose; so back they sailed to Pitcairn, where it was used for trading purposes with Mangareva.

"George also held the position of Govt. Assessor for a time. His long experience with boats proved in later years to be a real help and benefit to the Islanders.

"He attended the first Sabbath services conducted by missionary John Tay and was baptised in the first baptism ever to be held on Pitcairn. This was when the missionary ship *Pitcairn* arrived from America. His passing severs a link with the past. . . ." Volume 1, Number 6 (30 September 1959).

"Wednesday, 29th December. Tragedy struck Pitcairn swiftly as Eric Young died accidentally when rock fell on him at Whiterocks, on the Edge to Landing track. Eric, while helping Pervis, Jimmy, and Pastor gather gravel for the floor of the new mission engine house, sheltered from the rain for a moment under a ledge and was struck by a quantity of whiterock which subsided without warning, thus causing his instantaneous death."

"The two-then-one-ring series, repeated, told the Island something was wrong; but all were greatly distressed at the suddenness and finality of this particular disaster.

"After a service at the Church on Thursday, 30th December at 12 noon, Eric Young was laid to rest in the Pitcairn Island Cemetery. Pastor L. A. J. Webster conducted the church service, and Church Elder Pervis Young officiated for the majority at the graveside ceremony." Volume 7, Number 12 (1965).

"On the 15th of September news was received from New Zealand of the death, in his 88th year, of Parkin Christian. Having suffered indifferent health for the past few years, Parkin departed for New Zealand for medical reasons in May 1970, accompanied by his granddaughter Marona and her husband Pervis and two children.

"During his lifetime Parkin was an active member of the community. When only 17, he was sailing as a crew member on French trading ships plying between Tahiti and neighbouring islands. He also sailed aboard two locally owned sailing ships which traded between Pitcairn and Mangareva, some 280 miles away (in the French Gambier group), early in the century.

"In 1933 Parkin discovered the rudder of H.M.S. *Bounty* in Bounty Bay, which was later recovered and after remaining on Pitcairn was finally sent to the Museum in Suva, Fiji, for safekeeping, where it still remains. He served a term of office as Island Magistrate from 1956-57. . . .

"PARKIN CHRISTIAN—A MAN OF THE SEA. By Roy P. Clark. From the years of his youth to the present, Parkin Christian has exerted his influence upon the other islanders. The strength of his character betrays itself in the strong Polynesian features of his browned face, and the strong, hard body towering six feet in height. He is a man subject to reverses in temperament as quick as a sentence can be spoken and exchanged. From a flash of anger and scorn to an ever-captivating, irresistible smile, the change is instantaneous and complete—and any passion of huffiness in his speech is forgotten immediately. His personality draws an individual unto himself with a charm amazing to behold.

"His religious faith is sturdy and shows itself in his willingness to lend aid to those in need of it—whether it be sawing lumber, building a house, shaping a canoe from hewn logs, or the giving of his time and means to the public welfare, even when not required to do so. The widow, the 'stranger at his gate,' the islander he has known since childhood—all have at one time or another had cause to feel his compassion.

"The sea is in his blood, and its call has made of him a natural seaman with an uncanny intuition for predicting weather conditions and navigating among these islands. There is a confidence in Parkin's judgment greater than in the chart or compass, whatever the distance from land. Many the time have I seen him defy the laws of navigation; and those who command our longboats have learned, sometimes through bitter experience, to heed his advice—even though it disagrees with chart and compass. Quiet and unassuming, he tells of sea experiences of the past, as he lounges with seeming indifference in the stern of the boat; but his eyes miss nothing of his surroundings. He sees the set of the sail and jib, the colouring of the sky, the shifting of the wind, the clouds above and out on the horizon, and the pitch of the boat as it makes five or six knots in a good steady wind or a barely perceptible headway in a light breeze.

"There have been a few times when the course for Oeno or Henderson has been given by the captains of the boats as they left Bounty Bay, and steadily kept until the mileage for the island has been run; yet land was not sighted, and the boats have had to give up their search for it and return to Pitcairn. But this has not been so when Parkin was amongst the crew making the trip.

"I recall one of the many times I have sailed with Parkin to Oeno Island as proof of his intuitive judgment at sea. Someone of the crew calls out to the coxswain, 'How we headin', Charles?' The coxswain looks intently at his compass box and calls back, 'Northwest by north, and headin' right for land.' Parkin lifts his body from its reclining position and looks seaward—first to windward and then to the lee of the boat. He scans the sea in all directions for a minute or two—looks up at the sails, and then again at the sea astern of the longboat. His decision has been made. He speaks, 'Wal now, I don't care what yawli tul (all of you), and I ain't going' by that no-use compass either; and believe me if you like, for land is nomusa (not nearly) out ahead. Yawli look where I'm pointin'. I'll bet land's there,' and he points a little to windward—his arm strong and steady, his eyes ablaze with certainty. Then again he settles down to his former position in the stern of the boat to doze off to sleep or continue his story telling. Two or three hours pass by, then the man on the lookout calls 'land ahead!' The course has been changed according to the pointing of Parkin's finger. He rises unconcernedly from his uncomfortable resting place and sees the distant land. With pleased satisfaction he remarks, 'There, I told you so. If we only follow that good-for-nothing compass we would be dead as a hatchet.' (From some reason, on Pitcairn a hatchet is considered a more likely comparison than a doornail.)

"Over and over have I witnessed such compassless navigation—and his predictions and directions have been thrilling, uncanny, and almost supernatural. To my knowledge they have never failed, and I should know as well as anyone, for I have sailed with Parkin as shipmate for fifty years." Volume 13, Number 9 (September 1971).

"It was with a deep sense of shock that we heard last Sunday that Anderson Gilbert Warren had passed away peacefully in his sleep in Wellington, New Zealand. We here on Pitcairn knew that Anderson, or 'Tonic,' as he was affectionately called, was not a well man; but we were of the impression that he was on the road to recovery, and that he may even soon be trying to find a ship to bring him home.

"I asked three Pitcairners who knew him well to write a few lines about him in his different capacities—as a man—as a workmate—and as member of the Church—Editor.

"THE MAN I KNEW. By Warren C. Christian. We were children growing up together with two years' difference in our ages. As little boys we were at school at the same time and studied the same lessons, at first under our local teachers. Then in 1928 came our first teacher from New Zealand, Luther Hare, who taught us physical exercises, which we particularly enjoyed.

"We were rascals together also, as youngsters will be, and then as young men we worked together and in 1934 learned the Morse Code and semaphore as a means of communication while in the boats or on land, and were also able to 'Moss' passing ships, as we didn't have radio communications in those days. I remember one night when Anderson and some of the other boys went to 'Flatrock' (to 'Ruma') night-fishing. They came home along the cliff around 'Goathouse' with their flashlights held high, resembling a ship coming around Matt's Rock. When the lights were sighted, the village came alive as the ship bell was rung and the men rushed off to the Landing to launch the boats to go out and meet the ship! Yes, he was a man of humor and could always take a practical joke for what it was worth.

"We were crew and sailed together in the same longboat for many years; and, as we approached Bounty Bay at night, it was always good to hear him call, 'Port,' 'Starboard,' 'Steady.'

"Anderson was an exceptionally good gardener, carpenter, a real fisherman, and one of the master wood-carvers—a man who will be greatly missed by our community.

"TONIC—MY WORKMATE. By Tom Christian. On July 1st, 1957, Anderson and I started working together—he having learnt the Morse Code in his youth, practising with flashlights and whistles (made from Papaya leaf stalk) and anything else that would signal the 'Code.' He operated the Radio station with Andrew for a year or so prior to my takeover in 1955.

"Daily for more than eighteen years, rain or sunshine, we would trudge up and down the track to 'Taro Ground,' enjoying each other's company. Nearly always he would be sanding a wood carving while we walked and talked. We would spend approximately two hours at the Radio station, training and studying, so that he would be able to take over should the need ever arise.

"Anderson was 19 years my senior, but he was eager to learn all he could. He was very enthusiastic, and within two weeks was a proficient meteorological weather observer. He did well in learning radio theory, and took only a few instructions to become a good radio operator using the Morse Code and key.

"He was a hard-working man, always making sure he had sufficient in the garden and elsewhere to support his family and others. He was an expert wood-carver, and must have made thousands of carvings in his time.

"On February 27th I developed signs of acute appendicitis. Anderson made the call for a doctor, and though it was four days before a ship came to take me to hospital in New Zealand, Anderson took over from then on, and though he was worried, he efficiently kept the Station in operation until I came back in October 1960.

"In 1964 when I became ill and had to stay at the Station in bed for two weeks, Anderson with his family hurried home from New Zealand to assist. He took over in 1967 with the aid of three other trainees, while Betty and I went to the United States for further training and a holiday. He again kept things going until we returned in November. He always worried about equipment failure, as he felt that his knowledge was limited in that field. Anderson was a religious man and had a lot of faith in prayer, and I can't forget his words that first day in December when we went to the Station. He said, 'Tom, in front of that transmitter is holy ground. On my knees we have solved many problems when I had nowhere else to turn.'

"When we had the launch disaster in 1972, it was Anderson

65

who stood by continuously for several hours calling for medical assistance and handling traffic to this effect. He faithfully stood his post while I, with one broken leg and the other injured, was completely immobile. With our departure to New Zealand, he with Irma kept the Station schedules, though with Mike Randall, or the R.A.F., on the Island to maintain the equipment in case of breakdown.

"The last month or so prior to his departure, I noticed that he seemed to be making unusual mistakes in his work, and when I pointed this out to him, he said his head and eyes were bothering him. We did not realise that his condition was serious.

"Anderson was a popular man, liked by all, and his presence will always be missed in this community—particularly for us at 'Taro Ground,' where he made his last entry in the Radio Log on 8th July, 1974. He, with his family, left on the 11th; and since he was able to climb up the rope ladder to the ship unaided, little did we realise that we were saying a final farewell.

"Those 18 years we've worked together leave pleasant memories. We have always got on well together, sharing our problems, whether radio or otherwise.

"Last Sunday (30th March) I rushed home to keep my 'Ham Radio' schedule with Nelson Dyett in Wellington, and was greatly shocked when Irma's voice broke in to say that Anderson had passed away. It seems sadder too, because he has a tape-recorded message in the mail en route to us.

"The other day, as I cabled Wellington for a bouquet, it wasn't just for a workmate—it was for a 'close friend and buddy.'

"AS A MEMBER OF THE CHURCH. By Ben Christian. Anderson Gilbert Warren accepted the teachings of the Seventh-day Adventist Church under the ministry of the late Pastor Butz in the year 1928. During the years that followed, Brother Anderson laboured in several capacities in the Church, such as Sabbath School Superintendent and Teacher for many years, and leader for the children's department, in which the children gained much confidence in him, as he loved working with children.

"Brother Anderson gave valuable service to the Church, where for many years [no record as to how many] he served as deacon; and he was a local elder until his health condition deteriorated and he was forced to give up that position and seek medical assistance in New Zealand.

"He loved music and singing, and his voice will be missed wherever singing is heard. His friendly smile, kindly interest, and loving ministry will be missed by young and old." Volume 17, Number 3 (March 1975).

Editorials

While not a regular feature, the editorials carried in *Miscellany* through the years have served to focus community attention, whether calling the Pitcairners to an appreciation of their heritage, or challenging them to the undertaking of an important project, or helping solve a serious problem.

"Editorial—The list of names of servicemen, as read out by Floyd McCoy, during the Anzac [Australia-New Zealand] Service is one that such a small community as Pitciarn Island can feel justly proud of. Of equal merit too was the war effort performed by those remaining on the Island during the War years, and it is with great pleasure that this paper publishes the following information contributed by Floyd McCoy:

Pitcairn's Contribution to World War II

"Boyd Christian served in Crete, was wounded and taken prisoner to Germany for the duration of the war.

"Clement Coffin served in Egypt for two years. Was wounded at El Alamein and sent back home. Discharged in 1943.

"Chester Young served in Crete, Egypt, New Caledonia, and Norfolk Island. Was wounded and discharged in 1943.

"Ray Young served in four ships carrying supplies and troops in the Atlantic and Pacific. He was wounded in the thigh in Algiers when the *Awatea* was sunk by a torpedo.

"Robert Young served in six ships carrying supplies and troops in the Pacific. He was injured twice, once coming from Fiji, and the other off the coast of New Zealand.

"Colin Warren served in the Air Force until 1945.

"Walma Warren served in the ground force for two years. Went overseas to Japan and Singapore after the war.

"Wilfred Warren was on final leave, ready to leave for overseas, when he was accidentally killed.

"Percy, Vincent and Burnell Young, Joe Christian, Sterling and Andy Warren served in the Home Guards in New Zealand.

"Included in the war effort on Pitcairn Island were 200 cases of oranges sent to the Red Cross in New Zealand. In 1943, 500 walking sticks (canes) were sent to the Lord Mayor's fund for disabled servicemen. The islanders helped in other occasions when the opportunity came their way." Volume 3, Number 4 (April 1961).

"Editorial, I LOVE PITCAIRN, by Roy P. Clark. I love Pitcairn, where one's existence can be lived this side of Eden according to God's plan; where the gospel has free rein; where there is no opposition to one's belief, no ridicule, and no hindrance to worship God after the dictate of one's own heart.

"I love Pitcairn, where homes are homes—not merely houses, where security of life and property is as safe at midnight as at the sun's meridian, where families are united as one family with a common bond between all.

"I love Pitcairn, where there is liberty; where there is freedom to live out one's life of choice without being continually slaves to time; where men wake in the morning, not by alarm clocks, but by the awakening of nature—the crowing of cocks, the peep of dawn—and by the exuberance of a vivifying atmosphere that induces men to exclaim, 'It is good to be alive!'

"I love Pitcairn, where food is certain as long as no act of God decrees it otherwise, where there is an abundance of fish in the sea, where there are fertile hills and valleys that produce bountifully of plantains and bananas, where there are fruits in season for the picking, where the indispensable coconut tree supplies food in several forms, where little children are not forced to suffer for want of bread withheld at the whim of some despot carrying out a plan of 'greater glory.'

"I love Pitcairn, where there is love, laughter, hope, and opportunity, and not hate, sorrow, dejection, and futility.

"I love Pitcairn, where man is master of himself in the way of the evils of life, such as hate, persecutions, and killings, because of his faith and belief in God; where there is no racial discrimination, or creed, other than 'love your enemies' and 'do good to them that hate you and despitefully use you.'

"I love Pitcairn, despite her problems and misfortunes in not having a doctor or dentist, and no stores, no outlet for island produce, no anchorage for vessels in the safety of a harbour, no beaches, and no song birds—but fortunate that we have no dance halls, no intoxicating beverages, no tobacco, and no taxes.

"I love Pitcairn, and would gladly yield up my life to preserve its freedom that our forefathers created out of chaos and rebellion, so that the future offspring of our children can ever enjoy what our forbears left us—a belief in the Word of God, and a belief that to heed its teachings is the way to eternal life." Volume 6, Number 5 (April 1964).

"Editorial, WHAT HAVE THEY SEEN IN THINE HOUSE? By Roy P. Clark. The above pertinent question should be an important one to every family on the island. Why is this a provocative statement?

"Firstly, because we are a Seventh-day Adventist community.

Therefore we have the highest standard of Christian living and perfection to uphold. . . .

"Secondly, again, we are a spectacle unto the world, which has been watching the result of a transformation of a few depraved people who made this island a hell-hole of murder, debauchery, and what not, to . . . one practicing the tenets of Christianity.

"Much has been said and written of our moral ethics and Christian living. We have been lauded and praised as a community emerging from darkness to light, accepting the Word of God as our rule of living. Our godly lives have been used as an example of what the teachings of the Scriptures can do to those who yield to its influence.

"In the past three years there has been, it seems, a hurried influx of visitors to our island home and thus an absorbing of influences that have either been good or evil. Have the words and actions of these visitors caused a breakdown of our religious barrier or an improvement thereof? This, of course, is for the individual to answer for himself; but it appears that in most cases worldliness predominates over Christianity in those we have made welcome among us.

"Now the question once more: 'WHAT HAVE THEY SEEN IN THINE HOUSE?' Has our Christian background proved strong enough to offset a worldly influence? Have they seen an example of Christian living? Have they seen the family altar? Have they seen instances of discipline and correction among our children? Have they heard 'sound speech that cannot be condemned?' Has the order and cleanliness of our village and in our homes been an impressive one, and in our social life have they witnessed a pattern of good conduct?

"As these visitors have gone their way, has our Christian influence and behaviour proved such that they 'took knowledge' of us that we have 'been with Jesus?' " Volume 8, Number 12 (December 1966).

"Editorial, 11:45 p.m., 31st December, 1974, by Tom Christian. Dear Fellow Pitcairners at home and abroad: 1974 has a few minutes to go. The sun sank behind Palva Valley Ridge some five hours ago—midnight is almost here. The generator has stopped, the street lights have gone out for the last time this year, and the bell at the 'Square' will soon be ringing out the old and ringing in the new.

"Let's think of the things we have done in the past 365 days. Have we accomplished much? Have we contributed to the well-being of Pitcairn and all that's here? Pitcairn could be dying—our numbers are few. What is the minimum number required to keep Pitcairn going? There is a certain amount of manpower needed to launch the big boats, keep the roads and trackways clear, and do the many other things essential to make life pleasant for all.

"The rowboats that took you to the ships have long since gone. We steady the launches through the 'Bounty Bay' surf with the oars which perhaps you once rowed. We are still going ahead, but the swells are heavy. Young folks are leaving, others still wish to go. What is our future? Today there are 56 Pitcairners and five outsiders here—the lowest population in 100 years. In 1874 the estimated population was 71 inhabitants. What has caused the decline?

"This year we have had two births and three deaths. Thirteen Pitcairners have left for New Zealand—some for medical treatment, hoping to return; some for other reasons; and some to see the world and perhaps to stay. There seems to be real concern by the few here that perhaps time is running out for Pitcairners and Pitcairn, if our numbers keep falling.

"It is true that shipping and mail services are extremely poor, and earning a living can be difficult—particularly buying the essentials with such inflated prices on such low incomes. However it is true that pineapples are right now going to waste, oranges are plentiful for a December crop, and melons are becoming plentiful too.

"It is true that we have to use insecticides and fertilizers to produce good crops; but it is also true that Pitcairn is still free of crime, vice, and drugs; and the climate, though rather humid and hot in the past few days, is generally very pleasant.

"You abroad—perhaps you are comfortably housed, located, and have all you need. You may not be able, or do not want to come back; but think for a moment. Would you be happy if everyone had to leave Pitcairn because the numbers are too small to make an economic proposition? Right now if things got bad, you'd probably pack up and head for home as quickly as shipping permits, but would this always be possible?

"Think of those happy years when you roamed the hills picking guavas, chasing the goats, or perhaps fishing, or swimming the seas at 'Isaac's' or 'Bounty Bay.' Have you some suggestions to help us? How low can our numbers go before we have to abandon? Or will these two square miles of fertile, habitable land be offered to outsiders—to an overpopulated world—and let others occupy what was once our home—home of our 'Mutineer' forefathers?

70

"We need to earn enough to keep everyone happy, and we also need some young folks to come and stay. We need an industry, or industries, to give a reliable regular income sufficient to buy the essentials—flour from England, butter from New Zealand, and clothing from the United States. Think it over, folks. Can you come back? Can you make a living—enough to support a family? If so, perhaps we can repopulate a dying land.

"Perhaps Pitcairn's greatest need is a good reliable supply of water. Whether this can be found by damming, drilling, or distilling salt water, remains a challenge; but with water we can grow more, perhaps freeze more, or preserve more garden produce, and become more independent of the outside world. The all-too-frequent dry spells and droughts have created many problems over the years, and very little has been done to overcome the 'water problem!'

"Fellowmen, if you are not able to return, can you help find a solution to keep Pitcairn going? 1975 is ahead—perhaps high winds and ruffled seas? No one man, woman or child can face it alone. Let's face it together, let's work together, and with God's help bravely face the challenges ahead and keep Pitcairn shining for Pitcairners—sons of the *Bounty* mutineers!" Volume 16, Number 6 (December 1974).

Forestry

Pitcairn's once-natural forest has today almost vanished. The island is largely covered by bush and grassland. Small bush trees include the turau, tapau, rose apple, guava, and tall weeds such as lantana. Before 1960 sporadic efforts failed to bring back Pitcairn's larger, more useful trees. The islanders found that before their efforts could be successful their wide-roaming predatory goats had to be brought under control. Legislation by the Island Council in 1960 fenced the goats onto one portion of the island, and serious reforestation efforts got under way.

"On May 30 the school pupils planted over 175 young miro trees in and around the school boundary." Volume 3, Number 5 (May 1961).

"Jacob Warren, who is in charge of the island's reforestation plan, with his assistant, has planted over 16,000 trees in different parts of the island, mostly though at St. Pauls. This in the last three years. As an enthusiastic forester, we think that Jacob has done real well." Volume 9, Number 1 (January 1967).

"Recent activity in the form of paid work at Tedside during the past month has drawn our attention to the efforts of the foresters once again. The clearing and burning of lantana and guava has made it possible to prepare the ground for planting—part of a well-planned programme to assist the reforestation of the island.

"The original forest cover of miro and rata has long since disappeared, and scrubby secondary growth covers large areas. The larger trees once provided building materials for homes and boats, or wood for carving, while the smaller varieties were used for firewood. Of the latter there is still an ample supply, but miro wood for carving now comes from Henderson Island, and timber for building normally comes in the form of dunnage from passing ships.

"In the late 1950's the Island Council became concerned by the situation; and with the encouragement and assistance of Mr. Reid Cowell, Pitcairn's Commissioner at that time, the Forestry Department was set up with Desmond Christian as Forester. Desmond received forestry training in Fiji, and on his return to the island he made a start with the development of an area at St. Pauls. With Desmond's departure for New Zealand in 1964 there arose the problem of finding a suitable replacement; and happily the choice fell on Jacob Warren, who, since that time, has approached the job with enthusiasm and pride. As the forestry programme grew, it became apparent that the job was too much for one man; and in 1967 Maynard Warren was appointed assistant forester. Sam Young joined the department in 1969, and these three are now responsible for the care of the trees. Special financial assistance is provided for annual development work.

"Three major areas are now being developed. At St. Pauls, where planting commenced in 1960, there are 50,000 young trees—mainly miro. At Tedside there are over 10,000 miros, and at Faute Valley there are 2000 miros. In addition, windbreaks of Monkey Puzzle have been planted, as well as rain trees, Norfolk pines, oranges, paw paws, and passion fruit. Jacob estimates that in his time as Head Forester he has seen the planting of close to 100,000 seeds in the forestry. Recent plantings of pinus radiata seeds brought by Commissioner Dymond last August have not been very successful, and it is hoped that Norfolk pine seeds or seedlings can be obtained from New Zealand. This indicates a continuing development of forestry, with the accent now moving to trees capable of providing timber for building.

"The acquisition of land for the forestry has been satisfactorily accomplished by obtaining the written permission of landowners who have agreed to their land being used for tree planting in exchange for one-tenth of the timber produced. It should not be many years before these people reap the benefit of their wise decision, as already the rain trees have supplied a small quantity of timber for the recently completed launch; and Jacob carved a hand vase for Her Majesty Queen Elizabeth II from the first miro trees he planted in the forestry. ('Actually, my wife planted the tree—I just dug the hole,' explained Jacob.)

"The forestry is a comparatively new part of Pitcairn's history; but the effects of wise planning and dedicated administration and care will benefit the island for many, many years to come. . . ." Volume 15, Number 1 (January 1973).

Gardens

Although the Pitcairners rely ever more heavily on foods from distant lands, the gardens maintained on the island remain their mainstay for food. Lying in an arc on the slopes to the south and west of Adamstown, the gardens provide fruit and a variety of root and green vegetables. In addition to the staple subsistence foods of yams, sweet potatoes, taro, and arrowroot, the gardens provide sweet corn, tomatoes, different kinds of beans, and carrots. Fruits abound with little or no cultivation: grapefruit, lemons, bananas, oranges, limes, mangoes, pineapple, passion fruit, and guava. Sugar cane and dwarf coconuts round out the island's remarkably productive food picture.

Any letup in the rainfall on Pitcairn is an almost immediate threat to the gardens, and two weeks without rain means that many of the garden plants are wilting and in danger of dying. One of the island's continuing problems is adequate facilities for storage of water against the all-too-frequent drought periods.

"The orange season is over, but now pineapples and watermelon are in. Pitcairn is indeed fortunate, for there is always one fruit or another in season.

"Gardening is a continuous occupation. The minute there is a letup, the weeds and grasses soon take over. With plenty of sunny days but some good rains, the crops of tomatoes have been excellent.

"November is the main planting season for arrowroot, and quite a quantity has been put in." Volume 4, Number 11, (November 1963).

"Strong winds have played havoc with the more exposed gardens. A few of the men have complained that their melons are being 'busted up.' Citrus fruit which this time last year was in reasonable supply is now very short, largely as a result of winds knocking considerable quantities to the ground to bruise and rot. Bananas are not so plentiful as they should be—in fact, there is talk that the people may have to do some serious clearing up and replanting of this crop.

"Cabbages, which have been large and plentiful, are tailing off a little but are still sufficient to meet the demand, as far as we know. Most families are finding their gardens a big help in providing food for their tables.

"Guavas are around in small quantities, yet are sufficient to keep the children going and making the odd pie.

"Recent wet weather will no doubt be of great benefit to the land." Volume 7, Number 9 (October 1965).

Goats

The first goats on Pitcairn, along with chickens, pigs, and rats, came off *H.M.S. Bounty*. Today the pigs are gone, a concession to the islanders' Seventh-day Adventist faith, which forbids the eating of meats the Bible calls "unclean"; but the goats remain, forming what the latest edition of *A Guide to Pitcairn* calls "a contentious problem." From the beginning the goats were allowed to roam the island freely. For granting this liberty to the goats, the mutineers and their descendents have paid a high price in soil erosion and ravaged gardens. In 1960 stiff island legislation finally brought the fewer than 100 goats on the island under control. The goats are not often eaten, and they are almost never milked, but to some Pitcairners they form a hedge against a sudden cutoff of supplies from the outside world.

"Goat owners spent three days mending the fence of the pen after damage was done to gardens and young miros at Faute Valley. Most of the regulations governing the keeping of goats are known to everyone. Perhaps it is necessary to remind goat owners of the following regulation: 'All goats kept on Pitcairn Island . . . shall be confined within fences or tethered so as to prevent them from straying, and any goats not so confined or tethered shall be deemed to be wild goats.'" Volume 14, Number 8 (August 1972).

"Anyone passing Big Fence on the morning of the 15th could be excused for thinking that he had tumbled back in time to mid-nineteenth century Cimarron. The 'cowboys' were mounted on steeds that wheeled and turned as if in anticipation of the chase. The trail boss issued his final orders as one or two late-comers thundered up; then, with a whoop, the men mounted and charged up the hill in a cloud of dust and spitting Honda exhausts.

"Eight hours later, a very tired bunch of men returned to the village. They had chased goats three quarters of the way round

74

the island in order to catch the kids for marking. From Tautama they went, through Faute Valley, Outer Valley, Ginger Valley, Orlior, Tedside, Goathouse, below Pulau, and finally caught the last of the bunch up at Anderson's place. The goats thoroughly enjoyed it. Thirty-four kids were marked, according to the Goatmaster." Volume 15, Number 7 (July 1973).

Quite a number of families must have goat meat on the menu for Christmas dinner if the number of hunters who were out shooting on the 23rd and 24th is anything to go by. As the men chased the goats below Christian's Cave, the rifle fire sounded like an army platoon on exercises with machine guns. Surely there couldn't have been that many poor shots out hunting! Perhaps it is time the Entertainment Committee organised another shooting competition." Volume 15, Number 12 (December 1973).

A Hangi

"As New Year's Day fell on Sabbath, the Entertainment Committee arranged to celebrate the New Year on January 2nd, with games and a 'hangi.'

"In the morning the young men of the village collected rocks from the Landing, cut wood for the fire, and collected a supply of routi for putting around the food.

"The fire was set and lit at 1:15 p.m. By 2:30 the stones were judged to be hot enough, and the food which had been prepared and wrapped was placed in the wire baskets, which were set on the stones. A covering of routi leaves and sacks, to keep in the steam from three buckets of water, went over the food, and finally a layer of soil to close down the 'hangi.'

"Since it was expected that the cooking would take two hours, a game of rounders was organised and played on the front lawn of Pastor Webster's residence. This was followed by a tug-of-war between the men and the women which was won, contrary to tradition, by the men. The women immediately issued another challenge but were doomed to failure once again, and for the first time ever the men had proved superior.

"Just before five o'clock, the 'hangi' was opened; and the food was found to be cooked, much to everyone's surprise. The wire baskets containing the food were placed on a trestle table; and everyone helped themselves to ample portions of food, which were eaten from banana-leaf plates with the help of the fingers. Bananas, carrots, beans, pumpkin, kumara, Irish potatoes, onions, cabbages, chickens, fish, goat—quite a banquet. We were grateful to Thelma and Len for their gift of a goat for the 'hangi,' and many agreed it was the most delectable part of a very full menu.

"No doubt the women doubly enjoyed their meal, as they were spared the chore of preparing the evening meal for once.

"The youngsters still had sufficient energy to play a game of 'Prisoners,' which requires much dashing about; then, as darkness fell, people made their way home—vowing that another 'hangi' should be held at some future date." Volume 14, Number 1 (January 1972).

Harbor

The channel leading into the harbor at Bounty Bay, through which all longboats leaving or entering Pitcairn must move, is narrow and fraught with danger. A hard left-hand sweep has to be made immediately after entering boats move between the rocks at the harbor entrance, to avoid running onto other rocks straight ahead. Even on calm days the little indentation is pounded by surf, and handling the boats can be tricky. For at least two decades small improvements have been made at Bounty Bay, mostly by blasting of the more hazardous rocks from the water. In 1976 and early 1977 a major harbor improvement effort extended the island jetty further from the open ocean. A special team of British Royal Engineers, headed by Captain Hugh Cowan, worked with the Pitcairners on the big project.

"By Captain Hugh Cowan. The purpose for which the Pitcairn Management Team of Royal Engineers was formed is to help the people of Pitcairn Island to improve the landing facilities and so make them safer and easier to use. . . .

"We have also been asked to investigate other things while we are on the island; and most important of these is to see whether it would be possible to build a small airstrip which could provide an airlink to Mangareva, this the nearest airfield to Pitcairn. Of course we will also carry out any other worthwhile tasks that we are able to do.

"Landing of stores and equipment was completed on 3 June after 11 days, but this was only made possible by almost uninterrupted good weather and very hard work by all concerned. Since then we have concentrated on sorting, checking, and securing stores and equipment, and reassembling machinery which had to be dismantled for unloading. However, by the time this appears in print we should have opened up the gravel pit in Tonina Valley and started work on improving the road to Tedside, which will be our main source of stone and sand.

"To do all this, 16 Islanders work at any time, but the number required will vary as the work proceeds, and it is hoped that individuals will be able to work as much or as little as they wish. . . ." Volume 18, Number 6 (June 1976).

The project having been completed, Captain Cowan presented in mid-1977 a complete report of the work done:

"HARBOR WORKS SUMMARY. The Project lasted exactly nine months, from 23 May 1976, when unloading started, until 23 February 1977, when the equipment and remaining stores were handed over officially to the Island Council.

"During unloading 350 tons of stores were landed in 10 working days. When this was finished, the first job was to reassemble the mechanical equipment, which had been landed in pieces, and sort out stores, after which improvements were made on the one and a half miles of track to the new stone-crusher site at Tedside and a start made on the Landing-Edge road.

"However, the main part of the Project was the jetty. Here the first steel piles were driven on 24 August, and the last, of 172, weighing a total of 38 tons, on 15 November. 450 cubic yards of rock-fill was placed inside the piles and the structure completed by placing 145 cubic yards of concrete to form the deck and wave wall, after the necessary timber framework had been built. Finally, 250 tons of rock was placed on the seaward side as protection. The incomplete jetty was used for the first time on 12 November, and was opened officially on Bounty Day, 23 January. . . .

"The one task which could not be completed was the repair of the seaward end of the slipway. A spell of really calm weather had been expected some time in late December or January but did not occur. When attempts were made on two consecutive days, the sea was too rough for progress to be made. However, the experience gained then showed the best way of tackling the job when sea conditions do improve. Sixty-five tons of crushed rock was left stockpiled for this work and also for the upper part of the slipway, which had not been part of the Project.

"All the concreting and stockpiling of crushed rock referred to previously required the gathering, crushing, and moving up to two miles of 220 tons of crushed rock; the digging and stockpiling of 60 tons of sand; and the movement of 25 tons of cement.

"Quite clearly none of this could have been achieved without a great deal of skill, ingenuity, and hard work; and that this was readily forthcoming from the Island men is proved by the Project's success. All 18 available men worked, including the one who was only visiting 'on holiday,' and between them they contributed the equivalent of 2353 eight-hour man-days. When mention is also made of the Medical Officers who looked after the fortunately few injuries, and the ladies who cooked and cleaned for the Team, brought the lunches to the site, and passed our official messages by radio, it will be seen that the Project really did involve almost the whole population.

"During its time on the Island the Team examined four main areas for possible future works. These were further works at the Landing, breakwaters to protect the Landing, an airstrip, and a public water supply. . . .

"The length of airstrip required by the airline operating out of Tahiti is 985 yards. The maximum length of strip which could be provided in Aute Valley is 660 yards; but even to do this would be a major construction task, requiring more plant than is on the Island and taking many months to complete. Clearly no such work could be considered unless it was known that there were aircraft willing and able to use it.

"The provision of a public water supply would be a much smaller task than the others but would be technically difficult to carry out. It would also require constant skilled maintenance once installed and would offer comparatively few advantages over the present system.

"I apologize if this summary seems to paint a gloomy picture, but it is better to do this than to leave false hopes!!!" Volume 19, Number 5 (May 1977).

Henderson Island

Lying 105 miles east-northeast of Pitcairn, Henderson Island was discovered in 1819 by H.M.S. *Hercules,* and is named after the master of the ship. The Pitcairners first visited the island in 1851. At that time it was known to them as Elizabeth Island, having been sighted earlier by the American ship *Elizabeth.*

Roughly four and a half miles long by three miles wide, Henderson is a plateau made up of coral outcroppings and dense brush. Miro wood, from which the Pitcairners carve their curios, abounds on Henderson, and so the island is visited when supplies of carving wood run low. Often a passing ship will pick up the Pitcairners and their longboats and take them to Henderson, thus avoiding the long open sea voyage in relatively small boats. There are two known passages through the reef to the beach at Henderson, either of which must be approached with great care. Skeletons have been discovered and rediscovered on Henderson, suggesting on close examination by experts that they are probably the remains of shipwrecked seamen of the 19th century.

"On Friday 15, March, 1963, at 6:30 a.m., the S.S. *Corinthic* arrived with a number of passengers to disembark and a considerable amount of cargo and mail as well. Our friend, Captain (Arthur C.) Jones, was going to hoist our two boats, fully loaded with supplies, onto the foredeck, as he had done on previous occasions during the past recent years.

"We had to bring cargo ashore, discharge it, and then load our boats with supplies for the Henderson trip. All this took time; and during the unloading and reloading we were thoroughly cooled off by a heavy shower of rain, which not only cooled our bodies but also our spirits, because no one liked the thought of landing in rain, particularly with no immediate place to store our items of clothing, etc., except to cover them with tarpaulin. However, the shower soon became a drizzle; and it was not long before the first boat was on deck without any trouble whatever.

"The second one was not quite as easy, and difficulty was encountered in getting it strapped alongside the ship. However, it was soon under control and made fast on deck. It was 10:40 a.m. before we were underway, though the Captain had hoped to get away an hour earlier so as to give us as much daylight as possible for landing at Henderson.

"The hours sped quickly by, and for a start we had a lot of rain, but it soon cleared. Henderson was in sight by 3:30 p.m., and at 5 p.m. the first boat was being lowered over the ship's side. By 5:30 p.m. both boats had landed on the reef, and luckily for us the seas were as calm as could be expected.

"Wading in water waist-high, we unloaded the boats, while some held them in the breakers. It took an hour to land all goods on the white sandy beach; and by this time the sun was shining its last rays upon us—men on an uninhabited island!

"The greatest task now ahead, and one that caused some concern, was the hauling of the boats onto the sandy beach. However, where there's a will there's a way, and after straining for 45 minutes in soft sand ankle-deep, we had both boats up out of reach of high tides and made fast to the trees.

"Darkness was now fully upon us; and, with a little gas power plant, lanterns, torches and 'Conks' (old kettles or similar with large wicks of oil), we made our way into the trees and shrub, pitched two large tents, and by 10 p.m. most of the 20 men were already asleep, resting after a busy day.

Next morning was Saturday, our Sabbath, and no one complained about a day of rest before our arduous task of gathering miro wood commenced. At 10 a.m. we held Sabbath School; and then the rest of the day was spent in wandering on the beach or around camp, because dark clouds and passing showers were around the island.

"We were not entirely isolated, as Tom Christian (Chief Radio Operator) had brought his 'ham' radio transmitter and portable transistor receiver and at 5:30 p.m. was in contact with Anderson Warren on 'Pitcairn Radio.' Naturally the folks were glad to hear that all landing operations went smoothly and that all was well.

"Just after the sun had sunk in the 'rosy west' and our Sabbath over, the men brought out axes, saws, and lanterns and went into the bush. Soon the quiet woods were ringing with the sound of axing. This continued until nearly midnight; then there was a silence, as tired men went to sleep.

"Early next morning after Scripture reading and prayer, wood-cutting activity was in full swing, some going nearly two miles out to get wood logs and drag them back in the sea with ropes.

"Just after midday, at high tide, we decided that we should have fish for tea, so with hooks and lines we went a few yards down from where we landed, and in a few minutes we had caught nearly two hundred. Man, this sure was good fishing! In fact, we all could have spent the afternoon at the sport, but we could not eat any more than this number! Desmond and Wiles speared a good number, and they too enjoyed the friendliness of the fish.

"After the fish had been cleaned and cooked they were thoroughly enjoyed by all, and then back to work again shaping miro wood into fish, vases, turtles, birds, etc., until nearly midnight again.

"The next two days, Monday and Tuesday, the weather was wonderful, with calm wind and calm seas; and work continued without interruption except for a daily radio contact with Pitcairn in which everyone was interested to hear of the activity at home, even though we had been away only a few days.

"By Wednesday morning most of the men had reached their allocation of wood which the boats could carry and now awaited wind to sail back to Pitcairn. At 8:30 a.m. Pitcairn was still having calm weather with only a light breeze, while we at Henderson were having a light breeze—fair for sailing, but calm for sailing loaded boats. However, at 10 a.m. it seemed that the wind was increasing; so it was decided to pack up and leave for home. This took some hours, and it was 3:15 p.m. before both boats were loaded and clear of the reef. Many of us were sorry to leave so soon, as we would have liked to explore the caves, etc., on Henderson, an island much bigger than Pitcairn—15 miles in circumference but only 100 feet high—with coconuts the only edible food growing on the coral-rockbound soil.

"Our course was set for Pitcairn at 3:40 p.m., in a calm breeze, which to our dismay kept falling as the evening wore on. For the first six hours we sailed less than ten miles, which was very discouraging; and by morning we were only just over thirty miles from Henderson. The night had passed peacefully except for a lot of lightning, but at Pitcairn they had a severe lightning and thunder storm with rain, and we learned that they were worried about us in bad weather. However, we drifted and slowly sailed until morning, when very heavy rain poured on us and the wind started to increase. It soon calmed again, and the men started to row—with Pitcairn 60 miles away! The calm was temporary, and in a few minutes the wind had started again and rapidly increased. The sea quickly roughened, but it was only a small storm, and soon the wind abated to a good sailing breeze. By 1:15 p.m. Pitcairn was in sight, and it was a 'wonderful sight' after so many hours in calm, lightning, storm, rain, and wind.

"It took a long time to reach shore. We landed at 9:45 p.m. and finally got home about midnight. A fresh-water bath was welcomed, as no fresh water was available at Henderson except what we carried.

"And so, after 32 hours of sailing, one of the longest times ever spent in our boats in returning from Henderson, the journey came to an end—a pleasant, busy week spent as part of life on Pitcairn Island." Volume 5, Numbers 4 and 5 (April-May 1963).

"No sooner had the *Gothic* gone than a visit to one of the outlying islands was discussed in earnest. Some thought of Oeno for a holiday, but many others felt the call to Henderson. Late in the afternoon of Monday 22nd March *Reid Cowell* and *Dolphin*, with *Ho Ho* in tow, set a course for Henderson. Those of us remaining were to listen in and keep in contact by means of the new mobile transceiver, which had arrived so recently on the *Gothic*. At first the link was hard to establish, but after a while most were able to tune in on the *transceivers* to Tom and Henderson and Betty (Christian) on Pitcairn. It was learnt that the boats had a good trip up and that they were anchored off the reef on the west side. A change of wind made it necessary for some of the crews to take the boats to the lee one night. Steady rain made conditions uncomfortable for much of the latter part of the stay. Some difficulty was experienced loading the wood; and at one stage there was considerable danger of *Ho Ho* being lost as she was spun around on the reef, tearing off the greater part of her false keel.

81

"From early Friday morning, excitement rose as Tom's voice came in louder and clearer as the voyagers returned. Naturally, Pitcairn was visible to the men at sea for some hours before those on the island could obtain even a slight glimmer of the three tiny dots well offshore.

"At the landing some extra hands helped unload and stack the cargo prior to shipping the boats. . . ." Volume 7, Number 3 (March 1965).

History

"Readers will once again welcome an article prepared by Roy P. Clark, in which he outlines and explains a few of the controversial points in connection with Pitcairn's early history:

" 'Of late among certain individuals on the island there has been some controversy over the date when the mutineers of the *Bounty* actually landed on Pitcairn's Island. According to the books on the island's history, the actual date of the landing is not known.

" 'It has generally been accepted that the date was January 23rd, 1790, and according to a native daughter of the island, Rosalind Amelia Young, who wrote *Mutiny of the Bounty and Story of Pitcairn Island*, this is so, but other authors do not agree.

" 'If the above day is the actual time of the landing, then the burning of the *Bounty* occurred on the same day, which, it would seem, was an impossibility, for how could the mutineers dismantle the ship of all its gear in one day. We can imagine the crew stripping the ship from the keel to the masthead, taking from it every conceivable object that could be moved, and cutting down and up other parts of the vessel that could be used in the building up of the new settlement.

" 'There is not the least doubt about the time the *Bounty* was burned. This can be proved by an entry in the MSS left by the mutineers. The very first entry reads thus—"January 23, 1790, H.M.S. *Bounty* burned." (Quoted from *Pitcairn: The Island, The People, and The Pastor*, written by Rev. Thos. Boyles Murry, M.A., F.S.A.)

" 'Charles Nordhoff and James Norman Hall, in their book *Pitcairn's Island*, in the Authors' Note prefacing the story, mention that the Bounty Mutineers settled on the Island in the year 1790.

" 'Owen Rutter, in his book *The True Story of the Mutiny in the Bounty*, agrees with the above authors, saying that "Christian reached the island in 1790, and states the month as January.

" 'The Rev. Thos. Boyles Murry says that on January 23, 1850, the Islanders voted that an annual celebration be observed,

Bounty Day. This day was observed as the anniversary of the settlement of this colony, 60 years since.

" 'Evidently the settlement of the island began on the day the *Bounty* was burned, and not when they first landed on the Island, a date no mention has been made of to my knowledge, other than by Rosalind A. Young in her history of the Islanders.

" ' "Sixty years since," again brings one back to the burning of the *Bounty* on the 23rd of January, 1790.

" 'So, Mr. Editor, all through the years I have maintained that the mutineers landed on the 23rd. I here correct myself of this error, and my guess now is as good as anyone's, and the landing of the crew of the *Bounty* on Pitcairn's shore could be at any time in the month of January from the 1st to the 15th or even to the 20th. Can you make a better guess?'

"Roy has kindly furnished additional information taken by Rev. Thos. Murry from the *MSS* left by the mutineers: 'May 1795, the first two fishing canoes were made on the Island. The first record of salting meat, and of the making of syrup of or from the ti plant and from sugar cane was in the year 1799. February 13, 1840, Moses Young fell from a coconut tree 40 feet high and was only slightly injured. January 19, 1845, during the past week were "finished-up" two of the *Bounty's* guns. The first steamer to call at the island was H.M.S. *Virago* on January 24, 1853.' " Volume 3, Number 4 (April 1961).

"Letters to the Editor—Sir: In the *Miscellany* issue of April (1962), the report about Fletcher Christian returning to England from Pitcairn Island and therefore not being murdered here awakens in me the desire to give a few facts culled from several authors. These seem in one way or another to throw no new light on the theory that Christian did actually return to England and was seen there. (In April *Miscellany* had reported on a widely heard radio dramatization in England which suggested that Fletcher Christian had returned to England from Pitcairn and had lived out his days and died there, rather than being murdered on Pitcairn as most historians believe.)

"From the following, one must finally (until greater evidence is forthcoming) settle in his own mind for or against the supposition that Christian was killed on the island or did return to England.

"1. John Adams: Fletcher Christian was murdered on Pitcairn Island, 1783.

"2. Report in Cumberland about 1859: 'that Christian had returned to England and lived in concealment.' So we wonder how Edward Christian, brother of Fletcher Christian, and a noted barrister, 'was able to stay the hand of justice, preventing arrest.' Editor's notes on 'Letters of Fletcher Christian,' published in London, 1796, gave this account: 'In the year 1809, Captain Heywood, who, as a midshipman, had been a mutinner but was later pardoned, was walking down Fore Street in Plymouth. A tall man walked past him. His height, figure, and gait caused Heywood to recognize him. Walking quickly until he was abreast of the man, Heywood said quietly, so passersby might not hear, "Fletcher Christian." The man wheeled and darted away into a side street.' Have it as you will, Christian's letters were published in 1796 when he was supposed to be in Cadiz, and three years after he was said by Smith, alias Adams, to have been murdered on Pitcairn Island.

"3. Boatswain's Mate Morrison, in his journal, stated that, 'Mr. Christian . . . hoped to live the remainder of his days without seeing the face of any European except those who accompanied him.'

"4. Lady Diana Belcher's book *The Mutineers of the Bounty and Their Descendants in Pitcairn and Norfolk Islands,* 1870, makes it clear, as Morrison did, that Fletcher Christian never had the least intention of seeing England again. Quote—'After requesting Heywood to communicate certain matters to his family which he felt might at least serve to extenuate his crime, he rowed to the Bounty and set her course out of the bay.'

"5. *The Saga of the Bounty,* edited by Irvin Anthony, has this to say: 'In 1794 the Otahetian women at Pitcairn were found playing with five skulls (supposed to be those of the dead mutineers). Smith, alias Adams, could never point out Christian's grave, and he varied his story at different times.

"6. Rosalind Amelia Young, a native daughter, in her book *Mutiny of the Bounty and Story of Pitcairn Island,* has this to say: 'The wronged and oppressed Tahitians, obtaining possession of arms, fell upon the white men while they were quietly working on their alotments of land, and hunted and shot them down. Fletcher Christian, John Mills, Isaac Martin, William Brown and John Williams were killed.'

"Once again the question has arisen—was Fletcher Christian seen in England, or was he shot and killed on Pitcairn Island? One theory is as good as another, Personally, I am inclined to agree with the descendants of the mutineers of the *Bounty* and to what Rosalind Amelia Young says—that Fletcher Christian, with four of his fellowmen, was shot down on Pitcairn Island. Yours etc., Roy P. Clark." Volume 4, Number 5 (May 1962).

"The question has been asked, 'Where has the small Bible come from that is lying in the case (in the Pitcairn Seventh-day

Adventist Church) with the *Bounty* Bible?' Vi McCoy has supplied the following information:

"In 1828 George Hunn Nobbs, accompanied by an American named Bunker, arrived at Pitcairn Island from Valparaiso. He had reached the last-mentioned place after having passed through several adventures, and while there, heard for the first time the story of the *Bounty* and how Pitcairn Island was settled by the descendants of the mutineers. The story so fascinated him that he determined, it if could be done, to reach the island and take up his residence with the inhabitants. Accordingly, obtaining possession of a launch, he, with Bunker, left Valparaiso; and in due time they reached their destination safely, where they received a cordial welcome from the inhabitants.

"Nobbs did not long delay seeking to woo and win a wife: and, with some difficulty, at length succeeded in obtaining the hand of Sarah Christian, a granddaughter of Fletcher Christian.

"The launch on which the voyage of the two men was made was run ashore, broken up, and used in building Nobb's house. In giving account of himself, Nobbs said that he was the unacknowledged son of a marquis. Being by a superior education better fitted than was John Buffet to fill the place of teacher among the youth of the island, Nobbs had not been long among them before he took charge of the school, taking the work almost entirely out of the hands of Buffet. Buffet was inclined to resent this act of Nobbs as a gross injustice; but the people in general favoured the change, chiefly because of a grave fault which Buffet had committed. Yet some of the parents remained faithful in their allegiance to the teacher who had first come among them and did not withdraw their children from his care; for, in spite of his fault, he endeavoured to the best of his ability to perform his duties faithfully to them, while he sought to atone for the wrong he had done by a lifelong repentance.

"The duty of officiating as Pastor was also assumed by Nobbs.

"In August 1852 the *Portland* arrived at Pitcairn Island, and Admiral Sir Fairfax Moresby was welcomed by all on the island. Among the earliest subjects that engaged his attention was the position of Mr. Nobbs as the unordained Pastor of the people; and he took on himself the responsibility of sending that gentleman to England with a letter of recommendation to the Bishop of London, requesting him to receive Mr. Nobbs as a candidate for ordination and telling of his faithful service to the people of his adopted home.

"When the *Portland* left Pitcairn, Mr. Nobbs left too, arriving in

85

Valparaiso, then took passage on the steamer Orinoco to England.

"On presenting himself to the Bishop of London, his lordship, in consideration of Nobb's long service at Pitcairn and of the high character recommendation given of him by Admiral Moresby, as well as by other competent persons, acceded to his request to be admitted to holy orders; and on Sunday, 24th October, 1852, he was ordained in the parish church of St. Mary, Islington, London by the Bishop of Sierra Leone.

"In May 1853 Mr. Nobbs reached home again, the whole time of his absence not extending over nine months. He resumed his duties as Pastor and Teacher.

"In the latter part of April 1856 the Moyarshire, commanded by Captain Joseph Mathers, arrived from Sydney to carry away the Pitcairn people to their new home on Norfolk Island.

"Our Division Secretary (of the Australasian Division of Seventh-day Adventists), Pastor L. C. Naden, has been in correspondence with Mrs. Alma Brossey, the wife of a one-time Registrar of the Court of Norfolk Island. Among the old books they acquired was a Bible which was brought from Pitcairn on the Moyarshire in 1856. Originally it was the property of Mr. George H. Nobbs. Mrs. Brossey sent the Bible to Pastor Naden, and at her request it has been dispatched to Pitcairn. It is a small, thick volume, beautifully bound in gold-embossed leather." Volume 4, Number 6 (June 1962).

"HORSES ON PITCAIRN. Mr. (Roy) Clark has supplied this information:

"Prior to 1918 or thereabouts, horses were unknown on Pitcairn other than by word or pictures, and were brought here by schooners from Mangareva, an island of French Oceania some 300 miles to the westward.

"My account of the equines of this island must of necessity be brief because of the transitory and short-lived lives of the Mangarevan steeds. With the exception of one, they were old, and were bought or exchanged for a mere song. On one trip a young foal was brought ashore in such emaciated condition that it was only skin and bones and could barely stand on its legs. Its food for days on the voyage was only what pandanus matting could be found on the schooner.

"In time, the islanders became accustomed to the lives and ways of the horses and put them to work in the way of grinding sugar cane, hauling wheelbarrows uphill, dragging logs and firewood, racing them as a pastime, and of course riding them to their distant gardens.

"Eventually, after only a few years, all the horses met death in one way or another, only one being by natural causes. Two were found strangled at the end of their tethers. One broke a leg and had to be shot, and still another became lame and met his death in the same way. A mare and its foal died at the same time—the mare at the foal's birth and the foal soon after.

"Perhaps because of lack of understanding in the care of horses, and inadequate and proper shelter (save that of overhanging rocks and deep shade trees), their duration on the island was limited.

"Possibly this was all for the best; for in time word was received from Fiji that all horses were to be taken out to the sea and drowned, the reason for this being tetanus." Volume 8, Number 8 (September 1966).

Hula Skirts

"MAKING A GRASS HULA SKIRT. By Noggie Young. Some of the overseas readers might be interested to know of some of the many ways the Pitcairn women fill in their days on this small island. The following is an account of the preliminary work that goes into the making of a grass skirt, which women make frequently for sale aboard the passing ships.

"Firstly, you locate a Burau tree, of which there are plenty on Pitcairn. Branches of about six feet long and two to three inches in diameter are chosen. There is a green layer of skin on the outside of the wood which must be scraped off with a knife, leaving the white bark underneath this skin. The sticks are then tied in bundles of about 15 or 20 sticks (two bundles would yield about six skirts), and then they are placed into a pool of salt water (generally down at the rock pools at 'Isaacs'), are weighted down with stones so that they will not easily be washed away, and left for about two weeks to skeleton. This means that the wood is left soaking so that any of the remaining green layer of skin rots away, leaving the white bark (about one eighth of an inch thick through to the wood). Even though the sticks are weighted down, a watch must be kept on them when the seas are high to make sure they are still secure.

"When ready, the sticks are removed from the pools, the resulting slime washed off, and the bark (about three layers to each stick) pulled off. The bark is then taken home, washed again in fresh water, and hung out to dry. When dry, the bark is a bone colour and is very often used as is, but sometimes too, the bark is dyed by dipping it into a hot dye solution of various colors—the dye being obtained from U.K. (United

Kingdom—England) and quite expensive.

"Only then, after many hours of preparation, is the bark ready for the women to commence working it up into well-made skirts which sell so readily. However, before the job is finished it will take the women about another five hours to complete one skirt." Volume 11, Number 9 (September 1969).

Impressions

"DO YOU THINK YOU'D LIKE TO LIVE ON PITCAIRN ISLAND? By Roy P. Clark. The beginning for me came over 60 years ago when I set foot on the same sandy beach that the mutineers of H.M.S. *Bounty* did in 1790. From that time to the present, within my mind, it has been an earthly paradise.

"This island, formidable in appearance, is a mighty rock of volcanic origin—a lone bit of land in the vast reaches of the South Pacific Ocean—rough, rugged, jagged, and oblique to the extreme, with its highest point being 1100 feet above sea level. In all its five miles of coastline there is no safe anchorage. Most of its valleys are sharp, knife-edged, and deep. In its early history, the island was dense-covered with a great variety of trees and a profusion of ferns, dense undergrowth, and vinelike creepers.

"Throughout the land there is scarcely a stretch of flatland sufficiently large enough to play a game of rugby, football, or cricket. Soil is deep and plentiful.

"Approaching land from the north in one of the island's longboats, and nearing Bounty Bay, one faces a breathtaking scene of tropical, charming beauty, exquisite beyond description, but partially disgraced by modern longboat and canoe sheds, with shimmering galvanised roofing that has taken the place of primitive South Sea Island pandanus thatched huts.

"At the very water's edge in the harbour begins a steep, twisting road sufficiently wide enough to accommodate a Mini-moke car. This road leads to the 'Edge,' some 200 feet above Bounty Bay, the scene of the wreck and burning of the *Bounty*. The view observed nearing the harbour has little comparison to the panoramic view seen from the Edge. It takes in what is seen coming ashore into the harbour, with the added beauty of Landing Point, a sheer drop of a precipitous cliff perhaps some 600 feet. Below Landing Point is a profusion of pandanus palm and coconut trees. The blue of Bounty Bay, with underwater patches of seagrowth (very little coral) is just simply lovely, never uninteresting or boring.

"The Edge is one of two common gathering places for folk, and whatever might happen at the Landing, one may be assured that folk will gather to discuss the whys and wherefores of almost any topic. The Edge is linked with the sea more so than any other parts of the Island except the Landing. On 'Ship' and 'Fishing' days, the Edge is the centre of attraction to witness the goings and comings of ship, longboats, or small, privately owned boats. The villagers congregate to witness boats and crew going through the narrow passage into Bounty Bay. When the sea is rough, making the entrance into and out of the harbour dangerous, the women and children accompany the crews to the Landing to help if the boats should fail to make the passage and be drawn back into the harbour and onto the rocks. In the past such an incident caused the total loss of a longboat, and on yet another occasion brought tragedy, with the death of two men and the injury of others.

"Within the village are three fairly good roadways which lead to other places of interest on the Island. The settlement of this fair little isle comprises 31 houses. Twenty-six houses are habitable, while five are either uninhabitable or dilapidated. Each house is either above or below the main road, and designated by the Islanders as 'Upside' or 'Downside.' The former means toward the land while the latter means toward the sea. Therefore any article or object's location is either 'Upside' or 'Downside' of something else.

"Each family cultivates several gardens that are scattered throughout most parts of the Island. If the gardens are fertilised and sprayed, the produce is good, but otherwise the yield of one's labour is meager. Most years, fruits and vegetables are plentiful, and so with coconuts. In the settlement, mango trees have overrun and outgrown many other species of trees. There is no shortage of firewood, and tons of firewood are consumed each month by fires for cooking purposes. Trees grow in abundance, although trees for house building and carvings are almost nil. The men must go to Henderson (Island) for their carving timber and acquire by trade from passing ships tons of dunnage lumber, which is used extensively for house building.

"The island's water supply comes entirely from rain, with the exception of a small spring that has a rather difficult access. There is no system of irrigation as an extra supply of water for the vegetable gardens.

"Fishing from the rocky shore and the longboats or canoes is excellent. One must really love the sport to make a good fisherman, and it may take years of learning to understand the habits of fish and when and where they are to be found. The adage is that there is 'a knack and a trick to every trade.' So it is with fishing. I must admit, however, that there have been instances of downright good luck when some people, even though they do not know how to bait a hook, have managed a good haul.

"In the late afternoon of a fishing day, many community members may be seen making their way from all parts of the village along the narrow pathways which merge into the main road that leads down to the Edge. Here they watch the fishermen come ashore. On any given fishing day from the longboats, seldom are less than 100 fish caught. The catch is divided equally among the fishermen and hauled by 'Flying Fox' to the Edge, or brought up the steep road by Honda motorcycle.

"The fish home—scaled, cleaned, and prepared for cooking—then the long awaited call, 'Dinner's ready' or 'Yorley come and set daon.' Thus another fishing day is over. A meal of freshly caught fish eaten with prepared island food must surely wet the palates of connoisseurs of native South Sea Island cooking.

"Seldom is fish salted, for they are enjoyed either boiled or fried. Rarely are they baked in underground stone ovens, native style.

"Pitcairn Island is entirely free from world conditions as they are today. Imagine—no crime of any description. Our doors and windows are open day and night. Of course, we have not escaped high prices and suffer because of them. However, our Cooperative Store is a beacon light in a stormy sea of unobtainable foods not grown on the Island.

"All who would like to live on Pitcairn Island, 'Hands up.' "Volume 18, Numbers 10 and 12 (1976).

Island Council

Pitcairn's Island Council, which is charged with the management of all internal affairs, meets during the first week of each month, with the Island Magistrate presiding. Those making up the Council are the Island Magistrate, two Councillors, the Chairman of the Internal Committee, the Island Secretary, three nominated and two advisory members, and the Education Officer, who serves as Government Adviser. Before applying new rules the Council normally passes all legislative actions through the island governor, who is resident in New Zealand. Pitcairn's officials are elected, the Island Secretary preparing the electoral roll in December for the elections, which are held on Christmas Day. The term of Island Magistrate is three years. Everyone having three years' residence on the island and being 18 years of age is required to vote in Pitcairn elections. Failure to vote may bring a fine.

"The monthly meeting of the Island Council was held on Thursday, 6th February, 1964, with the Chief Magistrate, John Christian, in the chair.

"Matters which might be of interest to readers are that (a) Thelma Brown was appointed office typist. (b) Margaret Young was appointed as Teaching Aide at Pulau School. (c) The old-age Pension Scheme was modified to allow both members of the family to receive the benefit, provided they qualified to the satisfaction of the Council. (d) Goat owners were requested to remove or destroy all goats in or near the area where reforestation is being carried out by Jacob. (e) Pastor was asked if he would oblige the Council by making enquiries concerning navigation lights for launches and longboats. (f) The Council approved of a grant of 10 pounds to any Island resident who obtained a Certificate of Navigation." Volume 6, Number 3 (March 1964).

Island News

"Many years ago an American man was shipwrecked off the small island of Oeno and found refuge on Pitcairn Island for some nine months before returning to America. So vivid were his impressions of the Island and the hospitality he received that he decided to return to Pitcairn after many months, with his 16-year-old son. Here they settled, and the lad soon married a very charming young woman.

"Over fifty years of happy married life have passed, and now Roy (Clark) has taken his bride to the land of his birth. It was a joy to all to see their excitement when they boarded the *Willem Ruys* on Tuesday. We try to imagine their reaction when May sees for the first time the big wide world of America with its modern contraptions—and shoes (most Pitcairners go barefoot).

"Roy and May Clark are visiting his only brother in Los Angeles. They expect to be away for at least six months. We wish them a very happy and joyous holiday and will look forward to their return." Volume 3, Number 4 (April 1961).

"A serious plague of caterpillars has stripped the leaves off nearly all the burau trees at Goat House. Desmond has used D.D.T. powder in an effort to control their movement into town." Volume 3, Number 5 (May 1961).

"On Friday 26th (October) we witnessed some of the most spectacular seas seen for a good long time. We had had a fairly stiff breeze for some days before, but this could not have accounted for the tremendous waves which pounded the coast. At Isaacs the huge rollers were crashing right up to the cliff face; and quite an exciting time was had by some of the children in rescuing 'Burau' (a species of hibiscus), which was soaking. (The bark of the Burau is used for making hula skirts.)

"The next morning at just after 1 a.m., many of the Island's inhabitants were startled by a sharp earthquake. Earth tremors are a rare event here; so needless to say this experience caused considerable excitement.

"Wild cats are causing quite a lot of death amongst young chickens; so any cat seen prowling around fowl is usually given a short shift. Roy has become so concerned over the 'trigger happiness' of some of the boys that he made a special trip down to the pictures the other night to give a full description of his cat so it could be recognized and spared." Volume 4, Number 10 (November 1962).

"Watermelons are still plentiful, and we understand that Anderson has a particularly good patch 'Up Grass.' A popular time for eating watermelons is after church on Sabbath, when people invite each other over to their homes to 'have some watermelon.' Mangoes have had a short season this year, but guavas are now beginning to ripen. Some have already been picked over at Tedside during last week." Volume 5, Number 3 (March 1963).

"The Bell at the Square has been replaced. For us at Pulau, this is most appreciated, as in most cases it is now possible to hear the calls closely without straining the ear, during the evenings when the diesel generator is making a much closer and louder noise." Volume 6, Number 4 (April 1964).

"For the first few days of May some rough weather was experienced. During a storm on Thursday, 7th May, the telephone wires became tangled with the Pulau power line, causing all the phone bells to ring wildly. Several were 'caught' by the hot line. From a reliable source we learnt of one gentleman who came from his bath, only to get a short sharp shock as he attended to his persistently ringing phone before the generator could be turned off. We hear that he returned to the warmth of the bath only to have the light go out; so we won't know if he came out of the event clean or not!" Volume 6, Number 5 (May 31, 1964).

"By the middle of the month water supplies were very low, with crops and ground crying out for a large drink. From Tom (Christian) and his associated radio operators we learnt with hope and envy that not too many miles away the skies were opening up and making the sea still wetter, but not a sign did we see. However, it would appear that our visitors, Dr. Joseph Marseu, Pastor R. W. Taylor, and writer Frank Clune, brought the weather; for once we had them safely ashore our long awaited rain fell in bucketfuls, filling up wells and stirring long dormant seeds in the ground. We are indeed thankful." Volume 6, Number 10 (September 1964).

"Jan. 16. Guess what happened on this day? Can you believe it? Tests and trials were given by Pastor Webster in the presence of the Police Officer, Vernon Young, for licenses to ride Honda motor-bikes. Tom, Bruce, and Betty passed. Len, we are sorry that you just could not make the riding test but hope you will with flying colours at the next trial. Len, Tom, and Noggie received their licenses for Tractor Driving. Tests for tractors, Hondas; well! Jeeps maybe next or even motorcars? Who knows?" Volume 9, Number 1 (January 1967).

"The wind was piping a stiff breeze as we left *Ceramic* at midnight on Tuesday 16th and battled home against rising seas with heavily loaded boats.

"On Wednesday 17th wind was blowing strongly from the east and had considerably increased in force. During the evening it blew with even more vigour and continued without abating through Thursday and Friday, until on Friday evening it reached an estimated Force 11 on the Beaufort Scale and caused considerable damage.

"Sheets of tin were ripped from rooftops and walls, a verandah collapsed at an unoccupied house; tree limbs were cracked, twisted, and torn from trees; hundreds of banana trees were scythed down as the shrieking wind funnelled up valleys; hundreds of ripe lemons, limes, oranges, grapefruit, and mandarins were wrenched from the madly thrashing trees and hurled willy-nilly; miro and pine saplings were bent double and the flayed leaves burned on the slender, whipping branches; coconuts and coconut leaves flew dangerously through the air; the village was plunged into darkness as wiring was severed and the wind howled on, shrieking like a thousand demons.

"On the morning of the 20th we awoke to what seemed an uncanny quiet. The wind had dropped to the gentlest of breezes, and the day was clear and sunny. However, the road to church this Sabbath was strewn with branches, fruit, roofing, and all sorts of wind-scattered bits 'n pieces.

"On the Friday morning, the half-finished hostel building had to be secured with strong ropes; and these held well. Conversation after church with some of the 'old timers' revealed that this had been the strongest blow for many a long year.

"Dobrey and Ivan had the humiliating experience of having the whole seaward side of their roof lifted bodily onto the other half, exposing them completely to the elements. It's no fun on a night like this, lying in bed staring at the open sky and wondering what's going to go next. A hasty switch around of sleeping quarters, some frenzied work with tarpaulins, a temporary lashing down of the flipping roof made do until permanent repairs could be effected. Intermittent rain driving in did nothing to help matters.

"As your editor fought his way down to the engine house in gusting wind and rain on Friday evening to turn off the generator plant, he quite forgot that directly opposite the door of the house was an open window facing the direction of the wind. Result: as he forced the door open the wind gusted, funnelled through the window and open door, catching his widespread umbrella. The fabric cracked like a pistol shot, leaving the ed. holding a handle and twisted mass of bare, black ribs.

"Surprisingly, the part of the island least affected was the highest point at Pawala Valley Ridge. Here, above the winds, hardly a blade of grass was out of place.

"On the following Sunday, Monday, and Tuesday, householders got busy cleaning up the debris, while the men worked together reroofing and securing storm-damaged houses.

"Huge seas accompanied the wind; and *Canterbury Star,* due to call on Saturday 20th, radioed to say she was in very rough weather and would not be able to stop. High seas at the Landing had ripped away much of the wooden slipway; and, although it would have been possible to take a boat through the surf during Saturday afternoon, it would have been extremely hazardous. *Canterbury Star* was carrying personal stores; 17 cases of electrical equipment; Hondas for Thelma, Irma, and Oscar (long awaited); and five bags of mail—none of which we will see until June 8th when the ship is due back.

"Late on Saturday 20th, the wind had switched around completely and was blowing quite strongly from the west. Another hard blow immediately on top of the last would be too much to bear; and, while the pessimists insisted that 'it was certain to blow just as hard again to even things up,' we all kept our fingers crossed and have been enjoying normal conditions since." Volume 10, Number 4 (April 1968).

"Since 1952 The Governor of Fiji has held the responsibility for the Administration of Pitcairn Island affairs.

"On 10th October Fiji became Independent, the post of

94

Governor ceased, and Pitcairn Island affairs are no longer administered in Fiji.

"Sir Arthur Galsworth, British High Commissioner to New Zealand, has been appointed Governor of Pitcairn Island and will be operating from the office of the British High Commission in Auckland.

"Mr. F. E. Warner, who was with the staff of the Commissioner for Pitcairn is Suva, has joined Mr. Dymond's staff in Auckland, where his knowledge of Pitcairn affairs will no doubt be of great value." Volume 12, Number 10 (October 1970).

"This month Pitcairn Island was honoured by a visit from Prince Philip, Duke of Edinburgh. This is the first time in the history of the Island that a member of the Royal Family has set foot on Pitcairn Island, and the community as a whole was delighted to be able to welcome such an important visitor to the island and have the opportunity for a few hours to show him what true hospitality is. His Royal Highness was accompanied by his uncle, Lord Louis Mountbatten, and Lord Loui's daughter and son-in-law, Lord and Lady Brabourne.

"On Sunday 21st November the Royal Yacht *Britannia* anchored off Bounty Bay shortly after 4 p.m. Fortunately, the weather was favourable; and all members of the community who were fit and able were invited aboard the Royal Yacht to welcome the visitors and attend a party on deck. After boarding the yacht all members of the community were introduced to Prince Philip and then, having moved onto the upper deck, were served refreshments and had the opportunity to meet and speak with His Royal Highness and other members of the party. During this interval the Royal Marine Band played light band music on a lower deck. Very appropriately, tunes from 'South Pacific' were featured prominently, turning the afternoon into quite a festive occasion. At 6 p.m. all members of the community disembarked and returned to the island to complete final preparations for the welcoming of our visitors ashore the next morning.

"At 9:30 a.m., Monday 22nd November, His Royal Highness and members of his party landed at Bounty Bay and were driven in the Island's Mini-mokes to the Village Square. The Square had been decked out with flags and the verandah of the Court House decorated with coconut palms and local flowers. Seats had been placed in the Square, and all members of the community who were able to attend were waiting in keen anticipation. After our visitors had been escorted onto the verandah the National Anthem was sung, and surely never had the Anthem been sung with such volume and pleasure on Pitcairn Island. The

Magistrate of Pitcairn Island, Pervis Young, then delivered a short speech of welcome on behalf of the community, mentioning that, particularly as this was the first occasion a member of the Royal Family had visited Pitcairn Island, the community as a whole was greatly honoured by the visit. His Royal Highness replied: 'Well, Chief Magistrate, Islanders, first of all, thank you very much indeed for your welcome to me and to my uncle and cousin and friends here today.

" 'Anybody who's had anything to do with the Royal Navy— and all of us here have had something to do with it except Lord Brabourne, who was, unfortunately, drafted into the Army!—has heard of the *Bounty*, and I suppose it must be the ambition of every young Naval Officer to visit Pitcairn, and of course once you have seen it, it's a great excitement and a great pleasure, and we're all delighted to have this opportunity to be here. We've been looking forward to it for a long time, and we're very happy to find you all so happy and flourishing.

" 'We've just come from another unique island, Easter Island; it's unique in a different way; but we've come now to this second unique island in the Pacific.

" 'There are people in the more populated world, in London and in the United States, who talk about "getting away from it all." Well, I reckon you can't get any further away from it all than Pitcairn; and this is one of the things that made it so attractive, I think, to Fletcher Christian when he came here.

" 'We are delighted to see you all here. You know, you read about the lovely weather and the beautiful trees and the fruits that grow in the south sea islands and what a marvellous life it must be just lying there letting the pawpaws drop into your mouth and catching a banana as you go past. But of course you know better than anyone else that isn't true, and if it wasn't for the hard work and the resourcefulness and the persistence of the community that's lived here you would not be here now. It's a hard struggle, we realise that, and that's why I think that every ship that comes past here wants somehow or other to offer a little help and to give you something to help make your life easier on this island. You do have certain advantages, believe me; I think there are probably fewer ulcers on this island than anywhere else in the world, and that's something to be grateful for.

" 'Now it's 181 years and one month since the *Bounty* anchored in the Bay here, and that's a long time. When they arrived here they must have been a little concerned about their future—although I imagine they were a little concerned about their past too(!) when they set up this little community. But I just wonder what would have happened if somebody had prophesied—they didn't have a Pastor in those days to prophesy—I wonder whether he would have found something in the Bible to prophesy that 181 years later a Royal Yacht would anchor in the same place as the *Bounty* had anchored and that here we would be all friends and all sunshine and all happiness.

" 'Well, it's a great pleasure for all of us to be here. Thank you very much for your welcome. As you see, wonders never cease on Pitcairn; and I hope that the wonders never cease in the future and that you will continue to have a happy, if hardworking, existence on this lovely island. Thank you for your welcome and the best of luck to all of you in the future.'

"At the conclusion of the welcoming speeches everyone met His Royal Highness in person and then moved on into the Court House, where morning 'tea' was served. The day was extremely hot; and our visitors obviously enjoyed Pitcairn's sweet, cool watermelons. Soon after 11 a.m. the visitors moved on and visited the Post Office and Dispensary before leaving by Mini-moke for the trip to Taro Ground to inspect the Radio Station. Lord Louis Mountbatten showed particular interest in this visit, being very familiar with 'communications' from his younger days. It was then time to move on and visit the school, where the Assistant, Marona Young, had all the schoolchildren quietly awaiting their visitors. After talking to the children for some time Prince Philip handed out a parcel of sweets to each of them; and they in return sang for him a song which had been written for the children of Pitcairn by one of the past Pastors here—Pastor Webster. All Pitcairn Islanders seem to be naturally good singers. The party must have enjoyed this aspect of the visit to the school, as the Education Officer was requested to tape the children's singing at a later date and send the tape off to Buckingham Palace.

"The party then moved on up to the schoolhouse, where our visitors were entertained by members of the Island Council and their wives at a Luncheon.

"Around three o'clock the party moved on again for an informal tour of the Island. His Royal Highness particularly wanted to meet all members of the community, and so those who had been unable to go to the Square and welcome him in the morning were visited by the Duke in the afternoon in their own homes. This must surely have been a great thrill for these old folk. The Royal party was then driven up to Pawala Valley and Big Ridge before returning to the Square at 5 p.m. for afternoon tea.

"In the meantime the population had been entertained in the

97

Square from 3 p.m. to 4 p.m. by the Royal Marine Band, which had come ashore for this purpose. Pitcairn being such a small island, the sound carried well; and those who could not actually be present could hear the strains of the band from their homes. Pitcairn certainly seemed gay on Monday 22nd February.

"Crew members of the *Britannia* and the escort ship *Blue Roger* also came ashore in the afternoon, and Pitcairn seemed to be fairly swarming with visitors. The ladies very kindly served afternoon 'tea' from 3 to 4 p.m. This was much appreciated by these visitors, who had come ashore expecting to entertain themselves, as they imagined everyone would be too busy that day to worry about them. However, on Pitcairn there is always plenty for everyone; and after these folk had been served there was still more than enough left on the tables for the official afternoon tea. In fact, the tables were still fairly groaning under the weight of the goodies.

"The Royal Party returned to the Square at 5 p.m., and afternoon 'tea' was served. At 5:30 p.m. His Royal Highness presented to the Magistrate on behalf of the community, a bell, and also a signed photograph to be hung in the Court House. Lord Louis Mountbatten also presented the community with a signed photograph as a memento of his visit. Gifts were then presented to our visitors from the community. The Duke received a carved walking stick (to match the one presented to Her Royal Highness, Queen Elizabeth, in Suva some years ago by John Christian, who was visiting Fiji at the time); a shark, which was signed by almost every member of the community; and a hand vase made from a piece of locally grown miro (the first piece cut from a tree grown locally by the Forestry Department). Lord Louis was also presented with a walking stick, and Lady Brabourne received a bouquet of flowers.

"The community then sang 'Keep to the Bible, My Boy,' 'Sinking of the *Vestris*' and the 'Goodbye Song'; and, sadly, it was time for departure. His Royal Highness and members of his party shook hands with everyone for the last time; and, all farewells having been said, departed post-haste for the Landing, where they departed in one of the Island's longboats for the Royal Yacht after 6 p.m.

"The day, it can safely be said, was a huge success. Although having to keep a fairly tight schedule in very hot and dusty conditions, our visitors were able to visit our Island in a very informal manner—which must surely be a welcome break from the usual Royal Visit.

"We trust they enjoyed their brief stay as much as we enjoyed having them here on Pitcairn Island.

"It was thought that overseas readers might be interested to read the words of the song 'We're From Pitcairn Island' sung by the schoolchildren for the Duke of Edinburgh:

We're From Pitcairn Island

1. We're from Pitcairn Island; we welcome you today.
   We're glad you've come to see us, but soon you'll sail away.
   We hope you will remember the love we tried to show.
   The friendships we have made today
   Remain, though you must go.

2. Our Island is so tiny, encircled by the sea.
   Its shoreline is so rugged, as you so well can see.
   Yet we so dearly love it, our homes are also there.
   But if you come our way again,
   Our welcome you may share.

Chorus
   We will miss you as you journey on your way.
   We do wish that you with us could ever stay,
   But we know that God will keep us in His hands.
   Perhaps someday we'll meet again on this far-distant strand."

Volume 13, Number 2 (February 1971).

"THAT LITTLE BLACK BOX. Tom (Christian) is regularly seen pumping air into a bedialed black box. He is carrying out measurements of atmospheric pollution as part of a comparative survey being organised by the University of New York. Tom's twice-daily readings will be of value in 50 years' time—perhaps of even greater value than they are now.

"Information provided by the U. of N.Y. authorities shows that in the city of New York, pollution can reach higher than 100,000 pollutant particles per cubic centimetre; Tom's readings show a pollution level of approximately 360 pollutant particles per cubic centimetre! Enough said." Volume 14, Number 4 (April 1972).

" 'THE STORY OF A DREAMER WHO MADE IT.' By Miss Kari Boye. When I was twelve years old, I read Mutiny on the Bounty, and my future was settled. I decided to become a sailor—although, I must admit, my parents tried to kill my romantic illusions of life on the seven seas. The fact that ships did not have sails anymore, that the men were no longer tied to the mast and whipped by the cruel captain, and that dissatisfied sailors consulted their trade unions instead of mutinying and settling on some isolated Pacific island in the good old way was disappointing; but I was not discouraged.

"A *Bounty* fever swept through my class at school after I persuaded the others to read the book; and we named ourselves after the *Bounty* crew, with our teacher as Captain Bligh, of course. I was Cadet Roger Byam, and was called Byam for years afterward. It was hard to accept the part of Byam, who did not even take part in the mutiny. Our parents and teachers had a difficult time while we were transforming our homes and the school into a make-believe world of His Majesty's armed vessel *Bounty*. We were experts on the rigging and sails of the ship, the British Navy in the 18th century, the winds and trades in the Pacific—anything that had any connection whatsoever with the *Bounty*. I even studied navigation on my own, and was furious when my parents refused to buy me a chronometer and a sextant for sun observation for Christmas.

"I had two big dreams as I stumbled through my teens: to become a sailor, and to visit Pitcairn Island. After college graduation at 19, I attended Oslo School of Commerce to learn typing, shorthand, and bookkeeping; but these tedious subjects strengthened my intent to seek my destiny on the seven seas.

"A year later I qualified for my radio operator's certificate, and during the past eight years I have been able to realise my ambition and see much of the world. I've been deer hunting in Canada, climbed volcanoes of Italy, and seen the Changing of the Guard at Buckingham Palace. In between voyages I spend some months at home with my family, working as a teacher of foreign languages; but always I feel the old restlessness and have to move on to see what life is like on the other side of the hill.

"And now I've finally arrived at Pitcairn after 15 years of dreaming and planning. In the last three years I have been in constant correspondence with the Island Council, the Commissioner in Auckland, shipping companies in New Zealand and England, and the British Embassy in Oslo, Norway.

"I am enjoying every minute of my life on the island, although everyone here keeps telling me each day that I'll soon tire of Pitcairn. But I'm not leaving yet. If Tom and Betty (Christian), my host and hostess, don't get sick of the sight of me, I'll stay until I have to leave to join my next ship." Volume 15, Number 11 (November 1973).

"At a graduation ceremony held at the Wigram Airforce Base in New Zealand on March 18, 1977, Pilot Officer Kevin Brian Young (23) was awarded the Astrolabe Trophy. This trophy is awarded to the navigator who graduates with the highest aggregate of marks in practical navigation and academic studies. . . .

"Perhaps it is coincidence; but when one looks back into Pitcairn's history, one of Captain Bligh's best-known mutineers was a navigator, Midshipman Edward Young, from England's West Country. Kevin is a seventh-generation member of Midshipman Young's family. . . ." Volume 19, Number 5 (May 1977).

"In the March '77 *Miscellany* we reported that Steve had found, in decomposed state, a bird, while on Oeno Island. We recently received from the British Trust for Ornithology in England the following information on the bird, which may be of interest: species—Southern Giant Petrel (Macronected giganteus); sexpull; ringed—25 March 1975 at Signy Island, South Orkney, Antarctica." Volume 19, Number 8 (August 1977).

"I'M AS FIT AS EVER! By Andrew Young. As young boys we often walked along the ridge from Big Ridge to Pawala Valley, picking guavas for our mums, who made jam and pies. In those days no thoughts were given to the fact that perhaps one day a road would be cut along the ridge to Big Ridge. Well, that time came over recent months when the men cut the said road; I have always had the urge to walk around the Island pushing my wheelbarrow, making use of the newly cut road. But a number of folk thought I was an old fool. . . . I'm only in my 70s now and am still as young as ever; and, to prove it, the following is an account of the trip I did make around the island . . . with my wheelbarrow.

"In the early hours of the morning of September 21 I decided to take my wheelbarrow from Adamstown around the ridge to Saint Pauls and back home again. The thought which entered my mind was, 'I wonder how long it might take me?' Having had my cup of Milo, I started my hike at 7 a.m. Due to a rain squall, the ground became rather sticky, but still I kept going; pushing my 'barrow until I reached Flatland at 7:15 a.m. There I stopped to clean the mud away from the 'barrow's wheel and of course to get extra air into my lungs. From Flatland I was able to make more speed, still puffing and panting until I reached Big Ridge at 7:30 a.m. It was here that the steepest part was reached. I took a well-earned short break, cleaning the mud away from the 'barrow's wheel once again, and then set off on the next stage of my hike at 7:32 a.m. I passed Matthew Young at 7:40 a.m. but did not stop to rest, as I was now travelling on firm ground. I arrived at Palva Valley at 7:47 a.m. From there on more speed was made. I had fair winds going until I almost reached Taro Ground, where I ran into headwinds, which slowed me down somewhat; but I finally

101

reached the Radio Station at 8 a.m. Without stopping, I turned off through McCoy's Valley from Hulianda, really moving quickly; and with only about 30 yards more to my next intended stop, a moth flew into my mouth. But still I kept going, spitting the moth out of my mouth; and my goal was reached at 8:15 a.m. I then turned off to St. Pauls; and I was still moving swiftly towards my next goal, St. Pauls Point, which I reached at 8:30 a.m. Turning round to come back, with Ships Landing Point as my next goal, was the trickiest part of my hike. Here I faced some strong headwinds, and the road was bad and stony, but nevertheless I reached Ships Landing Point at exactly 9 a.m. There I stopped for 20 minutes to load my 'barrow with firewood. I commenced my final run home to Adamstown at 9:20 a.m. and finally reached my starting place at 9:40 a.m.

"Travelling time was 2 hours 20 minutes." Volume 19, Number 9 (September 1977).

"The arrival of Medic from New Zealand couldn't have come at a more opportune time. Pastor Ferguson (chairman of the Co-op store) is reported to have said that prior to the Medic's arrival, the only articles left in the store for selling were: Rinso washing powder, balls of string, and glue . . . not very appetising. And indeed had Medic not happened along when it did, who knows, the editorial team may have run a cooking competition to see who could turn up with the most palatable, gooey-ooey, string spaghetti?" Volume 19, Number 11 (November 1977).

"Wasps seem to be increasing and causing a rather painful problem. Several of the locals have had stings. Ronnie Christian's face was unrecognizable for three days because of swelling through wasp stings." Volume 20, Number 2 (February 1978).

"Rats—these seem to be becoming a bit of a problem around the Island again. Most people are trapping or poisoning them, but when our boy Nig discovered one trying to climb in his bedroom window, in true western style he shot it between the eyes. P.S. Anyone calling at the Browns' house at night should call out in a loud, clear voice before entering." Volume 20, Number 3 (March 1978).

"Many of the men returned from Oeno sporting beards. Although wives protested, children cried, dogs fled in terror, and hens went off the lay, some beards continue to flourish." Volume 20, Number 3 (March 1978).

"Black Jack, the young frigate bird which Nig brought back from Oeno Island, has become a familiar sight in the sky above Adamstown.

"When Black Jack first arrived, he had only recently acquired his flight feathers and was yet too young to fly. In those days Black Jack's favourite method of transport was on Nig's motorbike; and it wasn't unusual to see Nig roaring around a corner with Black Jack on the handlebars, wings partially outstretched to help him keep his balance. But the rest of the time he spent on a perch outside Browns' house.

However, the time came when Black Jack spread his wings, all six feet of them, and took off. Some concern was felt for him, as frigate birds have a somewhat complicated feeding pattern: they obtain their food by flying close to gulls, terns, and gannets, and forcing them to drop the fish they have recently caught. The frigate bird then swoops and catches the discarded fish, usually before it hits the water.

"But Black Jack had no parental instruction in this art, and he was found a few days later in rather poor condition. Regular feeding soon had him back in good condition, but once again he took to wing. By this time Nig had taken to standing on the house roof and holding up tempting pieces of fish. Finally this ploy worked, and Black Jack flew down and plucked the fish from Nig's fingers. This was truly an amazing sight—to watch this very large bird swoop down and take the fish, avoiding obstacles such as trees and radio aerials. Since then he has continued to call twice a day for fish. You may well imagine that a bird of this size needs a lot of fish, and all of the Brown family are doing a lot of fishing to keep up with his appetite. Black Jack has even been known to visit the Browns as they are fishing at the Landing or Tedside to have a meal of really fresh fish. . . ." Volume 20, Number 5 (May 1978).

Island Transport

Until 1964 the only wheeled vehicle on Pitcairn was the traditional wheelbarrow, Pitcairn style. As roads were made on the island, however, interest in other vehicles increased—tractors, motorcycles, and Mini-moke cars. Today the Island fairly buzzes with wheeled transportation.

"Some months back, Tom Christian and the Forster family ordered two Honda 90 Trail motorcycles as an experiment, to reduce the time taken moving around the island. After several frustrating holdups, these machines finally arrived on the *Ceramic* and were assembled a day or so later. Both have proved an outstanding success, going practically anywhere there is a formed track. None of the new owners had had motorcycling experience, so learning to ride was also part of the fun. Even so, spills have been confined to a few minor slides in the first day or two. Interest in motorcycles as a new mode of transport for Pitcairn is high; and, judging by the enquiries received, it will not be long before others are seen here." Volume 8, Number 3 (March 1966).

"To anyone who does not know this small island, the movement of persons or goods on a mere two square miles does not appear a great problem; yet to those who live here it has far-reaching effects, governing in many ways everyday life here.

"When Fletcher Christian, at the head of a small band of mutineers, first came ashore, he and his companions faced a task which lesser hearts would have termed impossible. Theirs was the problem of transporting all redeemable goods from the wrecked *Bounty*, up an exceptionally steep and virtually unformed track from the Landing, to what we now know as the Edge. How did they do it? The answer is simple and straightforward—on their own two feet.

"On their own two feet? Yes, for generations Pitcairners have relied on the sole transport medium of two feet—and plenty of energy. Ask passengers on passing ships what they notice most about the Pitcairners, and very likely the answer will be 'the size of their feet!' At various times artists and photographers have portrayed hands to reveal a life-story of service; but locally, feet could well be the more dominant focal point. Feet that have helped move many tons of goods—fruit, vegetables, timber, and firewood—from one part of the island to another part, up steep slopes, down into muddy gullies, and even across the few relatively flat parts that exist on Pitcairn.

"As a supplement to 'footwork only,' time and necessity brought forth a massive . . . boxlike arrangement. . . . These wheelbarrows could well have been termed 'Pitcairn Waggons,' for in them the majority of the bulky or heavy items were moved. They are still a necessity here today, only in a slightly lesser degree. Very recently, a visiting party brought two rubber-tired, metal-bodied 'barrows. It will be interesting to see if this type gradually supersedes the originals—we doubt it. Rather would we venture the opinion that future Pitcairn 'barrows will possibly retain the old design but use metal frame and sides. . . .

"For a limited time at the end of World War II a crawler tractor was ashore to assist with certain projects being undertaken by a party from New Zealand. Within a few years of its being taken away the main evidences of its activities had vanished, and it became but a memory. So things remained until very early 1965, when a Bristol crawler tractor, made available by Colonial

104

Development and Welfare assistance, was assembled at Bounty Bay. This was followed on the next ship by a Massey wheel tractor, from the same source. These two units virtually began the era of mechanisation on wheels. Within a short space of time, 'barrow trackways were improved up to dry-weather vehicle roads. The cycling craze caught the younger folk, until now mostly all the school children use these two-wheeled concerns. . . . Further advances were made with the advent of two motorcycles, one of which is often employed to tow a small trailer unit.

"Inquiries are in hand for government diesel-driven vehicles in the jeep or landrover class; and, although the definite time of arrival is still uncertain, this type of conveyance should further speed up transport within the next year or so. At least one private inhabitant is also very interested in obtaining a four-wheeled vehicle in the near future. However, before it is possible to operate motorized transport in all weathers, further improvements will be necessary to consolidate the existing clay roads. Therefore, negotiations are also being made for the early delivery of a semi-mobile rock-crushing plant, which, if used wisely in conjunction with our present roading-development programme, will further reduce the necessity for the use of manpower in the shifting of goods and chattels over the uneven face of Pitcairn." Volume 8, Number 8 (August 1966).

Ivan's Teeth

"Kay was nosing around the tiny pieces of sand in the Bay on the 30th, when she saw someone's upper denture. On closer inspection she found that several of the teeth were missing, but one with a gold filling was in good shape . . . and helped to identify the owner as Ivan. But hadn't Ivan noticed that he had lost them? Sure he had, but he had given up hope of finding them. You see, he lost them when *Reid Cowell* went down on June 23rd last year!' Volume 15, Number 10 (October 1973).

Letters to the Editor

"Dear Sir: I am now an old man (83) and started my life as a sailor. One event in that life I have never forgotten: . . .

"I came in February 1901 as Able Seaman on board the four-mast bark *Clan McPherson* of Glasgow (with Captain McDonald and wife) up under your island in the morning, and stayed there the whole day. On shore the people (as usual) made holiday and came out in their boats and brought with them fruit, vegetables, and a friendly humor; and soon our decks were very full.

"As I said before, we lay-to the whole day and everything was very, very pleasant for us and I think also for our new friends. In the afternoon we couldn't, however, stay any longer but had to part again and pursue our long voyage to London. Many a time since then I have had thought of this beautiful day with those fine islanders and couldn't let more time pass without sending a few words to someone on Pitcairn Island as a thanks for this remembrance. Yours faithfully, Sten Roing, Malmo, Sweden." Volume 5, Number 1 (January 1963).

"Dear Editor: What strategic position has Pitcairn Island as a British Crown Colony under the administrative jurisdiction of the South Pacific Office? Why is it that the authorities are expending large sums of money on the island's economy and maintenance when it can be plainly seen only decadence is its future? Is the exodus of the islanders to New Zealand giving the South Pacific Office grave concern because the population has dwindled to less than a hundred inhabitants today, whereas three years ago they numbered 140 or thereabouts? What has caused this departure to an existence in city life?

"One factor of dissatisfaction is that more than half the island homes receive government pay, while the others have no regular income. Fifteen families draw pay cheques, while 14 do not.

"Other reasons for leaving the island are:

"1. The lure of money. The high wages paid in New Zealand.

"2. Labour on the island has become too arduous and increasingly toilsome. This has been brought about by the multiplicity of blights, destroying insects and weeds, not to mention the destructiveness of termites and wood borers that are working havoc in the island dwellings, and the lack of trees for lumber to rebuild or repair.

"3. The lack of ships to supply the islanders with a substantial income to secure the necessities of life.

"4. Complaints of no future on the island by both young and old. The same routine of life, with no advancement or improvement in personal achievements. On this point the question may be asked, 'What future do they seek to acquire in New Zealand?' Examine the lives of these dissatisfied people after a few years of city life. Have they improved their aspirations in enterprise or conduct? Have they bettered their lives by city life more so than the rural life of their forefathers? Actually what have Pitcairners accomplished in New Zealand to give them a better way of living?

"5. Of late years there seems to be an increase of sickness—an epidemic of different illnesses that has caused the islanders serious thought; and many have had to leave for New Zealand for medical attention. Once in New Zealand these individuals are reluctant to return home again.

"6. Has the breaking up of homes anything to do with the situation? There is an answerable underlying uneasiness among the people—a break-up of communal life. Perhaps the government is losing its hold on the islanders for stability and contentment, and this may apply to the church also. The whole situation may be summed up as a soon-coming disintegration of Pitcairn as a community of people.

"Perhaps South Pacific Office has sensed this in the years past, because of their many attempts to meet the problems by sending representatives to the island to meet the question at issue. Evidently this has failed; and now they are at their wits' end to meet the difficulties and do not know what to do with 'the fly in the ointment,' as Pitcairn may be called in its island affairs.

"Pitcairn has not escaped the general downfall of civilization as it is today and, with the world, has entered the vortex of unrest and uncertainty that, so it would seem, cannot be unraveled so as to restore peace and contentment and a well-balanced political and ecclesiastical situation. Yours etc., Roy Clark." Volume 5, Number 8 (August 1963).

"Seeing a film 'Mutiny on the Bounty' recently brought back vivid memories of a call our old troopship made at Pitcairn after the first big row.

"Another bloke and I were mess orderlies that day, and an Islander came with a glorious sea shell which he wished to sell.

"Neither of us Diggers had funds, but my cobber, quicker than I, offered the seller a loaf of white bread for the trophy.

"Never was a sale made quicker, but I was left lamenting till another Islander poked another glorious shell through the porthole, and another white loaf disappeared from the mess table.

"I still have that wonderful shell (a lovely irridescent thing), and it is the joy of my wife's heart. But I don't suppose the Pitcairner still has the loaf—hard as Army bread was! A. R. K. Tauranga." Volume 6, Number 6 (31 May 1964).

"Dear Editor: After reading Volume 6, Number 6 of *Miscellany* there were some remarks regarding liberty on Pitcairn. The remarks were dubious, and uncertain about man's liberty on the island because of hard work and the long hours, compared to the 40-hour week in most of the British Colonies and in the United States.

"Yes, the community of Pitcairn does work hard and have long hours, and here is where I want to emphasize the meaning of the word 'liberty'—suppose we were under a communist regime. The work would be more arduous, the hours longer; and instead of liberty it would be compulsion, oppression, and slavery to the wills of others.

"May I offer to our readers another aspect of Pitcairn's freedom and liberty.

"It is the English flag. It is to be able to sing 'God Save the Queen' without controversy of strife and words. It is to greet your neighbor in jest and goodwill banter, to condemn or approve right or wrong legislative power, or praise each other before dictatorship laws that may mean banishment, prison, or even death.

"It is to be able to do the job you like—to have your own garden; to catch your own fish; to plant your own seed and harvest the crop; to own your own house, and to build or destroy as one sees best; to come and go as one pleases; to raise families in ideal surroundings and environment; to walk the island pathways day or night without fear of molestation in any form; to enjoy around-the-clock pure, clean, fresh sea air; to have access to acres and acres of hills and valleys wooded with trees and vines, flowers and ferns, where your children can romp and play 24 hours of the day if need be.

"Where families can live together without fear of separation, except by accident or death—not living in fear of parting by despotic powers because of some trivial wrong or of unguarded speech.

"Where man's house is his palace.

"Where there are no recognized differences between the rich and the poor. In fact, there are no rich and no poor.

"Where, if you're out at the elbows, you stand on an equality with the man by your side.

"Where, in conclusion, we on Pitcairn are practically a self-ruled community, laying down our own laws to our manner of living.

"Hereafter, with diffident thought, let us not say there is little or no liberty on Pitcairn. Rather, let us say, 'Give me Pitcairn, or give me death'; for the island has the very essence of freedom and liberty. Respectfully, Roy P. Clark." Volume 6, Number 9 (31 August, 1964).

"On Pitcairn the Florida Orchid is known as the Hattie tree, and there are various stories which explain why it is so called. The most likely of these is that the original tree was brought from Norfolk Island by Harriet McCoy (nee Christian), wife of Edmund.

108

"The possibility of this being so could be confirmed by the knowledge of whether Bauhinia variegata exists, or has existed, on Norfolk.

"Regardless of its background, the Hattie tree provides the basic material for a beautiful memento of Pitcairn." Volume 15, Number 4 (April 1973).

"A short article in the April issue (of Miscellany) on the origin of the Hattie tree brought this delightful reply from Hilda Young in Auckland. (Hilda is 'Mrs. Pitcairn' in New Zealand, the person everyone turns to in times of trouble.) 'The Hattie Flower tree was brought to Pitcairn by Miss Hattie Andre from the U.S.A. She was a fully qualified teacher sent to the island by the Seventh-day Adventist mission in Washington. Homesick Hilda.' " Volume 15, Number 8 (August 1973).

Mail

"Open three days a week, Pitcairn's Post Office must surely be one of the world's remotest. The Post Office bursts into life whenever a ship is calling at the Island, as folk rush about madly to get letters and parcels ready for posting. When mail arrives on the Island, again the Post Office becomes the centre of attraction, as everyone waits with great anticipation for 'Outside News' from relatives and friends.

"With those opening remarks, let us pause for a moment to give a thought to the significance of June 7 as far as Postal services for Pitcairn are concerned. Most readers should receive, with either May or June's Miscellany, a special cachet on envelopes, signifying 50 years of Postal service. Up until 1926, because there was no Postal service available on the Island, Pitcairn overcame this situation by having its letter franked: 'Posted on Pitcairn Island: no stamps available.' Then from June 7, 1927, up until 1940, the stamps and postal rates from New Zealand were used. On October 15, 1940, the first Pitcairn stamps were issued; . . ."

"Although Editor was unable to ascertain who posted the first letter on the Island and to whom it was went, records do show that the first recorded parcel for dispatch from Pitcairn belonged to (the late) Mrs. May Clark. For your information, the parcel weighed seven pounds and was being sent to E. J. Williams of Wellington, New Zealand for the sum of a little over four shillings (that same parcel weight today would cost $1.20). The date recorded was 7/11/1940. Pitcairn's first Postmaster was Roy P. Clark, who held the post until he retired in 1958. His assistant from 1950, until he assumed the post of Postmaster in 1958, was

Oscar Clark, who has held the post since.

"As one correspondent wrote, 'The idea that a letter from Pitcairn was handled by the descendants of the *Bounty*, by way of longboat, and travelled halfway around the world is exciting. . . .'

"PREPARING OUTWARD MAIL. As well as being open three times per week, the Post Office is always opened prior to the arrival of a ship (provided that the arrival does not coincide with the Sabbath) whose Master has indicated he is willing to take the mail. With his staff, Warren Christian (as present on sick leave in New Zealand) and Reynold Warren, Oscar commences by informing everyone when the Post Office is to be opened for receiving mail (this is usually five hours before the ship is due or five hours before sunset). A last-minute rush by everyone to capitalise on what is usually an unexpected caller takes place; and, for perhaps a day or two beforehand, folk busy themselves packing parcels and writing letters, so that when the Post Office is opened for business they have got their last minute chores completed. Believe me, it is hectic.

"Following the closing of the Post Office to the public, the busiest time for the staff gets underway, in which registering, cancelling, and sorting of letters and parcels is carried out. When items have been sorted, documentation begins as parcels being set are entered in a Parcel Bill (a record of parcels leaving the Island), a Letter Bill is filled in (a record of registered articles leaving the Island), and an Airmail Statement is filled out. Then parcels and letters are placed in appropriate mailbags and sealed with a lead sealer, with the marking PIT/PO. Pitcairn does not have its own mailbags; and, as all mail arrives from either United Kingdom, U.S.A. or New Zealand, mailbags from these countries are used, although mailbags from the latter country tend to be used more often. So in essence a New Zealand mailbag may be used to deliver mail to Panama. Mail sent from the Island will always end up either in New Zealand, Panama Canal Zone, or United Kingdom. As one may gather, it is necessary to resort to Pitcairn mail in these places once again.

"When all mailbags have been sealed, they are taken to the Landing by tractor (if the roads are dry), or by shoulder if the roads are wet. Once the motorboats are launched, the mail is loaded on board and covered with canvases to help keep waterspray (at time buckets of water) off the bags. Once the mail has been safely hoisted aboard the ship, the Postmaster asks the Master of the ship to sign the Waybill and Mail Receipt. A copy of the Waybill is handed by the Master to the Mail Officer at the port of call.

"The mail is now out of the hands of the Postal staff, and it is up to the various Post Offices around the world to ensure safe deliveries of mail.

"Sorting Inward mail—Usually the Postmaster, along with everyone else on the island, knows how much mail is to be brought ashore before the ship arrives. The radio staff has made contact with the vessel a day or so beforehand. Once out at the ship, the Waybill is signed by a Postal staff member only after the mail is safely off-loaded into the motorboats. Mailbags are covered with canvases and usually come ashore among the cargo. At the Landing the mail is separated from the cargo, and there it waits until all cargo is delivered or secure. Should mail come ashore on Sabbath, it is left at the Landing along with the cargo until Sabbath evening or the following day. If the roads are wet, the mail is placed on the Flying Fox tray, sent up to the Edge, and manhandled in slushy mud to the Post Office. With barely a chance for a well-earned rest, the Postal staff begins sorting the mail. As they go about their task, the Square gradually fills up with folk who wait in earnest for their mail. In the Post Office, staff members are busy sorting the letters and miscellaneous papers (pamphlets, booklets etc.) first of all. When this is completed, Pitcairn's unofficial Mayor, Morris Warren, is asked to ring the bell; and then the once-patient crowd surges forward to receive their letters. After receiving their letters, folk go out into the Square to catch up with news. Again the Post Office staff begins sorting parcels. All parcels must be accounted for and are entered in a book set aside for the purpose alongside the names of the lucky recipients. Then the announcement is made for the lucky folk whose names have been called out to sign for and collect their parcels.

"The weary staff have at last the opportunity to take leave of their work, and one can imagine how eager they are to catch up with "Outside News' like everyone else.

"Further Information—join Postmaster Oscar Clark on a guided tour: On entering through one of two doors, you will see on the wall facing the entrance two framed pictures of Her Majesty, Queen Elizabeth II, and H.R.H. Prince Philip. The hardboard walls are bamboo in colour and the ceiling white. On the serving counter are two metric scales for parcels, and on a working counter is a metric scale for letters. There are 27 individual P.O. boxes (private but not locked) and one Private Bag. A Public posting box is built into the Post Office similar to those found in 'Outside' Post Offices. On the wall to the right of the main entrance you will see on display stamps which have

111

been issued over the year. Please note that these stamps are not for sale. On sale at present are the current definitives (soon to be replaced), British Postal Orders, Aerogrammes, and ordinary and special envelopes. With the exception of the envelopes, stock and money are kept in three fireproof, strong safes. There are also town nonfireproof safes and a filing cabinet for storing miscellaneous items. . . .' Volume 19, Number 6 (June 1977).

"Twenty-nine weeks since the last northbound supply vessel from New Zealand . . . 19 weeks since the last batch of mail from/via New Zealand: Yes, that is what the inhabitants of Pitcairn have had to contend with.

"And despite the gloomy mail service, among the many letters received . . . was one from an English correspondent, . . . who says, 'Many thanks for your letter dated 17 January '77. It took exactly six months to arrive.' Furthermore, the writer's letter, dated 29 June '77, arrived at Pitcairn on November 24 aboard our supply vessel, *Medic* from New Zealand.

"It is frustrating, isn't it? We can only ask that you continue to be very patient while waiting for replies to letters written. More often than not, replies to your letters are not forthcoming simply because they have not been received on Pitcairn. Unfortunately, there is nothing for the present time, at least, which can be done to improve the present mail situation.

"Island Secretary Ben Christian informed us that he was pleased to note that most personal cheques sent to Pitcairn for various reasons were undated, thus saving the embarrassment of returning cheques to the senders to present again due to their being out of date. . . .

"Why, even we here on the Island are most anxious to hear from the 'outside world'; and who can blame us if we think. . . 'nobody loves us anymore?' Editor." Volume 19, Number 11 (November 1977).

Making a Well

Wells on Pitcairn are not the deeply dug affairs to obtain a supply of underground water that are seen in many parts of the world. They are used for the catchment of rain water. The once thatched roofs of island homes are now made of corrugated iron designed to catch rainfall and bring it to the well.

"How often have you had water shortage problems? And how have you or your Water Authorities coped with such problems? I realise that water shortage is a serious problem we all have to face sometimes, but if we have at our disposal good reservoirs or holding tanks, such problems may be alleviated considerably.

"On Pitcairn we have our water shortage problems, for we have no rivers from which to draw water during drought conditions and consequently are left to the elements of nature for our water requirements. To add to this serious problem, we cannot run off to the nearest tank manufacturer and place orders for water tanks, because the closest manufacturer is approximately 3000 miles away.

"How then do Pitcairners deal with water catchment problems? . . . The following is an account by Steve Christian on the building of his well:

" 'It all began on the 15th March, and with the help of some of the men we carefully selected soft grey rock, which abounds the Landing, and carted it all by tractor up to my house a mile away and 200 feet above sea level. The rocks, of about five-inch thickness, were especially selected for their straight seams, which could make them easy to split with wedges and thus make our job easier. Getting the sand from Tedside by tractor was also a big job when the climb back to my house (half a mile away) is 350 feet above sea level. Approximately 30 bags of sand were collected; and, to complete the list of ingredients, one drum of cement was acquired for making the necessary mortar for joining the rocks together.

" 'The task then was to mark out the well's size, eight feet long by six feet wide, on the ground and then proceed to place the first layer of rocks around the perimeter of the marked site. This being carefully done, it was then a matter of building onto these foundation rocks up to a height of three feet, ensuring that all rocks were shaped in such a way that the wall was built up squarely and level. Following this stage, soil was dug from within the framework of the rocks to a depth of two feet. A slight hollow was dug in the floor to allow debris to be swept into it and thus make it easier to clean out when the well was finished.

" 'When all the rocks were neatly cemented into place, the men plastered the inside of the well, leaving a two-inch-diameter hole in the appropriate place for the outlet supply for the house. The floor of the well was also plastered; and, after the plaster had dried, water was poured into the well to clean the well out.

" 'The well being completed, the final job was to dig a trench two feet deep and 18 inches away from the sides of the well. This was done to prevent the roots of nearby trees from trying to work their way into the well in search of water. Past experience has shown the damage to the wells that these trees are able to do if their roots are not cut back.

" 'And after 11 days of hard and patient work, the well was

113

completed, ready for the rain.' " Volume 18, Number 4 (April 1976).

Medical

The Pitcairn people are a healthy lot. Dr. David Gibson, a Texas physician who visited the island in 1972 and examined a number of the islanders, reported:

"It would be difficult to find a comparable population anywhere in the world as healthy, robust, and physically fit as these people. I am amazed to see 50- and 60-year-olds trotting up and down the steep paths of this little island. And it is nothing to see Pitcairn men of more than 70 scrambling up rope ladders to the decks of ships like only 20-year-olds elsewhere might do. Apart from minor surgical procedures, there really isn't much to do."

For all their good health, though, the Pitcairner's life is a hazardous one. Records going back a century reveal that about one in every five Pitcairners dies accidentally—at sea, in falls from cliffs, or in shooting mishaps. Yet the life expectancy on the island is as good as, or better than, in the United States.

Pitcairn's isolation seems to have kept much of the disease that has been a problem on other Pacific islands from its shores. When the isolation is broken by visitors, however, even casual contact may be enough to lay the entire population low with such common infectious ailments as colds or influenza.

"We are very sorry to say goodbye to Sam and Vula and little Terry, who recently left for New Zealand for medical purposes. Although thousands of watermelons have been consumed on this island, Terry was the first that we know of to swallow a seed that lodged in the windpipe. Everything was done that we could possibly do, without effect. Tom (Christian) spent many long hours at the radio station trying to locate a passing vessel. Eventually, after much persuasion, the captain of the *Glanely* took Sam, Vula, and Terry on board. Sam was one of our faithful bell ringers.

"The Church business meeting was held last Tuesday evening with splendid reports from all departments of the church. It was duly voted at this meeting that Reynold and Bruce be appointed bell ringers, to assist Clinton. Bernice was also appointed to the office of Deaconess." Volume 3, Number 3 (March 1961).

"Our readers will remember in our last *Miscellany* the report of little Terry Young, who had to go to New Zealand for surgery because of a watermelon seed in his windpipe. We are happy to report that Terry and his parents had a really wonderful time on board the tanker that took them to New Zealand. The party was

114

met out in the Wellington harbour by a Police Launch and taken quickly ashore, where the Free Ambulance took them straight to the hospital. The operation was performed the same day, and we are all so happy to know that once more we have proof that God cares for His own." Volume 3, Number 4 (April 1961).

"The coming of a ship to the Island is always marked with great interest. Is all the mail ready that should be? Are there as many souvenirs for sale as the ship demands?

"The public fruit that goes on board has to be gathered; this being exchanged for such items as flour, rice, milk powder, potatoes, or sugar. Ships bring with them much of interest, and sometimes infection from the outside world.

"Recently a ship with measles aboard called here. No one was permitted to go on board, and all trading was done over the side of the ship. If an outbreak of measels had occurred here, future ships could refuse to call. All such infections must be reported.

"Mishaps too, sometimes accompany the visits of ships. Just two weeks ago Clifford was unloading timber from a ship into the longboats below, when his left little finger was almost entirely severed, as the rope slipped. An officer close at hand quickly notified the captain, who in turn notified the ship's doctor. For reasons best known only to himself, the doctor decided to stitch the finger back into position, and sent the patient ashore with instructions that it was to be left for three days before redressing. Four hourly injections of Pethidine were given and the latest of antibiotics; but, when the wound was examined on the third day, gangrene had set in.

"By ham radio the Medical Officer (on Pitcairn) contacted doctors in America to see if she could get any further advice to prevent the gangrene from spreading before the finger could be amputated by the doctor on the next scheduled ship. We then received word that a Star ship would be passing close sooner than the other ship, and it is generally known that these ships have highly qualified doctors on board, who either are returning from, or going to England for specified study.

"Once more our radio operators sent a medical S.O.S. across the waves, and the captain of this Star ship was very willing to stop. On board was a surgery specialist, who offered to attend to Clifford. The offending gangrenous finger was skillfully removed and today Clifford is doing very well. Once more we are grateful for radio and the ships that come to our Island." Volume 3, Number 5 (May 1961).

"Where did it come from? How did it get here? These are questions that almost the whole populace of the Island has been asking about the recent influenza epidemic, which hit us with all its fury.

"Your guess is as good as mine. We do know that many other places are suffering from the same scourge; so it does seem rather apparent that passing ships must be our downfall for collecting infections from the 'outside.'

"There were 112 people on the island when the flu first started, and there are only six or seven who can boast of having missed out. Some had only slight infections; others were sure they were going to die. We are very glad to report, however, that no one has done that; and now it would seem that the worst is over. The extreme weakness that has persisted for so long after the fever subsided is the general complaint of every patient.

"There have been several influenza epidemics in the last four years, and we sincerely hope that we collect no more such maladies for many years to come. Medical Officer." Volume 3 Number 12 (December 1961).

"28th January—At 9:15 a.m. the alarm bell, followed by the 'Man the Boat' bell, rang out; and there was a frantic rush to the Landing. Word had come in that Warren had had a bad fall while fishing at Tedside. In very quick time all available men had the launch in the water and we were out of the harbour. Conditions at Tedside were not easy; so four of the men—Bruce, Charles, Desmond, and Radley—dived overboard, two of them with the metal stretcher, and swam ashore. Warren had been standing on a rock, fishing, when it gave way. He fell heavily onto the rocks below and then into the water. Fortunately, he was not so seriously injured as was first thought. He was carried round to Rat Hole, where he was safely passed into the launch and brought to the Landing. From there he was carried to his home, where he was attended to by Mrs. Davies (Medical Officer). It was amazing how quickly the whole operation was completed, for Warren was in his own home within two hours of the alarm having been rung." Volume 5, Number 2 (February 1963).

"Little Glenn Clark had a serious fall from a tree and hurt his eye, but we are glad that he recovered well and is now back in school.

"We have just completed a six-monthly (health) inspection of all homes. Mr. D. F. Bradnam and Ratu David Toganivalu (Executive Officer at South Pacific Office, Suva, Fiji) came with me on an inspection day. Some homes were growing old, but neatness compensates for that. Others have spent a lot of money in making their homes more modern and comfortable. It would be good if all the people could be so nicely housed and cheered by beautiful flower gardens. Lloyd's garden of flowers was beautiful. First, second, and third places will be announced next Saturday night and prizes presented.

"Please guard your homes, for 'health is wealth.' M. M. Ferris, Medical Officer." Volume 5, Number 7 (July 1963).

"3rd. As Pastor Ferris was carrying Merian down from the Church to the Mission House after the usual Tuesday evening prayer meeting, Pastor slipped and fractured his left leg. With the assistance of some of the men, he was carried to his home, where he was made as comfortable as possible.

"6th. The *Athenic* arrived from London. At the request of the Chief Magistrate and Mrs. Ferris, the ship's surgeon was brought ashore to attend to Pastor. Once a proper splint had been applied to the injured leg, the patient was transported out to the ship. Accompanied by Mrs. Ferris and their daughter Merian, he sailed for New Zealand. Also travelling out as patients were Floss Young and Elsie Young. Floss's two children, Glenda and Donald, were also passengers. The island is certainly having a very bad run with sickness." Volume 5, Number 10 (October 1963).

"MEDICAL REPORT. By Mrs. M. M. Ferris. . . . It is a pleasure to work in the new dispensary, which has louvre windows and curtains. We are proud of the new adjustable examination cot which has just arrived. It is a personal gift from Mr. Bradnam, and it is very much appreciated. Glen was the first to use it, when he had three stitches in a leg wound. We thank Mr. Bradnam for his very kind and valuable gift.

"Last week Jacob had a very nasty accident to his eye. He was hammering a steel peg to pin down a line, when it sprang up and hit his glasses. His glasses broke, and pieces of glass cut his eyeball. Fortunately, the Expedition boys, on the spot, were able with the aid of a camera lens, to remove most of the glass; and the last piece came away on the way home. The eye soon healed over, with care; and we are thankful to God for His protection. We are sorry to have had a casualty on sports day, when Mr. Hardwick Knight of the Expedition party was badly hit with a cricket ball. . . . During the past few weeks the 'flu' has been affecting most homes. Some were affected by laryngitis, some had bad backs and aching limbs, and two were tonsillitis cases. They all seem to have recovered now, with Mimi and Fred being the last to shake it off. Bert and Charles left on the *Atlantic* for New Zealand, where they will get good medical attention. Mr. and Mrs. Cowell left on the same ship, and we are grateful for their sincere interest in the medical welfare of the people of Pitcairn Island." Volume 6, Numbers 1 and 2 (February 1964).

"NANCY'S FALL. On Thursday afternoon, June 24, the telephone rang, asking for the nurse to go to the clinic immediately. She was simply told that Nancy had fallen down a cliff.

"I followed to the clinic to find out what was the matter, and there learned that Nancy was down Tautama, stranded on the cliff. I enquired of several children standing there where Tautama was, and they had no idea where the direction was.

"I rushed off in the general direction of Hulianda with a bag of bandages and a bundle of splints. The boys had gone ahead with the stretcher. When halfway up the hill, I met Donald running down. He told me they couldn't bring her around the cliff on the stretcher and would have to go down in the boat. So down to the Landing all hands rushed, with most of the old men to help push the launch down the slipway.

"The seas were fairly rough; but the *Dolphin*, with the spray flying in all directions, quickly made the distance to Tautama As we approached the cliffs, there were big waves rolling in, and it was quite evident that it would be difficult getting Nancy aboard.

"Nancy had been on a fishing trip with Charles, Charlotte, and Les; and, in trying to negotiate a crack in the cliff wall, she slipped into it and would have fallen right down into the sea had she not wedged herself tightly into the crack, with her back to one wall and her knee to the other. Charles had great difficulty in lifting her out of this predicament. He then discovered that her knee was very badly cut, and her back was badly lacerated over a large area. Les ran back up the cliff and gave the alarm. Help quickly came, but it was impossible to carry the patient back off the cliff.

"The *Dolphin* backed in, with all the men manning the oars; and ropes were thrown to the folks up on the cliff. These were attached to the stretcher. Charles, Noggie, Lloyd, and Melva held the ropes and slowly lowered Nancy down the cliff, while the other men in the boat pulled their ends of the ropes, swinging Nancy out over the waves onto the launch.

"I hope that my Kodachrome pictures will reveal something of the terror on Nancy's face as she swung out from this 30-foot cliff edge, over the tossing waves, onto the rocking launch! The helpers then dived into the sea, following the launch out through the surf. Two sharks were reportedly swimming close by.

"I commend the men for their bravery in handling the situation so well in spite of the rough seas, and in getting Nancy safely back into Bounty Bay. The men called me 'sugar' because I tried

118

to dodge the spray! All hands were soaking wet when we reached the shelter of the Bay. Nancy was quickly taken to the dispensary.

"Melva had cared for Nancy on the cliff, and her bandaging had prevented hemorrhaging. It took several hours to get her bandaged up properly, and the knee wound required six stitches. All felt that Nancy had come off very well, considering the dangerous fall she had suffered. Now she is slowly recuperating and should be up and around soon.

"Her husband, Bruce Young, especially requests that a special thanks be given to all who worked so hard and long and in such a dangerous place to rescue his wife, following her unfortunate accident. He especially appreciated the help of the older men who rushed down to Bounty Bay to help launch the boat. . . . W. G. Ferris." Volume 7, Number 6 (June 1965).

"Tuesday 13th September: N.Z. Shipping Co's *Otaio* called in the early evening with a considerable quantity of cargo, including timber for the proposed new launch—also fuel for government use and dunnage for the community. During loading, Cairn slipped and damaged his ribs against the gunwale, so requiring the doctor's help." Volume 8, Number 9 (September 1966).

"Accident at the Square—Steve Christian met with an unfortunate accident whilst playing in the Square on the evening of 4th Oct., injuring his thigh and apparently fracturing it at the joint. Our Medical Officer and her husband treated Steve and did their utmost to relieve his pain but felt that a doctor should examine the patient and if necessary advise on further action. Radio messages to ships at sea and to London were followed a couple of days later by contact with *Port New Plymouth*, placed well south of here. After an exchange of messages this ship agreed to call and send her doctor ashore for the following Monday.

"It had been thought likely that Steve would have to leave home and travel to Panama, but the doctor was able to reassure Mrs. Webster that they had done all that was possible. He also recommended that later on an X ray be taken. . . .

"Steve's parents, Ivan and Dobrey, and all on Pitcairn greatly appreciated this vessel calling. The Island Council resolved to write a letter of thanks to the Port Line." Volume 8, Number 10 (October 1966).

"Brian's heavy fall from his bicycle left him with a greenstick fracture of the left forearm and considerable pain. When it was suspected that he might have internal injury, the *Adelaide Star's*

Doctor was called and recommended hospitalisation in N.Z. We certainly miss Brian about the island and hope that he has a speedy recovery.

"We have had to put out calls for medical assistance on three occasions and often wish that some retired G.P. would spend part of his retirement on Pitcairn.

"November 17th, *Adelaide Star*. This ship answered a radio call for medical aid for Brian, who had fallen heavily from his bicycle. Returning from the Henderson area, the ship arrived at 4 p.m.; and the Doctor and two officers wasted no time getting ashore. While the Dr. attended Brian (and Mrs. Reeves, who was suffering from pneumonia) the two ship's officers were Honda'd about the island by Craig and Steve. The boats returned to the ship at 5:45, and the ship sailed at 6:15. We are very grateful to all concerned for their prompt assistance." Volume 9, Number 11 (November 1967).

"On Sunday, May 12th, *Cap Vilano*, calling for the first time, radioed to say she would stop for one hour, if there was mail to pick up. Two mailbags were ready for forwarding, and the ship gave her ETA (estimated time of arrival) as 1 p.m.

"Two launches were put to sea in moderate conditions, and the ship appeared well to the westwards of a rainstorm at 1:30 p.m. The ship hove to two miles off Matt's Rock; and soon we were mounting the single rope ladder, at the top of which was a landing platform—the steps arrangement being held steady by two of the ship's crew. This heavy steel contraption was hooked over the rail of the ship and apparently was not secured in any way at the base. However, all scrambled safely aboard and began their trading with the officers, crew, and 10 passengers.

"After what had been to this time a very pleasant visit, the whistle blew, summoning us all to the boats. Only a few men were actually in the boats, when Albert appeared at the top of the ladder. Turning around and facing the ship on the top step, Albert grasped the two handrails and leaned back, looking down to find the rope ladder with his feet. No one was holding the steps at this time. Suddenly, the whole piece of apparatus came away from the ship's side, flew across the five feet of water between the boats and the ship, then across the first boat (*Boxhead*), to land with a crash on the outside boat, *Reid Cowell*. Albert fell 20 feet down the side of the ship, landing on his back across the gunn'el of *Boxhead*, from where he bounced into the water between the ship and the boat. He was quickly pulled out of the water by Len and Pervis in a state of severe shock and wrapped in canvas on a bed of oars placed across the thwarts of *Boxhead*.

"The ship carried no Doctor, but pain pills were obtained from a very concerned Captain and administered to Albert as the boats left the ship's side at 3:15 p.m. All speed was made for Bounty Bay, where luckily reasonable surf conditions prevailed.

"A hasty phone call from the Landing prepared the Nurse, and with minimum delay the patient was warmly wrapped in a stretcher and carried by six men to the Edge. From there, a short ride to the Square by car, where Nurse Ferris and Royal were ready to do their best for the patient.

"With no previous experience and only the skimpiest instructions, Tony, Pastor, and the Editor untangled the intricacies of the new X-ray machine well enough to expose two plates to assist with diagnosis. Results were good enough to show a broken neck of the femur, with possible dislocation, plus fractured ribs on the left side. These findings were later confirmed by visiting medical practitioners.

"While under medication, Albert was moved to Dobrey's house, where he was made as comfortable as possible, with his right leg in traction. At this time, Tom was beginning what turned out to be a marathon spell of duty at the radio station, attempting to contact a ship carrying a doctor. *Corinthic* (Captain Anderson) and *Rakaia* (Captain Cosker) were contacted that evening, the former northbound with a Doctor on board and the latter southbound with neither a Doctor nor facilities for nursing. Captain Anderson indicated that he would stop at 5 a.m. the next morning and put his Doctor ashore, while Captain Cosker's ship was 400 miles off and headed on a course to pass close to Mangareva, but he indicated his willingness to call if *Corinthic's* Doctor recommended immediate removal of the patient to New Zealand.

"*Corinthic* arrived at 5:45 a.m., and Dr. Hutcheson (a young Canadian woman medical practitioner) and the ship's Fourth Officer were taken ashore. Progress ashore was reported to the ship every 15 minutes by Pastor, operating a walkie-talkie from Dobrey's. . . . The Doctor confirmed Mrs. Ferris' findings, but said that the patient could not be shifted to New Zealand at this time because he had contracted pneumonia. She prescribed treatment, examined and treated four other folk, then reboarded the ship, which sailed at 8:30 a.m. . . .

"*Rakaia*, meanwhile, had been very active by radio in attempting to contact any southbound ship carrying a Doctor, as well as alerting the U.S. Marine Search and Rescue organisation. Pitcairn Radio had also asked for assistance from Wellington Radio.

"Albert's condition fluctuated considerably over the next five days, and 'round the clock' watches were organised among the folk so that he had constant supervision and attention.

"*Port New Plymouth*, northbound with a Doctor on board, was given all the necessary information; and, after consideration, the Doctor decided that, as the patient had been seen by a physician, all he could recommend was removal to New Zealand at the first opportunity. The ship's master said that he would attempt to contact any southbound vessels.

"*Port Albany*, (Captain L. Brown) was contacted on the 22nd, when, on detailed information sent, Dr. Jackson of Adelaide decided that he should make an examination, Captain Brown notifying that his ETA was 8:30 a.m. on the 23rd. The ship arrived at 9 a.m., and the Doctor was immediately taken ashore in rough seas. Ship-to-shore walkie-talkie contact was again established. From the detailed medical reports received from Mrs. Ferris, Dr. Jackson had a very good idea of the patient's condition and had had a special splint constructed by the ship's carpenter. This was carried ashore by the Bo'sun, but unfortunately this apparatus proved to be too short. The Doctor agreed with previous findings, but also noticed from the X rays that the broken head of the femur had rotated 180 degrees; and he rcommended transferral to New Zealand as quickly as possible for surgical treatment. A further recommendation was that the patient be accompanied to N.Z. by a medical attendant. The Doctor rejoined the ship at 12:30 p.m., and the ship sailed at 12:45 p.m. We are grateful to Captain for his kindness in sending ashore two dozen fresh eggs for the patient, as well as sweets for the children.

"Our quandary now was (A) to contact a southbound ship; and (B) who to send as attendant. Nurse Ferris was the only one filling the requirements, and we could ill afford to send our Nurse and leave the island without a qualified person to attend day-to-day needs.

"The first problem was overcome when Tom contacted *Laurenthic* early in the evening; and the second was solved when we received word from Dr. Jackson on *Port Albany* that he was satisfied that the First Officer on *Laurenthic* had sufficient medical experience to look after Albert, providing that he was accompanied by someone from the island to assist generally. Warren had earlier indicated that he would willingly go with Albert if it were necessary; so that the only problem immediately facing us was to get the patient safely onto the ship, which was to arrive at dawn the next day.

"*Laurenthic* was off the island at 4 a.m. on the 24th; but no attempt was made to get a boat through the heavy surf until it was quite light, at 6:45. Once again six willing men gently carried a well-wrapped Albert in the stretcher, this time in the opposite direction of his first journey, and placed him across the stern thwarts of *Reid Cowell*.

"The whole community turned out to see him safely on his journey, to wish him Godspeed and a quick return to his homeland.

"Hoisted over the ship's stern by derrik, Albert was soon being made comfortable by Nurse Ferris and Dobrey in a very-well-set-up sick bay. Warren was quartered with him so that he could be immediately on hand when needed. The ship left at 8:30 a.m. bound for Wellington. AS WE GO TO PRESS (JUNE 2nd) WE ARE ABLE TO STATE THAT WORD WAS RECEIVED YESTERDAY THAT ALBERT PROVED TO BE AN EXCELLENT PATIENT ON THE VOYAGE, THAT HE HAD A COMFORTABLE JOURNEY, AND THAT HE IS NOW IN WELLINGTON HOSPITAL.

"The People of Pitcairn have asked me to express—to the Masters, Officers, and men of *Corinthic*, *Port Albany*, and *Laurenthic*, who stopped and gave practical help; to the *Rakaia* and *Port New Plymouth* (for their advice and radio contacts); and especially to the various Radio Officers concerned: Wellington Radio, Govcom, Suva, 'Voice of Prophecy' Radio in U.S.A. (who were prepared to go to a great deal of trouble and effort had it been required); and to the Shaw Savill and Port Lines for allowing their vessels to stop and give so much of their valuable time—the sincere and grateful thanks of the whole community.

"It goes without saying that we sincerely appreciate the advice and expert attention given by Dr. Hutcheson and Dr. Jackson, who were both willing to risk life and limb in a double journey through the surf to Bounty Bay.

"This paper would also like to commend the folk of Pitcairn for their helpfulness and community spirit in a time of stress—particularly Mrs. Ferris for her long hours of patient nursing; Dobrey for turning her home into a hospital; Pastor and Tony for their work with the X-ray equipment; and the radio staff, particularly Tom, who worked long hours sending and receiving long, involved medical reports as well as efficiently maintaining the normal schedules.

"We can only hope now that Albert will successfully recover from his injuries and that he will soon again join us here on Pitcairn." Volume 10, Number 5 (May 1968).

"Fred Brown had a fall at Tedside on the 14th, and it was

necessary to take a boat around to bring him safely back. After a few days in bed Fred was all right, but had one foot bandaged up. A few days later, Laura, his wife, was shifting furniture, when she dropped the end of a bed on her foot, breaking a small bone. Consequently, Laura spent the anniversary of Ivan's birthday in bed, with Fred still hobbling about. The birthday guests had to fend for themselves, although as usual Laura had everything prepared." Volume 10, Number 7 (July 1968).

"On 8th April, around 5 p.m., the peace and quiet of Pitcairn was shattered by the urgent ring of the St. John Ambulance bell strike: Ding-Ding . . . Ding. Ding-Ding . . . Ding. On Pitcairn all public events are announced by certain strikes on the public bell. Fortunately, this St. John Ambulance bell strike is seldom heard, as it announces an accident.

"When the 'accident' bell rings, all the able-bodied men drop whatever they are doing, make straight for the Public Square, and organise a rescue party. On 8th April when the men arrived at the Square, it was to be told that Tom Christian had caught his big toe in the chain of his Honda whilst trying to get home from a day's fishing at Tedside. When Tom and Betty set off that morning, it was beneath a clear blue sky, but during the afternoon dark clouds rolled quickly over Pitcairn, and before long heavy rain was falling. It does not take much rain to turn our tracks into treacherously slippery mud. When the weather appeared to be turning bad, Tom and Betty headed for home. Unfortunately, they left their run too late; and the road was very slippery.

"Meanwhile, Warren (Betty's father) had set off for Tedside with a canvas. He thought Tom and Betty would decide to leave their Honda at Tedside till the roads dried and would wish to cover their bike from the elements. He met Tom and Betty, who were by this time about halfway between Tedside and Big Ridge. (For those who do not know Pitcairn, the track up from Tedside is quite rough and very, very steep in parts.) Tom and Betty were managing quite well at this stage; so Warren turned around and started on up. However, he had hardly gone 100 yards when the accident occurred, and he was recalled. He took one look at Tom's toe and set off quickly for help. Fortunately, Tom had not lost the whole of his toe—just a goodly portion on the end of it.

"Tom, of course, was in great pain; but decided to start crawling as best he could. He felt the men would find it extremely difficult to carry him up the steep incline in such muddy conditions. (Tom, by the way, is no 'flea'—6'1" high and weighing about 175 lbs.)

"Somehow or another he managed to crawl along (Betty having wrapped his toe as best she could with what was available) and in this manner reached the top of Big Ridge. By then his toe was very, very painful; and, as the grade was now to be downhill, he decided to try getting along in a sitting position, Betty pulling him as best she could. Although far from comfortable, it was at least easier on his toe. By the time the men arrived with a stretcher, Tom and Betty had come about half a mile from the scene of the accident.

"The men got Tom settled onto the stretcher and set off with small jogging steps (this helps one not to slip in the mud) for the Dispensary. Here Mrs. Parker and Royal Warren (her assistant) were awaiting their patient. The men waited whilst the patient was attended to and then carried him home to bed, where he remained for several days. . . ." Volume 13, Number 5 (April 1971).

"Many people were fishing from the rocks or launches on the 5th; Ben was fishing at St. Pauls and expected his wife, Irma, to join him presently.

"While crossing the rocks to Glennie, Irma suffered a fall and landed on jagged rocks 12 or 15 feet below the route she had been following. Royal was first on the scene; and she examined Irma to determine the extent of her injuries and then called to Ben, who was unaware of the mishap. Leaving Irma in Ben's care, Royal contacted Anderson, who was fishing in the same locality. He tried to attract the attention of the men in the boats, but it was not until he had made his way to the goat pen that he succeeded in conveying his message. Anderson's frantic waving was first interpreted as an indication that there was a ship passing at the time, and the men were already aware of this. Finally they realised that something was amiss and came about to return to the bay. Meanwhile, Royal made her way to the village and alerted Mrs. Webster, who hurried to the Landing.

"Len and Tom were fishing at Isaac when they heard of the accident and immediately raced up the steep track. Thelma was waving a sheet from the Edge near her home in the hope of attracting Dave's attention (perhaps this is why the ship stopped). Len and Tom decided that they would have to launch a canoe to convey Mrs. Webster and a stretcher to the scene of the accident, and this they did with all speed.

"When the launch arrived at Glennie, Oscar, Pervis, and Reynold swam ashore to find what needed to be done; then the boat headed for the Landing. They were met by Len and Tom with Mrs. Webster; then a quick transfer from canoe to launch, which then landed the medical officer on the rocks at Glennie.

"Mrs. Webster gave Irma on-the-spot treatment; then the patient was carried to the longboat and brought to the Landing. Stretcher and patient were taken to the Dispensary, where full medical treatment could be administered. Fortunately, Irma's injuries were confined to severe bruising and cuts, which required nine stitches; we say fortunately, because anyone familiar with Pitcairn's rugged coastline will know that it could have been much worse.

"Irma spent three weeks in bed as a result of the accident, but we are happy to report that she is now well on the road to complete recovery. It is grand to see you out and about again, Irma." Volume 15, Number 4 (April 1973).

"While still Medical Officer, Mrs. Newman was grateful to hear that the ship *Zealandic* was going to call in at Pitcairn on the first of the month, going north from Auckland, and that if sea conditions were favourable, the vessel was not going to stop, but the Master of the vessel was going to arrange to have the antibiotic (Bactrim) dropped close by in the vast Pacific. On the morning of the 1st the vessel duly arrived at 7 a.m.; and, slowing down in near-perfect conditions, executed a successful drop, which two of the local men collected and brought ashore.

"Many thanks go to British High Commission in Auckland for organising this 'drop' and thanks to the Master of *Zealandic*." Volume 18, Number 9 (September 1976).

"Ships have been the lifeblood of Pitcairn since settlement first came to the island. As time has gone on, this dependence has become greater, until today it is doubtful if life could go on on Pitcairn without ships. We rely on ships for basic supplies, fuel, sale of curios, and medical aid in event of serious injury or illness. However, the tables were turned rather dramatically on the morning of January 8th.

"None of the lookouts were aware of the 'mystery' ship until she was close in. Even Andrew Young, who checks the horizon before his wash, had failed to do so that morning. To begin with, we thought she was just one of those ships which come in close for a look but do not stop. But as she came closer she fired a distress flare, indicating something was badly amiss. We could now make out her name: *Maaskroon*, from Antwerp.

"As soon as the first Pitcairners were aboard, the mystery was explained. There had been a fight on board between two seamen the previous evening. One of the seamen had pulled a knife and stabbed the other seaman in the lower abdomen. The injured seaman was in a serious condition in the ship's sickroom.

"Our nursing staff, Mrs. Ferguson and Royal, were sent for and were soon aboard the vessel. They did what they could to make the injured man comfortable. The captain was very relieved to have such an experienced medical staff on board and requested that they accompany the injured man to hospital facilities in French Polynesia. This turned out to be Mururoa. The nursing staff agreed. This unselfish action by our staff probably saved the injured seaman's life, as the medical knowledge of the officers and crew was almost nil. They eventually had the injured man lifted off by helicopter at Mururoa, from where he was flown to a French hospital. Our nursing staff were returned three days later by a grateful Captain. . . ." Volume 20, Number 1 (January 1978).

Miro Wood

An Austrian wood carver named Laeffler, who lived on Pitcairn earlier in this century, is credited with teaching the islanders to carve curios, which they sell primarily to those on passing ships. Using wood brought from Henderson Island, the Pitcairn men fashion their handicrafts or curios in home workshops, with bench and lathe, chisels, gouges, axes, planes, broken glass, and sand paper. For decades the Pitcairners have called the wood they use for their carvings "Miro" wood. They also consume quantities of a chocolate drink called "Milo." It was, therefore, something of a surprise when the islanders learned from the Amercian Wood Collectors' Society that what they thought they were carving was really what they were drinking.

"Miro, or Milo? The first we recognize as the wood used here for carving curios, and the second as a beverage often used in Pitcairn homes.

"The American Wood Collectors' Society, however, has other ideas; and the following appeared in their bulletin of August 22nd, 1967:

" 'In stories about the Pitcairn Islanders' carvings, statements are made that the wood they use is Miro and that it comes from Henderson Island. The *National Geographic* concurs in this, but does not apply any botanical name. In their December 1957 issue, they state that the wood is wine-red; and they show a picture of a fallen Miro tree in connection with the story, "I Found the Bones of the Bounty."

" 'Research in *Standardised Plant Names* shows only one reference to Miro wood, which it asserts is Podocarpus ferrugineus. This is definitely a New Zealand tree, and its range does not extend over into the vicinity of Henderson Island. While the wood Pitcairners use is called Miro, it is properly identified as Thespesia populnea. This is the tree that the Hawaiians call Milo. The Indian name is Portia Tree, and in Tahiti it is called the Bendy Tree. *Standardised Plant Names* lists only Portia Tree for Thespesia populnea.

" 'Let us not dispute the Pitcairn name of Miro for their wood, but rather add it to Thespesia populnea as another common name for it. Although this might seem to create additional confusion in the minds of some people and cause disagreement among others, I believe that in fairness to all concerned the Pitcairn name Miro should stand as is. And for this reason alone: the name Miro has become so deeply implanted, as the wood used in their products and associated with them, that to urge any change in nomenclature at this time may affect their sales and reputation.

" 'We often find that common names are misleading like this in many parts of the world; hence it cannot be too strongly urged that the correct botanical names be used.'

"(An interesting article. The first time I hear anyone being asked to 'Pass that piece of Thespesia populnea,' I'll let you know.—Ed.)" Volume 10, Number 2 (February 1968).

Navy Gift

"Another link in the chain of events which has associated Pitcairn Island with the Royal Navy for over 180 years was forged recently with the arrival of an Aldis signalling lamp and accessories aboard the *Majestic*.

"This generous and expensive gift was made to the island on behalf of the Royal Navy by Admiral Sir Anthony Griffin, the Controller of the Navy, following enquiries made by His Excellency, Sir Arthur Galsworthy, Governor of Pitcairn.

"Sir Arthur has asked that the lamp be presented to the people of Pitcairn on his behalf, and this will be done as soon as a suitable time presents itself.

"The Island Council will doubtless arrange for the safe housing of the lamp at the radio station, for ease of access and to ensure that it receives suitable servicing from the station staff.

We feel sure the lamp will be of great benefit to the island's communications." Volume 14, Number 9 (September 1972).

Oeno Island

Oeno is Pitcairn's "Holiday" island, and the islanders make at least one trip to it each year. Located some 75 miles northwest of Pitcairn, it is named after an American whaler, which sighted the low atoll in 1824. The island is the graveyard for a number of

128

ships. About two miles in diameter, Oeno has a strip of land on the western reef that is about one and a half miles long and less than one mile wide. The reef around the lagoon is entered from the north, the reef itself teeming with fish. Coconuts and pandanus grow well on Oeno, but the only water is brackish and can be obtained only by digging for it.

"OENO. By Roy P. Clark: It happened on a Tuesday in the late afternoon of January 3rd, 1961. Three boats crowded with 73 souls—men, women, and children—left Bounty Bay for Oeno Island, grounding on its white sands at 11 a.m. the following day.

"To tell of all the events and happenings during our nine days' visit would take far more space in our *Miscellany* than could possibly be spared, but not to mention something of the trip would be an impiety both to Oeno and our monthly paper. Memory brings to my mind several scenes that to me were joyous, exciting, unusual, ludicrous (and even ridiculous), sad, and painful.

"I see groups of women and children, overcome with seasickness, lying on the sand beneath cabbage trees, languid and weak, glad to be free from the rocking and tossing of the boats during the night and early morning. I recollect the signs of thankfulness and gratefulness on their faces as they relaxed and drank sweet water from the young coconuts, so refreshing and cool, which were handed down to them by those more able to climb the trees.

"There was the unloading of the boats. Personal belongings were put in three piles, waiting for the tents to be erected—by using masts, oars, sails, and three special canvas coverings—so that each individual could choose his bed and space for his or her own impedimenta. Men and women slept in the same tents as per family, friend, or relative, and even as they so desired.

"I see the men scattering in all directions with spear and spear gun, with hook and line, seeking fish for the evening meal. Then there were the happy meals eaten together, standing or sprawled on the ground, or sitting on fallen trees, while some, with pannikin [tin cups] and plate in hand, visited the camps of others perhaps to compare meals.

"Tropical squalls of rain brought dismal hours of inactivity, when the entire community would lie huddled in their tents bemoaning their lot and longing for the sunshine so as to allow them to fulfill their desires and duties such as fishing, gathering coconuts, going on the shallow reefs for shells and coral, and allowing the women cooks to attend to morning and evening

129

meals, even in downpours of rain where there was little shelter over the open fireplaces.

"I see men rushing to the water's edge with spear and line to kill sharks that had ventured in close to the sand—men all tense with determination and excitement to kill their hated enemies. On one occasion a shark was cuaght and dragged up on the beach. It was caught by the hand of Len Brown, who, snatching its tail, lifted it from the water onto the beach, where it lay heaving and slashing the sand. I see the onlookers scattering in all directions and then timidly returning to get a closer view of its last throes in death. The nerve required to even attempt to catch a five-foot shark by its tail proves Len a fisherman from the crown of his head to the soles of his feet—every inch of him. . . .

"Then there were the Sabbath School and Church Services held beneath the trees, with Pastor using as a pulpit some biscuit tins and the congregation sitting on the sand carpeted with leaves.

"There was Jacob, who does not boast of being a fisherman, coming home highly elated over his catch—a basket almost full to the top. 'That's the way to do it,' he says, and holds up a large kingfish.

"I see men and women fishing in Sharky Hole—women inland with their long knives, slashing at the pandanus palms for their long leaves, later to be used for weaving purposes. My memory brings back swimmers in the lagoon; . . . the children becoming as black as natives of other Polynesian Islands.

"Then there was the loading of the boats for home—the pull to and out through the passage to the open sea, before the hoisting of sails and the setting of the homeward course. When the winds had become dead, the launch was called in to tow the other two boats. I recollect very clearly the torrents of rain that fell during the night, soaking through canvas in the boats—much to the discomfort of the people.

"Then at last I recall the joyful voices of 'Land Ho' and the safe passage in from Bounty Bay to the harbour. All is well that ends well." Volume 3, Number 1 (January 1961).

"1st-6th March, 1964. Because timbers from the wreck of the *St. James* had been uncovered on the Oeno sandbank, the men decided to make a quick return visit to reclaim them before the sand again covered their position. With one launch and one sailing vessel, a dozen men left Pitcairn on the evening of Sunday, 1st March.

"Their visit proved well worthwhile, with some good pieces of timber retrieved and more coconuts brought home.

"From what we hear, the homeward journey proved rather trying, with headwinds and rough seas—24 hours for the return! However, this gave the men an opportunity to try out their skill in keeping on course under less than favourable conditions." Volume 6, Number 4 (April 1964).

"OENO, HERE WE . . . UH! OH! . . . NOT THIS TIME. At 4 p.m. on Wednesday, 23 March, 26 local adults and children began the task of taking their food supplies, clothing, and miscellaneous items down to the Landing in anticipation of a holiday at Oeno.

"By 7:20 p.m. both longboats were loaded and in beautiful sea and weather conditions. The boats and holiday makers were on their way, with Carl and Marilyn aboard their yacht (the *La Desirade*, which was visiting Pitcairn—the skipper had decided to accompany the people to Oeno) looking after the navigational side of things. The evening seemed to be like one of those uneventful ones where everything was going according to plan. All one could hear was the drone of the engines, the water rippling past the boats, and the chitter-chat among the folk. The excitement was soon overcome by tiredness, as passengers nestled down for the evening.

"Then at 3 a.m. on Thursday 24th, weather and sea conditions began to roughen; and, by 8 a.m., because the boats were heading directly into strong northwesterly winds conditions, the decision was made to head back for Pitcairn rather than continue to make for Oeno Island. This decision, of course, was not known by those of us who had remained on the Island. So without having sighted Oeno the boats turned back, and what followed was drama on the high seas, so often read about but not often experienced. Within 10 hours of setting out from Pitcairn in calm conditions, the holiday makers were now being tossed about in the boats by a cruel and angry sea. During the latter part of the morning wind speeds around the Island were reaching gale-force strength, with speeds between 30 and 37 knots, at times reaching 40 knots.

"How are our voyagers getting on? Where are they? Have they reached Oeno?—these were some of our thoughts. It wasn't until 11 a.m. that Radio Officer Tom Christian placed the long (telephone) ring around the village telling us that he had been in contact with the longboats and that they were heading home. We were relieved to learn that despite the terrifying sea and weather conditions, at least everything was well meantime. But observing the appalling sea conditions from the Island and listening to the strong winds in the trees, one could only hope that our seafarers would return safely. Visibility was getting poorer, and with mist hovering over the Island and with many whitecaps on the waves, it was difficult to pick up the longboats out at sea, despite the fact that Tom thought that the seafarers could spot the Island.

"Our first ray of hope came at 1:15 p.m., when Brian placed the long ring to inform us that he had spotted one of the two longboats about two miles off. One longboat?—where's the other one? Most folk hurried down to the Landing to lend a hand, and then further good news spread that the second longboat had been spotted.

"As the longboats reached the Harbour entrance, many hearts, both on land and in the longboats, were saddened, seeing the force with which the huge waves were pounding the small harbour relentlessly. As the old saying goes, 'So near and yet so far.' The one thing our seafarers wanted at this time was to be ashore. Minutes seemed to tick by so slowly. And then, all of a sudden, there was a momentary calm. Seizing his opportunity, coxswain Steve Christian screamed out for 'FULL AHEAD.' Responding to his cry, Engineer Kay Brown immediately revved up the engine, which responded splendidly; and the longboat gathered sufficient speed to get into the harbour safely before huge breakers began crashing in once again. Children, women, and supplies were quickly whisked from the boat; and the longboat was hauled into the Boathouse.

"Then the eyes turned seaward again to watch the second boat. Again the minutes dragged; a lull; a scream from coxswain Charles Christian for 'FULL AHEAD,' and the engine again responded splendidly to Engineer Oscar Clark. Gathering speed, the longboat made the harbour safely, with the roaring breakers coming in almost simultaneously. Once again children, women, and supplies were quickly taken from the boat, which was then hauled into the Boathouse.

"I leave it to your imagination—the relief and joy expressed by the folk who watched from land and especially the voyagers, when all were reunited safely." Volume 19, Number 3 (March 1977).

"THIRD OENO TRIP. It may surprise you to learn that the boys made a third trip to Oeno [Island] on Wednesday the 22nd of March for a couple of days. However, it was not a pleasure trip (So they tell me!) but a trip to recover some timber from some of the old wrecks there. Although some of this timber is 50 to 60 years old and is buried in the sand, most of it is in perfect condition. One piece measured 12" by 12" by 30'." Volume 20, Number 3 (March 1978).

Painted Leaves

"In the year 1828 George Hunn Nobbs, accompanied by a friend, reached this Island from Vaparaiso, Chile, in a very small cutter. He so endeared himself to the islanders that not long after his arrival he was made leader of the Pitcairn Island Church, as well as Sunday School teacher.

"In 1852 Mr. Nobbs was sent to England by Admiral Moresby of the British Ship of War, *Portland*, where he was ordained minister of the island church. On his return to the island by way of Valparaiso he brought the islanders a young seedling—the soap-seed tree.

"This same tree is still growing here, sheltered by a huge, spreading banyan tree. Though the enormity of the banyan dwarfs its old friend, the soap-seed is in reality a very large tree. The longevity of this tree is attributed to the protecting care of the banyan, which has protected it from the frequent northerly and westerly winds that blow hard enough to cause considerable damage to the other trees in the locality from time to time.

"There are a few scattered soap-seed trees, progeny of the original, in the village, but there are none in any other part of the island.

"The tree obtains its name from the round, black, marble-sized seeds it bears once a year. From the outer husks of the seeds there exudes a sticky, offensive-smelling substance that seems to have some propensity to act as a cleaning agent, though a very poor substitute for our present-day soap. For the past two generations and more no such use has been made of the seeds, but in earlier years the husks of the seeds were crushed, and the resultant frothy lotion was used as soap—and particularly as a shampoo. It seems to have been a safeguard against lice and other vermin and various scalp irritations. The same lotion was used for a like purpose in Valparaiso many years ago.

"The old granddaddy soap-seed tree, now well over 100 years old, still bears thousands of seeds, which continue to yield forth their frothy, foul-smelling goo when placed in water.

"However, the soap-seed tree has reached a higher pinnacle of dignity and usefulness since its fall from grace as a soap-making agent. The leaves are picked at a certain time of the year, placed in earthen jars with water, and left to rot for a period of 14 to 16 days. At the end of this time the leaves are taken from the jars and are separately rubbed between the palms of the hands, thus cleaning off the outer surface of green and leaving only the ribs and veins intact. This cleaning process is an unpleasant task as

133

the stench of the putrified leaves and the stagnant water is very offensive.

"Now they are washed in plenty of clean water and then left to soak for a further two days. Afterward they are washed in soap and water until the veins become clean and white and delicate as old lace. They are now known as 'skeleton' leaves.

"Each leaf is ironed and becomes flat and crisp, though not overly brittle, when dried.

"Delicate flower designs are drawn on the lacy surface; and the leaf—once a green, growing thing; then a stinking, rotting mess—becomes a fragile ornament of lasting beauty. The painted leaves have been used as an article of trade since the days of the sailing vessels and have proved to be one of the finest commodities of trade that the islanders have ever produced.

"Thank you, George Nobbs. Contributed by Roy P. Clark." Volume 14, Number 7 (July 1972).

Population

The question of how many people are required to maintain Pitcairn as an inhabited island has been asked and answered by many persons, both expert and otherwise. At one time the question was important, when there seemed to be too many people; recently the fear has been that there are too few. The first estimate of the island's population came from Captain Mayhew Folger of the American sealing ship *Topaz*. When he visited the island in 1808, Folger estimated there were 35 people living there. By 1856, just before the emigration to Norfolk Island, the population had soared to 194. A total of 43 people returned to Pitcairn from Norfolk in 1864. The island's all-time high in population—233—came in 1937. Since that time there has been a decline in numbers. *Miscellany* has faithfully recorded the composition of the island's population, sometimes even giving semiannual reports.

"By Roy Clark. There are 27 families (comprising husband, wife, and children), six widows, and seven widowers. Those of marriageable age are 14—eight men and six women. In addition there is one divorcée, one spinster, two bachelors, two grass widows, and two husbands with wives abroad. Children of school age number 37. Of these, 35 attend school—13 boys and 22 girls. There are 10 boys and 11 girls under school age, making a grand total of 147 people on the Island.

"Occupied houses number 57, vacant 29. A few of the latter are dilapidated. Below the pathway from the landing place to the school are 36 houses, while above this pathway are 50. To this amount have not been added canoe and engine houses. There are 14 engine houses and seven canoe houses, making a total of 107.

"Among the houses are a church, post office, dispensary, and a public hall, all of which are in the Public Square.

"Below are itemized a miscellany of odds and ends that make up our social life: One petrol and 14 diesel engines. Six outboard motors for the canoes, 37 stoves, 12 refrigerators, 7 washing machines, 42 telephones, 57 sewing machines, and 14 typewriters.

"To catch water we have 80 cisterns; 12 or more of these are out of use. Musical instruments which keep us in tune with God and man are: 11 organs, 4 pianos, 1 violin, 1 mandolin, 12 radios, 2 recorders, 3 radiogramaphones, 17 phonographs, 18 ukeleles, 6 guitars, 1 piano accordion, and a few mouth organs. The Island Band comprises 1 trombone, 4 cornets, E-flat bass, tenor horn, kettle drum, and one instrument of unknown name. To top this, we have nature helping us out with 25 dogs, cats unnumbered, poultry by the hundred, but not a single singing bird. There are a few goats and sea birds, as well as a scattering of sparrows.

"We have a wireless station, 1 launch, 4 longboats, and a number of canoes. There is electricity on the island, produced from private generators.

"No TV, no buses, no trams, cars, trains, planes—in fact, nothing that carries except wheelbarrows. No taxes to pay and no bills to foot. No store to buy from and no money in circulation. We have a rock in the Pacific five miles round and two miles through. We have beautiful hills and valleys and plenty of fish.

"We could do with a few more trees, especially coconuts. Are We Pitcairners Satisfied? I wonder why all the old-timers come back to their homes or want to come back, with the desire to be buried in the little cemetery near the Edge close by the sea."—Volume 2, Number 3 (March 1960).

"Annual statistics for the year 1961 include: Population 127, including 10 temporary residents. There are 39 males, 38 females, 20 boys under 16, and 30 girls. Only 19 of the men are under 60. During the year, 50 ships stopped off the island. The present tally of dogs is 19." Volume 3, Number 12 (December 1961).

"During the month we have said good-bye to Maude Dyett, who has been spending a short return visit to her homeland and to Parkin Christian, who is off to visit his friends in Florida, United States of America. Tomorrow, 2nd November, we say farewell to another seven of the community, who are leaving for New

135

Zealand on *Ceramic*. In addition to Wiles Warren and his family, Radley Christian and Clinton Warren are also departing.

"With these people leaving, the population of Pitcairn will be as follow:

	Males	Females
Under 15 years	15	11
15 years to 60	16	18
Over 60	13	12
Total Males	44	
Total Females	41	
Grand Total	85	Pitcairners
	5	Strangers

Volume 5, Number 11 (November 1963).

"Dec. 23. As of this date, the population of the island is as follows: Married men 25. Married women 23. Widowers 4. Widows 3. Bachelors 5. Single boys 2. Single girls 5. Schoolboys 11. Schoolgirls 10. Nonschoolboys 2. Nonschoolgirls 3. Pastor Webster, Mrs. Webster, and daughter Rosemary . . . Total 96." Volume 8, Number 12 (December 1967).

"CENSUS, 31st December, 1972. Total population, 84—includes seven non-Pitcairners. Age distribution of permanent inhabitants (1971 figures in parentheses):

Age in years:	Male	Female	Age in years:	Male	Female
0 - 10	4 (4)	5 (5)	51 - 60	7 (7)	2 (4)
11 - 20	8 (11)	8 (8)	61 - 70	5 (6)	2 (2)
21 - 30	1 (1)	2 (4)	71 - 80	7 (7)	6 (6)
31 - 40	1 (1)	3 (1)	81 - 90	3 (3)	1 (1)
41 - 50	5 (6)	8 (8)	Totals	41 (46)	36 (39)

Volume 14, Number 12 (December 1972).

"WHO'S WHO. Following is a list in alphabetical order, according to heads of families, of people living on the island as of 30th September. Overseas readers may find it helpful in solving some of the problems caused by *Miscellany's* (and Pitcairn's) use of first names only. In most cases the Christian name in common usage is given, sometimes in shortened form; names by which some folk are more commonly known are given alternately. Occupations, where applicable, are shown. In parentheses we also show ages grouped according to the following table: (1) under 5 years; (2) 5 to 15 years; (3) 16 to 19 years; (4) 20 to 29 years; (5) 30 to 39 years; (6) 40 to 49 years; (7) 50 to 59 years; (8) 60 to 69 years; (9) 70 to 79 years; (10) 80 to 85 years.

BROWN - Len (6) (Supervising Engineer); Thelma (6); Dave (3);

Kay (Trainee Tractor Driver) (3); Clarice (2); Yvonne (2).

CHRISTIAN - Ben (7) (Island Secretary); Irma (6) (Radio Operator III); Julie (4) (Assistant Typist); Dennis (3) (Trainee Radio Operator); Marlene (2).

CHRISTIAN - Charles (6) (Landing Supervisor); Charlotte (6) (Cleaner); Carol (4) (Councillor); Ronnie (1); Dean (1).

CHRISTIAN - Elwyn (8) (Dentist and Assistant Engineer); Evelyn or Nurse (9).

CHRISTIAN - Ivan (7) (Councillor); Verna or Dobrey (7).

CHRISTIAN - John (9); Bernice (9).

CHRISTIAN - Lloyd or Jimmy (8).

CHRISTIAN - Ninette (9).

CHRISTIAN - Steve (4) (Engineer); Olive (4) (Typist); Trent (1).

CHRISTIAN - Tom (5) (Radio Officer); Betty (5) (Radio Operator II); Jackie (1).

CHRISTIAN - Warren (7) (Assistant Postmaster); Millie (8).

CLARK - Oscar (6) (Postmaster); Norma (6); Glen (3) (Cleaner).

CLARK - Roy (10); May (9).

WARREN - Anderson (7) (Radio Operator I); Royal (6) (Assistant Nurse); and Michael (2).

WARREN - Calvert or Caddie (10).

WARREN - Christie (9); Mima (10).

WARREN - Jacob (7) (Head Forester); Mavis (5) (Assistant Postmistress); Jay (3) (Assistant Tractor Driver); Meralda (2).

WARREN - Morris or Mento (8).

WARREN - Virginia or Gina (9).

WARREN - Reynold (6) (Assistant Postmaster); Nola (5) (Librarian) and YOUNG - Barry (3) (Roadman).

WARREN - Maynard (8) (Assistant Forester).

YOUNG - Albert (9).

YOUNG - Andrew (9) (School Committee).

YOUNG - Henry (8) (Chairman of Internal Committee); Floss (6); Noggie (4) (Tractor Driver); Donald (3) (Roadman); Alison (2); Pamela (2).

YOUNG - Norris (10).

YOUNG - Pervis (6) (Island Magistrate); Marona or Pussy (5); Janet (2).

YOUNG - Sam (7) (Assistant Forester); Vula (6); Terry (2); Ann (2).

YOUNG - Theo (10); Lila (9).

"In addition there are seven non-Pitcairners, being the families of the Pastor and Education Officer. How many is that all told? 78. ... This is not an official census; ... please accept our apologies for any mistakes." Volume 15, Number 8 (August 1973).

"POPULATION CENSUS AS OF DEC. 31, 1974. Although this is unofficial, we have endeavoured to be as accurate as possible. In addition to those listed, there are five outsiders, being the families of the Pastor and the Education Officer:

	0-4	5-15	16-19	20-29	30-39	40-49
Males	3	1	4	1	1	3
Females	3	5	1	2	3	6

	50-59	60-69	70-79	80-89	
Males	4	4	7	1	
Females	1	2	3	2	Total: 56

"CHRISTIAN STILL LEADS: Surnames:

CHRISTIAN	25
YOUNG	13
WARREN	11
CLARK	4
BROWN	3
Total	56

"Let's look at some interesting statistics:

	1954	1964	1974
Population	136	90	61
Shipping	69	40	30
Passenger Ships Carrying a Medical Officer	46	30	5

Volume 16, Number 6 (December 1974).

"CENSUS. The following is a breakdown of the population as of 31 December. As you will see, CHRISTIAN still leads. . . .

CLARK - 4   CHRISTIAN - 27   BROWN - 5
YOUNG - 12   WARREN - 15   OUTSIDERS - 11
                Total—74."

Volume 18, Number 12 (December 1976).

"PITCAIRN'S POPULATION. The last count was taken in December last. To bring everyone up to date, Jackie Christian, age six, as has been working hard at this task at her teacher's request. The population now stands at 65, as compared with 74 when the last count was taken." Volume 19, Number 6 (June 1977).

"FIFTEEN PERCENT INCREASE. No, that's not our annual inflation rate; but rather, with the nine folk who arrived at Pitcairn during the month, Pitcairn's population of 63 was boosted by 15%. The unofficial population now is 72." Volume 19, Number 12 (December 1977).

Power on Pitcairn

"FROM CANDLEPOWER TO KILOWATTS. Whatever the *Bounty* mutineers brought ashore with them to illumine the dark

138

night hours, be it tallow-dip candle or lantern, we may be sure that supplies were soon exhausted and that they soon had to look about them in the land of their choice for some suitable substitute. The Tahitians in the party would certainly know of the Candle Nut tree, and it is probable that this nut (known locally as Doodwi or Dooeedee Nut and scientifically as Aleurites triloba) has been in use from the very early days of Pitcairn's history.

"In the early 1900's, before the opening of the Panama Canal, it was possible, on rare occasions, to obtain small supplies of paraffin or candles from sailing ships, but generally the Doodwi was the sole source of lighting.

"The green fruit grows in profusion on the slender Doodwi tree, and inside each fruit are two nuts. These are easily cut from the soft flesh of the fruit and are stored and dried until ready for use when the hard outer husk of the nut is broken open and the combustible seed within exposed. These have the texture and feel of a peanut, are about the size of a walnut, and are even edible in small quantities. When properly aged and dried, these are skewered onto a Ni-au (the firm, narrow stalk of the coconut leaf), one on top of another, until a dozen or so are firmly fixed into place. Three or four of these stalks, similarly loaded, are bound tightly together with Pulau bark; and you have ready to light a torch that will last for hours.

"Difficult to light at first, these primitive torches have the saving grace of being difficult to extinguish, even on the windy nights when the women would line the cliffs and the lights of many Doodwi torches would guide the men in from late-calling ships. . . .

"May (Clark) still has two full wooden boxes of Doodwi nuts stored away, while her husband, Roy, has found that the hard outside bark of the nut can be rasped, papered, polished, and brought to a smooth, glossy finish resembling mahogany.

"After the opening of the Panama Canal, when supplies of kerosene became available, Roy and his father evolved the 'Conk.' This was a teapot-sized container with a straight spout, down which a wick was pushed to draw up the oil. When filled with kerosene and lit, a satisfactory light was produced, together with a quantity of black smoke. The homemade Conk had a straight handle angled up from the base opposite the spout, but it was not long before old kettles and teapots were found to do the job satisfactorily.

"With increased supplies becoming available due to the increased shipping, kerosene could now be ordered by the drum;

and this ushered in the use of hurricane lamps, kerosene lamps, and torches. These replaced the Doodwi and the Conk and are still in use today.

"In 1928 two young Americans arrived on Pitcairn to install a petrol generating plant to assist Andrew with his duties as radio operator. Intended in the first place as a battery-charging unit, it was not long before its other capabilities were recognized; and Andrew soon had the plant providing lighting to his near neighbours and the church.

"Then in 1951 the first diesel plant to be installed for house lighting was installed at the new schoolhouse, and a year later Elwyn set up the first privately owned diesel generating plant. Others soon followed; and most homes enjoyed the pleasures of electric lighting, either from their own plant or from power supplied by a neighbour. The supply from most of these plants was irregular, depending largely on fuel stocks on hand; and a typical situation would be that a plant owner would supply power on three nights a week to all those on his circuit who shared in costs. A walk around the village at nights, when all plants were operating, and one would hear a variety of poppings and splutterings as the different types of engines vied with each other to distrub the evening hours. Each had its own particular beat and rhythm, easily distinguishable one from the other; and everyone could tell just by listening what plants were operating on any particular night.

"When the schoolhouse received its 4.25 k.v.a. single-phase Lister Generator, this provided power not only to the schoolhouse, but to the homes of some Government officials, government buildings, and street lighting from Pulau to the Landing. Operated by the Education Officer, this plant supplied power seven days a week from dusk until the E.O. decided to go to bed—never early, I might add.

"On January 14th of this year, *Gothic* arrived from U.K. with the largest diesel lighting plant ever. This was a three-phase, 70 k.v.a. plant, weighing 56 cwt and, together with ancillary equipment packed in separate crates, providing quite a problem in loading and landing on the island. *Ho Ho* was prepared for the extra-heavy crate by removing thwarts and strengthening bearers. Once the crate was loaded into the boat, the main difficulty was over; for the seas were calm.

"Since that time, the engine has been bedded down and test run by Maika Vosinabula, PWD engineer from Fiji; poles and wires have been erected from Pulau to the Landing, and most homes have been rewired and connected to the new supply by

Tony Hermans, who is under contract to the Government, and who has been assisted by Steve. In the meantime, power is supplied to all homes, street lighting, and Government buildings from 6 p.m. to 11 p.m. on all nights except Friday, when it is turned off at 10 p.m. Started at 6 p.m. on Friday October 4th, it has had a month of trouble-free running, and we hope that careful checking and maintenance will ensure many years of good service from this lastest acquisition." Volume 10, Number 10 (October 1968).

"ENGINE REPAIRS. The diesel engine on the main generator supplying electric power to the village refused to start on the 20th. Candles and kerosene lamps were soon in evidence, and life went on as usual for most.

"That the engine should come to a halt was no surprise, as a major overhaul has been due for some time. We are fortunate that it has kept going for so long.

"The following day, Len, as Supervising Engineer (a new post created at the beginning of the month), with Steve, Oscar, and Dave to help, started the job of dismantling the engine. The sludge and rust they removed from the cooling system had to be seen to be believed. The six cylinders were stripped in pairs, and the whole operation was performed in a well-organised and efficient manner.

"One half of the cylinder head was found to be severely burned, but this was removed by grinding. Replacement of cylinder linings, connecting rod bearings, pistons and rings, and several gaskets was effected.

"Four working days later, on the 24th, the engine was started again and run up on successive nights until we once again had our normal hours of supply.

"We are grateful to the men who did the job so quickly." Volume 14, Number 10 (October 1972).

"On the night of the 29th, Steve Christian went down to the engine shed to shut off the main generator, when he noticed that the floor was all covered with oil. He turned the generator off and then with the aid of a torch saw that the side casing of the engine had a huge hole in it where the con-rod had smashed right through it. How the engine kept going is still a mystery to all concerned. The next morning a closer inspection showed that the con-rod had broken off inside and then in pieces had smashed its way through the side of the engine casing. Worse was to be found out. The crankshaft was badly scored and possibly warped, and we found to our dismay that we did not have the necessary spare parts to repair it.

"A hurried cable to our Head Office was sent that night, ordering the necessary parts. We were informed that only some of the parts were available in New Zealand, and that the rest would have to be ordered from England. This of course meant that we had to wait for a ship from New Zealand to bring the parts from there, and then wait for one from England to bring the parts from there. With luck, we could have all the parts here by the end of March. In the meantime, for those without an alternative source of power, it's back to candles and kerosene lamps. Which brings up an interesting point. Do you realize that it costs just over one New Zealand dollar to land one gallon of kerosene on Pitcairn? So the lights are used sparingly. Let us hope that everything goes according to plan and that we may have our main power back on as soon as possible." Volume 17, Number 1 (January 1975).

"Imagine a typical Friday evening on Pitcairn—people settling down in preparation for the Sabbath, the domestic fowl finding their usual perches among the trees, the peace and quiet being disturbed only by chirping crickets and the waves lapping against the rocks, and everyone awaiting the sound of the Main Island Engine between 5:30 and 6:00 p.m., as this means we will have power for the evening until 10 p.m.

"Friday 11 June was no exception from any other Friday. The wind had been blowing rather strongly during the day, but seemed to quieten down toward dusk. The moon the previous night had not been quite full, and it was something to look forward to.

"The moment we had all waited for arrived—5:45 p.m.—a low drone—and then, 'LIGHTS'—the power was on at last! I guess everyone settled down for the evening dinner and the peaceful evening at home within their own family circles. However, the night's quietness was suddenly interrupted by all the lights on the island going off at 6:35 p.m., followed by the 'Long Ring.' What could it be? The 'Long Ring' (on the telephone) means news for everyone. On picking up the receivers and listening . . . it was certainly not the type of news that one expected. 'The Engine shed's on fire!' shouted Dobrey Christian, who lives closest to the Power shed.

"With dismay, disbelief, and utter shock, we heard the news; and within minutes many of the locals had congregated in the vicinity of the Power shed to see for themselves the roaring flames engulfing the shed like a lion feeding on its prey.

"For almost two hours the local men, aided by members of the Royal Engineers, fought the fierce flames—which at times rose to at least 30 feet into the moonlit sky—and without proper fire-fighting equipment, risked their own lives in so doing.

"The fire put out, all resigned themselves to the fact that, unless they had their own private generating plants (and there aren't many on the island), they would be without power for a long time to come. These fears, however, were shortlived; for, after sending a telegram to Head Office in Auckland telling them of this catastrophe, a reply came back stating that, all going well, a back-up plant (which they were going to send as a result of the Council's request to His Excellency, Mr. Smedley, while he was on Pitcairn) would be sent on the next supply ship from New Zealand.

"The cause of the fire—unknown. Extent of damage . . . recommended that the Generating plant, including the engine and shed, be written off." Volume 18, Number 6 (June 1976).

Princess Alice

"When the *Athlenic* called on Saturday, 24th March, amongst the passengers was Her Royal Highness Alice, Countess of Athlene. The Chief Magistrate, John Christian, and the Government Advisor, Mr. Kinder, were presented to her. John, on behalf of the people of Pitcairn Island, presented her with a Pitcairn basket filled with flowers. At the same time he asked Her Royal Highness to convey to Her Majesty Queen Elizabeth loyal greetings from all of us here.

"Quite a few of the local people also met Her Royal Highness, and it was interesting to hear their comments. All were thrilled to be given the chance of meeting a member of our Royal Family." Volume 4, Numbers 2 and 3 (March 1962).

Public Work

By law all men between the ages of 16 and 60 are required to do public work on Pitcairn. Directed by the Internal Committee, operating under the Island Council, the work includes maintenance of the public boats and the island's roads and paths, public trading (on ships), the landing of cargo, and the "share out," at which supplies obtained from public funds or through gifts are shared out equally among all families on the island. As is true almost everywhere, public work is unpopular on Pitcairn; but it is recognized as a necessity under the island's basically moneyless economic system.

"Public work took up about eight days, and during this time roads were weeded and some work was done in maintenance of the slipway at the landing.

"Two rain-trees (monkey-pods, to our American readers) were cut down in the school grounds; and the limbs were dragged to the Landing, where they have been used to provide some protection for the launches when they strike the base of the slip-way. Some of the remaining wood from these trees will now be used to renew the foot-bridge on the old road to Pulau. Over recent months this bridge has become quite dangerous, and we are fortunate that no one has had a quick trip to the creek bed below." Volume 15, Number 8 (August 1973).

"PUBLIC WORK. By Brian Young, Chairman of the Internal Committee. Public work started on May 8. It was planned to cork and putty all three motorboats and weed all the public roads. One and a half weeks was spent on the hard work of repairing the motorboats; and, at time of going to Press, all boats are completed and in fine shape.

"Launch No. 1—(Readers may recall that this boat had a major overhaul March/April last year) had a cork and putty job.

"Launch No. 3—had many rotten planks which had to be replaced, corked, and putty applied.

"New launch—required a five-foot false keel and work done on the stem. This took three days to do.

"At this stage I would like to thank the men for their hard and efficient work—especially Len and Jimmy for fitting the pieces of timber in place in the new launch.

"With the motorboats completed, the men changed their saws, planes, and hammers for hoes and cane knives and commenced work on the roads. For the benefit of readers, there are only 14 working men between the ages of 16 and 65; so it is a hard and lengthy job." Volume 19, Number 5 (May 1977).

Queen's Birthday

"This year the Island Council declared Monday 14th June a holiday to celebrate Her Majesty's birthday, and the Entertainment Committee made arrangements to hold sports at Pulau. However, a few days of heavy rain turned the playground at Pulau into a quagmire; and, although Monday dawned bright and sunny, it looked as though we would all have to miss our outing.

"Chairman Steve had other ideas. A few phone calls, a quick trip to the top of the island to study the weather and surf, and our programme was changed to a trip around the island.

"By 10:30, two boats were underway with happy crews, made up mainly of school children, parents, and teenagers.

"The day, as it turned out, was a perfect one for cruising, with a calm sea, gentle breeze, and a cloudless sky.

"Aute Valley, viewed from the sea, looks like an impossible place for a landing. The cliff rises in the shape of a buttress for a thousand feet, but tucked in behind a gigantic rock one finds a natural shelf, just at jetty height, and here we made our first stop and scrambled ashore. Some teenagers tried their hands at scaling the almost sheer cliffs to find suitable jumping-off places, whilst others disappeared over the side with masks, flippers, and spear guns. Those not so active threw in a line or searched amongst the rocks for bait.

"An hour or so in the shadow of Aute Valley cliffs, and we were off again, headed for the sun and Water Valley at Tedside. Riding in a boat is no novelty for Steve and Glen; so they took turns bouncing along behind one of the boats on homemade surfboards.

"At Water Valley there is an inlet that makes a perfect natural harbour for small boats. One simply has to step from the boat onto flat, solid rock, which looks for all the world like a low concrete wharf. It is a perfect place for a picnic. Few Lidos can offer the facilities found there.

"Small children have shallow, warm pools to splash in. Learners can take their pick of pools of various depths to suit their abilities; and the water in and beyond the inlet is crystal clear—deep enough for the deepest of divers—sheltering marine life of all descriptions—offering sport to satisfy the most adventurous underwater fishermen.

"The advantages offered by Water Valley for picnicking do not end with the swimming facilities. There is a fresh-water shower and soft drinks laid on too—if you know where to look.

"The shower is situated only a few yards from the mooring place for the boats. It has its source in a spring high up in the hills above Water Valley. This spring finds its way over the rocks and tumbles from a height of about eight feet in a clear, warm cascade. It is only a step or two from the salt water to the shower. Nature, it seems, has laid on all 'Mod Cons.'

"It is believed Water Valley derives its name from this miniature waterfall.

"The soft drinks, however, are not quite as accessible. I wonder how many of our readers have read accounts of the sparkling lemonade to be found in coconuts at certain stages of their development. In R. M. Ballantyne's *Coral Island*, the following is found:

" 'I immediately drank, and certainly I was much surprised at the delightful liquid that flowed copiously down my throat. It

145

was extremely cool and had a sweet taste, mingled with acid; in fact, it was the likest thing to lemonade I ever tasted, and was most refreshing.'

"Some of you may think that such stories of tropical islands are exaggerated a little. Well, in this case the account is true. The liquid in a coconut—when it is at the right stage—and it must be just right—is for all the world like lemonade. It even effervesces.

"To return to our picnic. Swimming, diving, and sun-bathing can be thirsty pastimes; and it was not long before some of the boys had scaled up the coconut trees along the shore and knocked a few nuts. These drinks just managed to round off the picnic lunches we had all brought along.

"During the afternoon the swimming and fishing continued, whilst some collected coconuts for use in cooking back home and young coconut trees for replanting on other parts of the island.

"All too soon the day was ending. The sun was beginning to creep over the hill behind us, and it was time to climb aboard the longboats and begin our journey home. The greater part of the journey had been completed in the morning. Matt's Rock was just around the corner and Bounty Bay only a short haul from there.

"It was a tired but happy crowd that jumped ashore at the Landing. A few years ago the walk to the Edge may have been just a bit much for the children after such a long day. However, thanks to our Hondas, there was no strenuous climb up the 'Hill of Difficulty' to take the shine off of a most enjoyable day.

"We hope Her Majesty enjoyed her birthday as much as we did on Pitcairn Island." Volume 13, Numbers 7 and 8 (July-August 1971).

Radio

Pitcairn's telecommunications can be traced to 1921, when Andrew Young began communicating with passing ships by lamp. Hearing of his efforts, the Marconi Company, in 1922, gave a crystal receiver to the island. A coil transmitter was donated in 1926 by a New Zealand radio enthusiast, and in 1938 two men from the United States installed transmitting and receiving equipment which had been purchased with private gifts.

Regular radio communications from Pitcairn began in 1940 with the help of the Navy Office in Wellington. By 1944, Pitcairn had become a meteorological station. Radio schedules were kept with Rarotonga in the Cook Islands until 1969. Since then the schedules have been with Suva in Fiji daily except Saturdays.

"From time to time readers and associates ply us with a series of questions concerning Pitcairn today. . . .

"By far the most common query is 'How do you keep in contact with the rest of the world?' Pitcairn may be just a tiny dot in the middle of the Pacific Ocean, but it does manage to keep in touch with the important world affairs in several different ways.

"Radio is obviously a most important medium, as nearly every Pitcairn family owns at least one transistor radio capable of worldwide coverage. Reception varies from place to place on the island, but it is most unusual for listeners to be unable to find a station of their choice. Probably the easiest located is Voice of America, which can be found in several places on the radio dial. Programmes from this and many other American stations give a wide coverage of news and views, of music and singing. The BBC and Radio Australia are often chosen for their wide coverage of news. Radio New Zealand is not so easy to pick up until around 10 p.m.; then a good programme can usually be assured. The broadcast band is full and often followed by many listeners. Again America predominates. Other Pacific stations are often in foreign languages. From Oeno Island, the N.Z. broadcast programmes are very distinct; but, unluckily for some, they are not so good in Adamstown.

"Pitcairn Island has its own radio station, staffed by several Islanders who are on the air morning and evening for sending and receiving cables through Rarotonga. Cost is a somewhat limiting factor in cable traffic, yet the rates to New Zealand (where the majority of the messages are sent) are reasonable enough for quite a full message to be sent for less than ten shillings. It is surprising how, with a little practise, one can eliminate all those unnecessary words, so condensing a cable to bare facts. It is quite possible to cable nearly anywhere in the world and receive an answer in 24 hours—in some cases only a few hours are needed.

"Radio Pitcairn also makes daily calls to nearby shipping, contacting around 20 vessels per month, very few of which actually stop. When it is known that a calling vessel is due, contact can be made up to five or six days away, although more frequently it is only three or four days prior to their arrival.

"No, the Pitcairn radio station does not, as yet, broadcast a local news and entertainment programme. It is hoped that 1966 will see the commencement of such a venture, as the idea was mooted earlier; and provision is now allowed for financing this. . . ." Volume 18, Number 1 (January 1966).

"By Tom Christian. 'CQ . . CQ . . CQ . . de ZBP . . ZBP . . QRU? . .ARK.' Twice daily, six days a week, the above signals are hand-pounded out on a brass key via radio transmitter and

147

aerial, intended for shipping in a radius of approximately 800 miles around Pitcairn. In International Radio Communications it means: 'Calling all Stations, Calling all Stations, Calling all Stations, from Pitcairn Radio, Pitcairn Radio, Pitcairn Radio. Have you anything for me? You are invited to reply.'

"Pitcairn Radio station—international registered call sign ZBP (or if on radio telephone, Zulu—Bravo—Papa) is located on approximately four acres of flattish grassland at Taro Ground, 870 feet (265.2 metres) above mean sea level. Join one of the operators—Tom, Betty, or Irma—on a guided tour.

"The time is 9:15 a.m. (Sunday to Friday). The operator on duty starts up one of the two diesel generators. . . . The operator then hurries across to the main building, enters the operating room, and switches the radio equipment on, allowing a few minutes warm-up time. While waiting, let us look around. The operating room is approximately 6 x 4.8 metres and has two 500-watt transmitters and two general coverage receivers. To the right is another battery-operated 50-watt transmitter and receiver which, though rather obsolete, is still operational and is used occasionally as an emergency unit or for short range 'Radio Telephone' with shipping. In the room are also the switchboards, which allow for 24-volt battery lighting as well as the 230-volt generator lights.

"The operator now checks the transmitter to the left, switching on the voltage (1600 volts). When the red light glows, the key is depressed; and the Morse code signal penetrates the ether waves. More often than not no ship replies, but at times an average of 9-10 different ships per month would reply, giving their positions, where bound/from, and quite often requesting a weather report.

"It is nearing 9:30—1800 GMT. The operator (also a meteorological observer) with pencil and weather observation book in hand, hurries outside to the meteorological enclosure and records the present temperature, the wet bulb, and the maximum and minimum since the previous day. Thermometers are reset; and the rainfall, if any, is recorded. Wind direction and estimated speed of wind, which can be checked inside the operating room on the anemometer indicator, is recorded. The visibility varies from day to day. Occasionally there is fog, when visibility may be as low as 150 metres; on a good day visibility may be over 50 kilometres. On a normal day the ocean is visible from North via East-to-West, only the small North-to-West sector being concealed by 'Big Ridge.' The present weather conditions are recorded, cloud type and amount (if cloudy, three types out of

27 are recorded), estimated height, and direction noted. Finally, the sea condition is recorded; and the observer hurries back into the operating room and 'Time Marks' and records the barometric pressure change on the Micro-barograph (which is a running recorder). The charts are changed weekly. The mercury barometer readings are recorded and corrected with correction cards to read the pressure at sea level; readings are also expressed in millibars. Generally, with average weather conditions, the pressures are fairly constant here, with an even rise and fall known as the 'Diurnal (daily) Variations.' With the comprehensive weather report completed and time moving along quickly, the operator codes the report into ten five-digit groups of figures—time now is 9:45—1815 GMT; time to communicate with Suva, Fiji, a little more than 3000 miles to the west of Pitcairn. The transmitter to the right is switched on; and within a few minutes contact is established (even though signals are generally weak), always in the International Morse Code. The weather report is sent first; and, although this is primarily done for the New Zealand Meteorological Department in Wellington, the report goes into the International weather service within a few minutes after leaving here.

"Two telegrams were sent this morning (1 November) to Auckland and Australia, respectively; and two telegrams were received from abroad. Because of the poor mail service, a reasonable number of telegrams (per capita) are handled. An average figure for this year, October inclusive, is: 547 sent and 413 received—a total of 21,078 words sent and 13,712 words received. By comparison, during the Bounty Bay project last year, 843 telegrams were sent and 633 received, or a total of 52,881 words. Schedule ended this morning at 10:07 local time, logged as 1837 GMT, just in time to make log entries and change the transmitter frequency to call on 12110 Khz and listen on the High Frequency Marine Bands for any ship which may be interested in calling us. As previously mentioned, most times no one replies; but occasionally a vessel which may have just left the Canal Zone, or is a little closer, will call and say they will pass by Pitcairn in a few days time, or even stop for an hour or two. If the latter happens, we are pleased; and within minutes a call is placed via telephone to the homes in Adamstown. And so, with an average morning's work completed, the operator types out the telegrams to be delivered and prepares to switch off.

"Before closing up, let us take a look at the rest of the main building. There are two bedrooms and a kitchenette to the right, and a battery room containing two 24-volt battery banks to the left. The building is 9.2 by 9.2 metres, including a porch and washroom, and entrance is from the west side through a reasonably equipped workshop. Although used mainly for storage, the bedrooms are for emergencies when an operator has to 'standby' for long periods; this has been the case in past years for a number of medical emergencies where advice or a doctor was being sought. Looking around outside, we see seven (50 and 60 feet) steel masts, nine white feeder poles, and a 7.6-metre mast with the wind indicator and anemometer, plus the 32-volt wind generator which was installed in 1953. There are four aerials currently in use; one being a 'diamond' shape (rhombic), which beams our signals to Fiji, the previous Administrative Headquarters. It was installed in 1964.

"Just having completed an average morning's work, we expect the evening schedule at 5:30 p.m. (0200 GMT) will be exactly the same, except that one of the three operators or the trainee, Kay Brown, would be doing the weather observation at 3:30 p.m. (0000 GMT) to be sent out two hours later. Quite often reception is poor; and, if 'traffic' is not cleared on the first morning schedule, contact has to be made again at 11:30 a.m., which is 8 a.m. in Fiji.

"Taro Ground is approximately half an hour's walk from Adamstown, or about seven minutes by motorcycle; if the weather is wet and the roads muddy, staff members have to walk up and down. It is not possible to miss a schedule, as recordings have to be made; and the operator would be listening on the other end irrespective of our local weather conditions. The station is not generally operated on Saturdays unless for emergencies—e.g., when a ship is due to call.

"The station building, though enlarged and renovated in 1964, was originally built in 1944 by New Zealand Military Engineers, who selected the site, installed equipment, and built accommodation to house the men who manned the set-up until World War II ended. With the military men returning to New Zealand, radio operator Nelson Dyett (who married a Pitcairn girl in N.Z.) came to the island in 1939, operating for approximately two years before returning home to Wellington. Another operator, Gilbert Long, came to the island with his wife but stayed for a few months. Self-taught Andrew Young, who, incidentally, operated amateur Radio Station VR6AY in 1938-40, contacted shipping at that time and operated as best as possible; but on a number of occasions the equipment broke down and ships' radio officers came ashore to effect repairs. So communication became unreliable for some years. Fortunately, mail service was reasonably good—at least once or twice a month.

150

"With the wartime equipment getting old and unreliable, our Administration purchased the battery-powered Marconi transmitter and receiver, along with batteries, and the wind generator, which was installed in 1953 by the late Floyd McCoy, amateur operator VR6AC.

"In 1954 Andrew and the last Anderson Warren started daily schedules with Rarotonga in the Cook Islands; but there was always the possibility of equipment failure, without someone to effect repairs. With my returning from a three-year training course in New Zealand, I assumed responsibility at Taro Ground on November 1, 1955; Anderson started a training course with me in 1957 and operated faithfully until his departure to New Zealand in 1974, where he regretfully became deceased in 1975.

"Since the new installations in 1964, there have been only minor changes or additions. We do not have an overseas radio telephone service; and the present equipment is quickly becoming obsolete, particularly since it does not cover single-side-band, which becomes compulsory for telephone communications in 1978.

"So whether you wish to send a telegram to or from Pitcairn, it will go via ZBP. Whether we zoom up on a motorbike or slosh up through the mud, we do our best to keep Pitcairn's official air service operational!" Volume 19, Numbers 10 and 11 (October-November 1977).

School

John Adams, the last of the mutineers on Pitcairn, was the island's first schoolteacher. His textbooks were a prayer book and the Bounty Bible. Adams was followed in 1823 by John Buffett, who had been a seaman on a whaling ship. In 1828 he was replaced by George Hunn Nobbs. Simon Young and his daughter, Rosalind, were teachers on the island following the return of the Pitcairners from Norfolk in 1864. Then in the last decade of the century the school was directed by teachers of the Seventh-day Adventist faith. Teaching of the children returned to the Pitcairners themselves between 1917 and 1938, and in 1948 the government took over responsibility for the school. The island's Education Officer, as the teacher is called, is named by Pitcairn's Governor and serves a two-year term.

From an average attendance of some 20 pupils in the 1950's, the number of students at the Pitcairn Island School rose to more than 30 in the early 1960's, then began a general decline. By 1974 there were less than 10 pupils. A simple pattern of education based on the New Zealand educational system is taught. All children 5 to 15 years are required to attend school.

"With possibly the lowest numbers ever, school recommenced on 27th January with a roll of eight. However, Marlene Christian will be leaving on the first available ship to go to Secondary School in New Zealand; and Kerry Young, who is here for a holiday with his grandfather, Andrew Young, will probably leave at the same time as Marlene. That will mean that the roll will than be at six, and two of that six are mine (the Editor); so there will be only four Pitcairners at school. The oldest child will be nine and the youngest five. There would not be many places in the world where the Teacher-pupil ratio is one to six. This of course has its advantages, as it allows for so much individual tutoring. This is a very well-equipped school, and the children are encouraged to use the equipment as much as possible. There are five more young Pitcairners coming on, but even with all of them at school it will still make it a very small roll." Volume 17, Number 1 (January 1975).

"SCHOOL NEWS. Children and teacher were delighted to receive letters and brochures from children attending Nord-Aurdal Ungdomsskole, Norway. The children here wrote to this school last August and are at present completing a project on Pitcairn which will be sent to the children who wrote." Volume 19, Number 3 (March 1977).

"SCHOOL NEWS. With Trent turning five during the month, the school roll has 'shot up' from 9 children to 10—5 boys and 5 girls. . . ." Volume 19, Number 8 (August 1977).

"With five of our children departing on the *Ionic*, the school roll now stands at eight. They are: Michael-14, Anna-12, Ronnie-9, Jackie Christian-7, Andrew-7, Dean-6, Jackie Cox-5, and Trent-5." Volume 20, Number 2 (February 1978).

Sharks

At Ducie, one of the Pitcairn Islands group, which is located 293 miles east of Pitcairn, the sharks are said to be extremely dangerous. In contrast, most Pitcairners seem to treat the variety around their island with general indifference if not downright trust!

"EDITOR COUNSELS. It seems to me that if the spear fishermen are not very careful, one may end up as a tasty morsel for a hungry shark. There have been a number of reports this month about the increasing audacity of these killers of the deep around Pitcairn. Len and Keen, out spearing one afternoon around the wreck of the old *Cornwallis*, were surprised by two snooping visitors with their wicked little eyes on the fish that the boys had speared. They shot at both but only managed to kill the one, after following it around for some time. A few days later they came in contact with some bigger ones, which appeared to be none too friendly. One made a pass at Desmond's flipper as he dived down; and Len, who was watching, feared for the worst. He said that it seemed as though Desmond's head was on a swivel as he looked from side to side for that shark.

"I think you spear fishermen should be more aware of the dangers involved and be especially on your guard when these man-eaters are around." Volume 1, Number 6 (October 1959).

" . . . Sharks are reported to be coming into Bounty Bay quite frequently. One was seen in the Bay last fishing day. Andrew tried to catch it, but the shark refused to bite and Andrew's line became fouled. Reports say that the sharks are harmless. Perhaps the children should be warned just the same to keep a sharp eye out when swimming—better to be sure than sorry." Volume 11, Numbers 1 and 2 (January-February 1969).

"FIRST SHARK CAUGHT. Len can proudly boast that he has caught the first shark from the new jetty. For the records, this happened on Tuesday 22 February." Volume 19, Number 2 (February 1977).

Ships

If anything can be called the lifeblood of Pitcairn, it is the ships that stop at the island. It is the ships that bring supplies to the Pitcairners; the ships on which trading or the sale of handicrafts and curios takes place; the ships which carry islanders to and from other parts of the world. . . . Near the turn of the twentieth century the islanders began to plan maritime ventures which would see Pitcairn developing trade with the Gambier Islands, the closest populated island group. A cutter, the *Pitcairn*, was purchased with funds loaned by the British, and the vessel, manned by Picairners, began carrying produce to Mangareva. In 1904 the ship foundered. A second cutter, the *John Adams*, was purchased, but it proved unseaworthy and was promptly sold. Then about 1919 the islanders built their own vessel, a 25-ton schooner named the *Messenger*. After making several runs to Tahiti the ship was caught in a hurricane, and the crew would have perished had not the American steamer *Sassenach* arrived on the scene at what seemed like the last moment. As with other areas of Pitcairn life, the ships that stop at the island have declined in number since the early 1960s. These days any ship that will stop off the island becomes an object of great interest and activity by the Pitcairn people.

"Did you hear about it? It proves to be one of the most dramatic

153

experiences I have witnessed for a long time. I really didn't know there were so many points to the compass where land could be found, but then, I am not a seafaring man.

"As we made our way homeward from the *Tata*, a heavy fog came down, blotting the island from view. Christie, with a firm grip on the tiller, made a sincere effort to hold in the direction of where our island ought to be. But where was it? Somebody pointed in this direction, and another pointed in directly the opposite, and before too long all of us were confused.

"In the meantime, Christie, trying to please all by setting a course somewhere between the two extremes, must have completed a full circle; and, when the fog actually did lift, we found ourselves blithely heading towards Easter Island, with most of us mute listeners to the advice of others.

"As sure as I am here on Pitcairn to tell the story, I am certain that if the hand of Providence had not lifted that fog curtain in time, it would have been like the year 1492 when Columbus sailed the ocean blue. But for us no happy landing in the Americas. As I recall this vivid experience, let me add in closing a plea in behalf of all passengers—next time please don't forget the compass, at least 'it' knows where north is.—Volume 1, Number 4 (31 July, 1959).

"On July 3rd, when the *Rangitane* came, she was accompanied by a not-unexpected southeasterly gale. At 11 a.m., when we cast off and moved from the lee of the ship, we faced the rising fury of the gale as we turned toward home, now some six or seven miles to the southeast. Radley's boat soon 'downed sail,' and the men took to their oars.

"The jib was hopelessly torn. Pervis and crew agreed to remain with them in case of more serious troubles, but it soon became apparent that the best course was for him to sail on home and return with the motorboat to relieve the tired oarsmen. After many tacks, much bailing, and volumes of calamity talk, we entered the Bay at 4 p.m., all tired, wet, and hungry. Within minutes the motorboat was off to the rescue; and words can hardly express the feeling of relief that we all felt when, at 5 p.m., it returned with the 'lost' boat in tow. . . . Volume 1, Number 4 (31 July, 1959).

"A very pleasant surprise awaited us on the morning of 3rd May, while everyone was assembled at the Square for Share-out from the *Rangitata*. Two ships were sighted at the same time, an unusual occurrence here, and evacuation of the Square was accomplished in less than 30 seconds.

"The *Boolagena*, the closest ship, was visited; and a very

enjoyable hour was spent on board. The captain of this Swedish vessel was a keen philatelist, and this undoubtedly (was) his reason for stopping. A little difficulty was experienced in trading, owing to the difference in currency. We did learn something, however. A Swedish krona is worth ¹/₅ in our money." Volume 3, Number 5 (May 1961).

"The *Rangitiki* called for the last time at 2 a.m. on Saturday 8th June. As it was such a shocking hour and also on the Sabbath, only a small party went out to say farewell to this, the last of the New Zealand Shipping Co. liners to call here. Our Acting Magistrate, Vernon, made a presentation to Captain Calcutt and expressed the appreciation of the people of Pitcairn Island for the wonderful service the company has given over many years. Captain Calcutt in reply said that, although his company's passenger ships would no longer be calling at Pitcairn, the New Zealand Shipping Co. had not forgotten Pitcairn and that the three cadet ships, *Otaio*, *Durham*, and *Rakaia* would make several calls each year. Once the people were back down in the boats, several of the well-known Pitcairn Island hymns were sung; then, as some rockets were fired into the air from the ship, her whistle hooted for the last time in a final salute. Volume 4, Number 6 (June 1962).

"*Willem Ruys*, unfortunately, arrived on Saturday, 7th July, a Sabbath day. As this meant no trading before sunset, the master of the ship took his vessel right round the island before stopping. It was nearly 4 p.m. before our boats were finally alongside. Conditions here were very rough, with quite a strong wind blowing and a very choppy sea. All got aboard without much difficulty and, once the Sabbath had ended, did a very brisk trade with the passengers and crew. Melva Warren and Noggie Young, representing the school children, visited the captain and gave him a present from the pupils in appreciation of his kindness on previous visits. Before we left the ship, two large cartons full of cakes and biscuits were given to the children. There was a grand share-out next day. In addition, John had been given a large quantity of sweets, and these too made another toothsome distribution for the children." Volume 4, Number 7 (July 1962).

"At 5:30 a.m. we were again answering the call of the bell. It was a fine morning, and we were aboard *Corinthic* by 7:30 a.m. Just after 8, Captain (A. C.) Jones, the master of the ship, accompanied by the Chief Magistrate and the Government Adviser, came ashore. The captain, although he has been calling at Pitcairn Island for over 14 years, had never been ashore; and now, on the eve of his retirement, he was at last achieving one of his ambitions. During his time ashore he walked to the Radio Station at Taro Ground and then over to the school, on the way visiting the grave of John Adams. At the Edge he was greeted by most of those who had not gone on board. Before returning to his ship, he lunched with the Chief Magistrate. As *Corinthic* was lying off for so long, the opportunity was taken of having the ship's surgeon, Dr. Cummings, also come ashore; and he examined several medical cases. It was finally 2:30 p.m. before we said farewell to the ship, and 5 p.m. before we were home. After a quick change and a meal, it was down to the Square for the mail." Volume 5, Number 2 (February 1963).

"We are truly grateful to the Shaw Savill and Albion Shipping Company for reducing the fare between Pitcairn and New Zealand to 50 pounds. This is a very substantial reduction, which will help greatly in removing much of the financial burden of travel to and from New Zealand.

"The New Zealand Shipping Company, too, is helping in many ways. Their most recent offer to take whatever handcrafts are available and place them on sale on their passenger ships is one which could easily provide another source for the trading of Pitcairn wares. This and their many other acts to assist Pitcairn are greatly appreciated." Volume 5, Number 7 (July 1963).

"Until the last week of the month it had been a very quiet time for shipping. Only one vessel arrived, the *North Sea*, a Swedish ship on its way from Australia to New York, stopping on the 23rd. The *Otaio* was supposed to have called on 15th, but the very stormy conditions which prevailed prevented it. There was hardly a day without strong winds, and most days also saw it raining at some stage.

"Because of the exceptionally bad weather in New Zealand, *Corinthic* was nearly four days late. It was just as well, for if the ship had been up on time it would have had to pass. As it was, because it was so far behind schedule, Captain Jones could not wait until daylight; so we had a night expedition. Conditions at the Landing were far from good, there being a very heavy surf running; so, rather than risk going out in the middle of the night, it was decided to take the boats out before dark and lie at anchor in the lee of the island until the ship came up.

"The run-out through the surf was accomplished without incident, and a reasonably comfortable time was spent at anchor. *Corinthic* came up at 1:30 a.m., and the task of unloading the considerable quantity of cargo commenced. Because of weather conditions it was decided that the stack of timber for the development scheme could not be handled; so this was left on board to come back sometime in the future.

"It was a great pity we experienced such bad conditions for this particular visit; for it was the last time Captain Jones was calling, as he retires from the sea on the completion of the voyage. It had been planned for a large gathering of the community to say our farewells, but such was impossible. Nevertheless, the captain, who has been a wonderful friend to everyone on Pitcairn for many years, was the recipient of numerous gifts and words of thanks.

"The boats finally got away from the ship about 3:45 a.m.; and then we headed back through the heavy swell to the shelter of Tedside, where we again lay at anchor waiting for daylight. Then, about 6 a.m., the launch and two longboats set off for the Landing. As we approached, it was very clear it was not going to be an easy run in, for large breakers were rolling in frequently. The shortage of men did not improve matters. To provide a full crew for the first boat, men from the second transferred, it being intended that they be brought out again in the launch to row in the second.

"The first run in was made without too much water being shipped, but just after unloading commenced, an extra-large roller swept the boat onto the slipway. When the water receded, the boat keeled over, the cargo slipped, and before anything could be done the next wave swamped the boat. Amongst the cargo which went overboard was a refrigerator, a stove, and two tons of cement, while floating about was an assortment of things, including a hive of bees! Needless to say the bees were far from pleased and expended their wrath on all who ventured near.

"Next to come in was the launch, and by skillful timing we reached safety in a fairly dry state. Once unloaded, the launch turned round; and, with the men needed to man the second longboat on board, headed again into the surf.

"After the men transferred, back came the launch; but just as it entered the breakers, a monstrous wave rose up as if from nowhere and, catching up with the boat, sent it charging in at a terrific pace. In the surging foam it failed to respond to the helm and, before the eyes of all watching at the Landing and the Edge, struck the end of the jetty a heavy glancing blow. Several in the launch, seeing what was coming, dived overboard into the boiling surf and came out without injury; but those who remained on board were not so fortunate—Vincent, Wiles and

Clinton all being injured. The way the boat stood up to the terrific crash is a credit to all who helped to build it here last year.

"After a short while the last of the boats came in without too much difficulty; then, once all the cargo had been unloaded and the boats hauled up, it was on to the mail, for some of the bags were wet. It was finally 3 p.m. before we were able to get home, 23 hours after setting out." Volume 5, Number 8 (August 1963).

"Monday, 20th January. Visit of U.S. Navy Supply Ship *Wyandot*. Great excitement was aroused by the Radio Operator's 'Everyone' call, telling us that the U.S.N.S. *Wyandot*, bound for the Antarctic via Lyttelton, would deviate from its course to visit the island and allow the men aboard for about two hours.

"Trading was brisk as the Americans proved to be both good buyers and generous givers. An announcement that the ship's store would be open for business proved very popular with the islanders, who took the opportunity to buy goods at prices hard to beat anywhere.

"There is quite a chance that the vessel will return to U.S.A. by the same route in late March—we look forward to seeing her again. . . ."

"Thursday, 23rd January. *Athenic*, travelling from London to Wellington, called (a few days later than anticipated), delivering mail and supplies from England. When returning to the landing for a forgotten basket, the launch struck a rock, which damaged the rudder. A new one was fitted in smart time and the trip resumed. Bert and Charles left for N.Z. to receive medical treatment. . . . Cowells also sailed away, to the sound of many fond farewells." Volume 6, Numbers 1 and 2 (February 1964).

"Thursday, 17th September, 1964. Once again a week ahead of originally scheduled time, *Ceramic* called from Auckland with a large amount of fuel and supplies. Among items of cargo were steel girders and hardwood planks—a forerunner of many more government shipments as the C.D. & W. plan of Development for Pitcairn gets underway, giving immediately plenty of opportunity to earn wages and, on completion, opportunity for an improved way of life; that is, if the challenge to develop and advance is accepted.

"*Ceramic* had a painfully small passenger list, but she did bring happiness here:

"Floss and Glenda returning from New Zealand were made most welcome again. We trust that they will continue to enjoy their life here.

"Dr. Joseph Marseu, of the Fiji School of Medicine and, until about a month ago, Medical Officer in the New Hebrides, came ashore to carry out a medical survey. He is staying at Pulau.

"Pastor Taylor, President of the Central Pacific Union of Seventh-day Adventists, brought the greetings of thousands of other Seventh-day Adventists to the tiny Mission on Pitcairn. Pastor Taylor hopes to get to know all the people and to gain an understanding of their problems. He is the guest of the Mission House.

"Frank Clune, an Australian writer of worldwide fame, has been around the world seven times, and has now called at our lonely outpost. Mr. Clune is doing final research for a comprehensive history of Pitcairn and its peoples. We look forward to seeing it in the not too distant future. Host and hostess to Mr. Clune are our policeman and his wife, Vernon and Lillian Young." Volume 6, Number 10 (30 September, 1964).

"ISLAND EVENTS. Tuesday, 6th October, 1964. Early in the morning the men down at the Edge observed a large yacht coming up to land. Most of the morning this yacht tacked back and forth, making little headway, so the 'five ring' was sounded, and the men set off in the launch to meet the visitors.

"On the way out, Charles, hopeful of bagging a 'couta (a barracouta), trailed a line, but he hooked more than he bargained for. A real monster—probably a swordfish or marlin (one was observed)—grabbed the bait and proceeded to make off in the opposite direction. Both Pervis and Charles tried in vain to hold him, but they finally had to let go because of scorched hands.

"The visiting yacht turned out to be the *Maylis*—a French yacht chartered from Tahiti by Doctor Harald Rheyder, a marine biologist of the Smithsonian Institute, Washington, U.S.A. With engine trouble and little wind *Maylis* was making no progress; so she was taken in tow and brought to anchor off Bounty Bay.

"On shore our visitors were just in time to witness the villagers turning out for their second typhoid vaccination.

"Dr. Rheyder expressed a willingness to take a party to Henderson; so a Council meeting was called. After taking into consideration the impending call of the *Athenic* and the doubtful condition of the *Maylis*'s diesel starting mechanism, it was decided by all parties that a trip was not practical." Volume 6, Number 11 (31 October, 1964).

"The . . . 17th, all were pleased to note the weather was fine, as the *Gothic*, with a very large quantity of cargo, was stopping for a limited time about midday. For the first time since the *Rangi* ships, four boats were taken out in order to handle the cargo as rapidly as possible so that Captain Campbell could get his ship moving again quickly. As well as stores from London, there was the MF35X tractor, a prefabricated workshop, paint for Pulau, and other items. Depsite great work by the men and the ship's crew, it was not possible to fill the boats completely by the time the whistle blew an hour and three-quarters after going alongside. The remaining shed sections and crates of spare parts were carried over to New Zealand (we hope they will be back on *Ceramic*).

"Coming ashore, there were some minutes of consternation and rapid action as *Reid Cowell* began to fill so rapidly with water that it was thought she would founder. The two longboats were cast off and left to their own devices, and *Dolphin* passed a line to *Reid Cowell* so that, with the two at 'full ahead,' more speed could be made for the safety of Bounty Bay. Meanwhile, the *Reid Cowell* crew was hurriedly shifting cargo to find the cause of the inrush—the cause, a knocked-out drain plug! With the longboats once again safely in tow, this incident did not seem too bad, but at the same time it was somewhat worrying.

"Unloading with the aid of the new derrick and the crawler winch was not so backbreaking, but it was still very late by the time all was cleared up. Sorting of mail was left until the following day." Volume 7, Number 1 (January 1965).

"Word was received by radio at Taro Ground that both Shaw Savill ships expect to be off Pitcairn at 3 p.m. on Thursday, 3rd June, 1965. As this is the first contact with either ship for this call, there is the possibility that one or the other will be earlier or later than the time given today, 31st May. But whatever the hour of arrival, it is going to be a full day for everyone, with two cargoes, two mails, and everything else that is entailed with ship day. *Gothic* had done exceedingly well to be here no later than five days behind the scheduled ETA, and *Ceramic* has been turned around in New Zealand in approximately four weeks." Volume 7, Number 5 (May 1965).

"June 18th. Radio contact with *Pioneer Gem* stated she was due to pass at 2 a.m. on Saturday morning, 19th. The Master regretted not being able to stop but said he would put the ship's mail (to be posted), over the side in a drum, as had been done on the way out to Australia. He was advised on the risk of doing so at nighttime, since our men were not very keen to go out hunting a drum at 2 a.m. with choppy seas. However, he said he was attaching the yellow drum to a 3-foot-diameter bundle of dunnage timber to make it more easily seen, and also as a reward for the searchers. So, as he was passing Pitcairn, a few men were launching the

Dolphin; and they went searching around until 8 a.m., when they returned without seeing a sign of anything and felt convinced that nothing was dropped overboard.

"Radio contact was made later, and *Pioneer Gem* said that the releasing gear got fouled and the ship was four and a half miles off to the northeast before the mail and timber was released. Searching around the heights of Pitcairn still located nothing, and by Sunday morning the visibility was poor with rain, so the ship was advised that the chance of recovering anything was very slim. Meanwhile the mail and cash for postage is probably being held in Davy Jones's Locker!" Volume 7, Number 6 (June 1965).

"On Saturday, July 3rd, the Cable and Wireless Ship *Retriever* called, on an official visit to show the British Flag. She was on her way from the South American coast to Fiji and, by request of His Excellency the Governor of Pitcairn and of Fiji, was asked to make the call. She came and dropped anchor at Bounty Bay. It was a perfect day, and most of the men went out in the longboats. Happy greetings were exchanged, and gifts of carvings and fruit were presented to the ship. Some of the leading men were entertained at an official lunch, and this was a very happy occasion. The officers were very anxious to learn of the welfare of all the people ashore.

"A pleasing feature of the visit was the presence on board of a Fijian crew, and I was delighted to find among them some old friends. Departure time came all too quickly; and, after the Pitcairn boys had sung their farewell songs, the Fijians thrilled us with a lovely rendition of their famous 'Isa Lei' song. Sadly, we waved good-bye. A telegram of farewell to the Master also included greetings to His Excellency the Governor. In reply, the Master, Captain Cross, graciously thanked all for the happy visit and promised to personally convey Pitcairn's loyal greetings to His Excellency.—W. G. Ferris."

"During Sabbath School (July 31st), the Barquentine *Verona* was sighted a few miles off, headed for Pitcairn. Her owner and master, Captain Christopher Sheldon, had written nearly a year before, telling us of his proposed visit; and now at last she had arrived. It had been a rainy morning, but the sky had cleared, and the wind was moderate. We were happy to see her coming in with her glistening white sails, and about 1 p.m. we were welcomed aboard by the Skipper and his 24 crew members. We also greatly appreciate goods that were ordered and which were so kindly brought to us freight-free. One of the items, a gents bicycle for Thelma's boys, was the envy of all the children.

161

Nineteen (crew) members came ashore with us and were taken into the homes of the people.

"Saturday night was thoroughly enjoyed by all, as Mr. Sheldon lectured on a most enjoyable 16mm movie film, 'The Last Voyage of the Yankee'—a vessel under command of Captain Irving Johnson. The night had its mishaps, though, because after many months of perfect running, our projector broke down, and the school machine had to be brought from Pulau to finish the evening. . . ." Volume 7, Number 7 (July 1965).

"The return trip from *Ceramic* was not without its worries. Both launches and the longboat were fully loaded, a fact which, linked with a near head-on sea, made progress very slow, to avoid shipping the seas over the bows. With the engine of *Reid Cowell* at such a slow pace, the pump was not operating fast enough to cope with shipped water. In the shelter of Matt's Rock, cargo and passengers were transferred to *Dolphin*, whilst the longboat was rowed toward Bounty Bay after being cast off when the *Dolphin* had turned back to lend assistance. Once the water level was reduced by hand bailing, *Reid Cowell* made a slow passage back to just outside the harbour, where still more cargo was transferred to the other launch, which had by then been unloaded and brought out again. Auxiliary pumps and a special fly-wheel shield are being fitted to this troublesome boat in the hope that such events will be avoided in the future." Volume 8, Number 1 (January 1966).

"For months we've thought and talked about the coming of it, and for the last few weeks the Islanders have worked steadily on curios and basketware, stockpiling against the day it came. On 28th February it finally arrived—and now, of course, it's gone on its way to Easter Island, Valparaiso, and other South American ports. Yes, for the past month or so we've lived with and by the *Bergensfjord*, counting down the days to its coming. Much of the village life has centered around this fine cruise vessel—ask when a job was likely to be done or perhaps a house alteration started and the reply was most likely to be 'after the Big Ship.'

"The closing few days of February were rather anxious ones as the wind blew persistently from the northeast, causing the Pacific rollers to build up and come piling into Bounty Bay with monotonous regularity, to such an extent that doubts were expressed about the women and children being allowed to go out. Somehow the situation never got too bad; yet by Sunday it was obvious to all but the most optimistic . . . that the children would of necessity remain ashore.

"Saturday night Tom (Christian) made radio contact with the

162

ship and heard about the stop at Rapa-iti (incidentally, the first cruise ship to call there), where 250 passengers were able to go ashore. The Master, Captain Gronbuht, sent in a message hoping for kind seas and expressing a desire that a small party could come ashore.

"Monday morning the bell rang early; and the boats cleared Bounty Bay in good time, with the men and women on board, leaving many rather sad little faces behind on the Landing, as sea conditions were not considered favourable enough. Due mainly to a half hour difference between ship time and local time *Bergensfjord* was a little longer coming up than expected. On board a really wonderful reception awaited us. After exchanging greetings the Pitcairners were escorted to the upper sun deck, where ample deck and table space was made available for curios to be displayed to advantage. Brisk trading was mingled with happy chatter, as various aspects of island life were discussed with the very pleasant and cordial passengers. At 11 a.m. the majority of the passengers gathered in the grand ballroom, where slides of Pitcairn were shown by the Pastor and Education Officer. These were received most enthusiastically.

"Readers will be pleased to know that *Miscellany* prepared an information pamphlet containing a farewell message, illustrated with a *Bounty* sailing ship in front of the outline of Pitcairn, a list of Island Officials, an outline of Pitcairn data, Souvenir and Stamp brochures, and a copy of January *Miscellany*. These were given to the Cruise Manager, who decided to distribute them in the grand ballroom. The demand far exceeded the supply of 300, which we had hoped would be sufficient. If through them some goodwill has developed, we, the Editors, will be more than satisfied.

"Shortly after 1 p.m., all gathered once again on the upper sun deck, where songs were sung by the Pitcairners and messages of thanks exchanged between Master, Magistrate, and Adviser.

"Julie Christian had the distiction of being the only child to go out to *Bergensfjord*. For some time Julie has been troubled by a growth under her foot. The doctors on board very kindly agreed to remove this during the stop. Had they been unable to do so, Julie may have had to go to New Zealand. We are indeed grateful for this service.

"In the happy expressions on the Pitcairners' faces as they made their way up from Bounty Bay, we could see reflected the success of the day, both socially and financially. And with the promise of the larger sister ship of the Norwegian American Line, *Sagafjord* calling in approximately 12 months, things indeed

163

appeared rosy." Volume 8, Number 2 (February 1966.)

"An old friend of many Pitcairn Islanders, Captain White, called (Wednesday, 8th June) in *Port Victor* from New Zealand about noon. Captain White has called here in other vessels over the years and has always proved to be a good friend and a welcome visitor. *Port Victor*, a cargo vessel with limited passenger accommodation, stayed almost two hours, during which time the men were able to sell a good quantity of curios and also obtain a further supply of surplus dunnage timber. Unfortunately, their visit was marred by an accident alongside the ship, when Fred Christian, who is in his eighties, caught his legs between the ship's side and the launch. Although no bones were broken, the skin was lacerated; and Fred was considerably shocked for some time. After treatment by the ship's doctor, Fred rested in the open air till towards the end of the visit, when he was lowered over the side in a special stretcher and brought straight ashore in one of the launches, whilst the rest of the men remained at sea to gather the wood. With Fred safely on land, Warren took his launch out again to assist in this task.

"We are pleased to report that Fred is now fit and well. In fact, he is very much his old cheery self again." Volume 8, Number 6 (June 1966).

"Nov. 22nd. *Ceramic.* At last, at last, at last . . . There were Tom and Betty (Christian) after their six-month visit to U.S.A., looking fit and healthy, with everyone so glad to see them home again. A fine day, with the ship arriving at 8:30 a.m. in smooth water. Medical attention again required, but instead of the ship's doctor, Sir Arthur Porritt, Governor Designate to New Zealand, came ashore to examine the pneumonia patient, Mrs. Reeves. Sir Arthur was accompanied by Lady Porritt, their daughter, Lady-in-Waiting, and Captain James Jones. All rode out to Pulau on the back of Hondas, where the patient was examined and pronounced out of danger. After a quick visit to Flora and an even quicker morning tea at Pastor's, it was time to return to the ship. Captain Milne's wife was also a member of the shore party and had to be watched closely, for she took quite a liking to one of the island babies and would have spirited it aboard ship had she been able. Brian left for N.Z. for medical treatment, accompanied by Sammy, together with Pauline and John Lindsay, who were to once again take up residence in New Zealand. With few stores to be unloaded, and a full ship of passengers, there was plenty of opportunity for trading and making purchases from the Barber's Shop. The ship finally sailed at 11:20 a.m." Volume 9, Number 11 (November 1967).

"We looked forward to *Amalric's* visit with enthusiasm. We'd had no ship for weeks; and the calm seas and good weather during the previous fortnight showed, each day, a clear, distant horizon, unbroken by any ships and reminding us of our isolation. We therefore welcomed *Amalric* as an old friend, calling this time with mail, Co-op stores, a few drums of fuel oil, and some power poles. We'd handled heavier loads before; so, although the power poles were an unknown quantity, we entertained no real concern about this one.

"The poles were required for our new electrical reticulation scheme and, as we knew only light poles were needed (even though there were 92 of them), no real difficulty was foreseen.

"Contacted two days away, we were surprised to hear that *Amalric* was in heavy weather and would be later than expected. The next day the ship was still in rough seas and now not expected to arrive until late in the afternoon. We didn't worry too much. It might mean working a couple of hours in the dark at the ship's side, but the seas were calm and the weather fine. We could handle it.

"March 7th dawned dull and warm with moderate seas. As the day progressed, the seas came up a little with the stiff breeze; and it seemed the ship might be bringing the bad weather with her. With *Gothic* due on the evening of the 8th and *Haperangi* calling with mail from London on the evening of the 9th, we were in for a busy three days and were certainly hoping for good weather.

"*Boxhead, Reid Cowell,* and *Ho Ho* were out of the harbour by 5 p.m. and headed out from the island to await the ship, which had been sighted from Taro Ground. As we waited, we speculated as to the size of the power poles; and it was with some amazement that we saw the actual size of them as they lay on *Amalric's* afterdeck as the ship hove to, three quarters of a mile off the island. Twenty feet long and three feet in circumference, these poles were going to take a lot of handling.

"Work began immediately, and the first 20 poles were simply dumped over the side, a method which proved most unsatisfactory. As darkness fell, the poles began to drift off into the murk; for it was found difficult to gather and lash poles into a towable unit. Both launches worked hard on these first poles, leaving *Ho Ho* tied up at the ship's side. Poles could only be towed ashore in groups of five at a time by each launch, taken through the surf into the harbour, winched onto the Landing, then rolled and manhandled as far as possible out of the way to leave sufficient room for those still to follow. Tony had thoughtfully rigged a large floodlight at the Landing, which helped handling considerably.

"When it took an hour to load and land the first 10 poles it was obvious that we were in for a long job just on the poles—the rest of the cargo wasn't even considered.

"After some organising, it was decided that a launch would tow five poles (already lashed together on the ship's deck), and *Ho Ho* would be loaded with 8 to 10 poles and be towed ashore by the second launch. This system worked and was the pattern of work until 7 a.m.

"The men worked magnificently in most difficult and dangerous conditions for 15 hours through the night—being continuously in the boats for most of that time in heavy seas. Soaking wet all the time, being doused by spray and drizzling rain for most of the night, they stuck grimly to the task. Praise too for the captain—continuously on the bridge, conning his ship all night through—and the First and Second Officers, who handled the unloading from the deck of the ship. This was a night for clear thinking and precise hand signals and quick reflexes on the part of the winchman, whose timing had to be perfect with each pole handled. With the boats bobbing and dancing beneath the ship's counter under the monstrous suspended logs, the situation called for teamwork. . . .

"As the boats left for the shore, the deck crew readied the next poles to be moved, while Tony and the Editor spent considerable time lassooing and making fast some of those errant poles from the first lot heaved overboard, which came bobbing back into the circle of the ship's lights. Four were laboriously retrieved in this manner, but it was thought at the time that as many as eight were still adrift on the high seas.

"Many of the island women and their families spent this night in the boatsheds, plying their men with food and hot drinks as they brought each load ashore. Never was a hot drink more appreciated by cold, wet, weary men.

"With the last poles finally ashore, the remainder of the cargo—24 drums of oil, 46 cases of stores, mail etc.—was distributed among the three boats; and *Amalric* sailed at 8:30 a.m. after what was surely the longest stay by any cargo vessel at Pitcairn, on what was certainly the longest night. . .

"(While) rock fishing at Tedside, Ben was surprised to find three of the missing poles washed up on the rocks. A boat was launched as soon as word was received in the village and the errant logs towed around to the Landing." Volume 10, Number 3 (March 1968).

166

"May 23rd. *Port Albany.* As we came alongside beneath an overhanging gangway, the ship's Bo'sun was almost caught between gangway and boat, as we lifted quickly on a high swell. As it was, he fell into the boat, where he stayed, and went ashore with the Doctor after getting a good wetting. These were very friendly folk, a very happy ship, and will always be welcome at Pitcairn."

"May 26th. *Birgette Skou* arrived at 3 a.m., carrying 11 bags of mail and urgently needed medical stores, in the worst possible weather. Giant breakers swept into the Bay, but it was decided to make an attempt to get out. For 35 minutes the men fought to straighten the boat in the narrow exit, but a drenched crew had to give up this hopeless task, and Tom contacted the Master, who agreed to stay until first light. In daylight it looked much worse, although it was decided to make another attempt, with Len picking the time from White Rock. A call from Len and the boat was off in a flurry of spray, with everyone cheering as it was seen that it was safely through. The seas were too high for boarding the ship, and the mail and stores were taken in the boat with some difficulty. A perfect time was picked for reentry, and we were glad that the men were safely ashore. The ship left at 7:50 p.m., taking green seas across her bows, and we are very grateful to the Master, who kept his ship for so long on our behalf." Volume 10, Number 5 (May 1968).

"A TRIBUTE TO MR. O. A. DALY. The Shaw Savill Shipping Company has long been friends of the Pitcairn community, and the names of some of the masters of the Line's ships are household words here. So much so, that geographical features (on the island) have been named after them.

"Foremost among those who have had this small community's interest at heart has not been a seafaring man, but a landlubber—tied to an office desk in far-off New Zealand—someone who has never even seen Pitcairn, but is known to every Pitcairner, whether they live on the island or in New Zealand.

"Mr. Owen A. Daly of Shaw Savill's Wellington office has proved to be a reliable and trustworthy friend to all Pitcairners over many years of service with the Company, and at the end of this month he retires.

"How many Pitcairners in New Zealand have turned to him in time of need? How many times have urgent cables been sent to him to arrange this, order that, send some urgently required article, book an air passage or hotel room, or send a fresh supply of eggs and butter to the island?

"Nothing has been too much trouble for him, and we can only hope that if anyone in New Zealand can replace him and do half as much, then we will be satisfied.

"The Government of Pitcairn is well aware of all this, as are those in the administration in Fiji; and, as a tribute for his prolonged efforts on our behalf, has extended an invitation to both Mr. Daly and his wife to visit Pitcairn as honoured guests for as long as they care to stay. We hope they can both take advantage of this invitation so sincerely made. . . ."

"The ships of the Shaw Savill and Albion Company started calling at Pitcairn as long ago as 1914, when the Panama route was first commenced. . . .

"To these men and other Masters, Chief Officers, Wireless Operators, Pursers, Engineers, Deck Officers, Stewards, crew and friends—we are sorry you are no longer calling; and we wish you well wherever you may be." Volume 10, Number 7 (July 1968).

"Whenever a ship leaves Pitcairn waters, it is a tradition to sing them a hymn, followed by the 'Goodbye Song.' It may interest the overseas readers to read the words of this 'Goodbye Song':

> "Now, one last song we'll sing—Goodbye, goodbye!
> Time moves on rapid wings—Goodbye!
> And this short year will soon be past;
> Will soon be numbered with the last;
> But as we part, to all we'll say—
> Goodbye, goodbye, goodbye.
> But as we part, to all we'll say—Goodbye, goodbye, goodbye.
> "We gather now to say goodbye, goodbye!
> We can no longer stay—goodbye!
> Thanks for your love and constant care,
> And kindness that we kindly share.
> We part but hope to meet again—
> Goodbye, goodbye, goodbye!
> We part but hope to meet again—goodbye, goodbye, goodbye."

Volume 11, Number 8 (August 1969).

"On the morning of the 9th the *Regina Maris*, a three-mast clipper-barquentine, arrived unexpectedly. This barquentine had been expected at Pitcairn in January of this year, but en route she was struck by a thunderbolt and de-masted and had to return to Norway for repairs.

"Wishing to visit Australia for the Cook bi-centenary

celebrations, she sailed directly to Australia and visited Pitcairn on her way home to Norway.

"The *Regina Maris*, a beautiful old sailing vessel built of oak in 1908, carries 34 sails, including 6 studding sails—about 7000 square feet of canvas. Highest mast is 115 feet. The owners have kept her fittings as near as possible to the original manner, but an auxiliary motor was installed in 1932. After being struck by the thunderbolt and returning to Norway, the majority of the crew left the ship, calling it the 'devil ship'; but about two of the original crew members remained on board. Including the Master of the ship, the crew numbers 18 whilst on her visit to Pitcairn, two short of the usual number.

"Unfortunately, weather conditions were not right for sails; and the ship arrived and left under motor. The crew members took turns in coming ashore, the first half coming in the morning and the second half in the afternoon, and visitors were allowed to go out for a visit when the last boatload of crew members returned to their ship about 5 p.m. When the time came for the longboat to return to Bounty Bay, a hymn and the goodbye song were sung as usual. Then, to our surprise, the crew of the *Regina Maris* gathered on the deck and returned the compliment with a rendition of a Sea Chanty. As she got underway about 7 p.m., several flares were let off from the *Regina Maris* as a farewell salute. Not to be forgotten too is the share-out of chocolate sweets, handkerchiefs, and pocket knives kindly sent ashore by the Captain of the *Regina Maris*. We on Pitcairn are certainly rather spoilt in this respect." Volume 12, Number 8 (August 1970).

"During a visit to Pitcairn Island this month by the *Sir Percivale*, the Master, Captain McLaughlin, made known the facts concerning the ship's movements at the time of the loss of *Reid Cowell*, and his actions following the subsequent calls for medical assistance. From comments which have been made to him by several people on the Island, he was led to believe that there was a general opinion held here that *Sir Percivale* did little to provide help when it was so badly needed.

"Captain McLaughlin stated that on receiving the request for medical assistance, he gave orders for his ship to leave station and make for Pitcairn. Radio reception during the next 24 hours was poor, and the exact extent of the injuries sustained by the two men involved was not clear. But he had been able to ascertain that help was required and for this reason he set course for the Island. With 12 hours until her E.T.A. at Pitcairn, *Sir Percivale* received the news that further help was not required due to the arrival of the *Enseigne de Vaisseau Henry*.

169

"*Sir Percivale* then returned to her original station, knowing that help had been provided for the injured men.

"It is easy for us here on Pitcairn to criticize the actions, or apparent lack of action, of ships in times of emergency; but it would be well for us to remember that there are many factors affecting the captains' decisions about the movements of their ships which are not known to us. It is apparent in this case that the ship which was able to give assistance first was closer to Pitcairn when the emergency call was received and was a faster vessel than *Sir Percivale*.

"In fairness to Captain McLaughlin, it must be stated that this information was given to the writer during the course of a conversation, and it was not the captain's intention to have his explanation published. However, we felt that readers on Pitcairn would be interested to learn the facts, and for this reason we have taken the opportunity to publicize Captain McLaughlin's comments." Volume 14, Number 7 (July 1972).

"*Majestic* (Captain Williams) arrived in the rain at 3:30 p.m. (on the 27th). Among the cargo she carried from the United Kingdom were the supplies which had not been landed from the *Port Montreal* in June. Two hours were spent unloading cargo into the launches; but, unfortunately, there was insufficient room in the two boats for the entire cargo. Dusk was approaching, the captain did not want to open his hatch in the rain, and time ran out with seven refrigerators, steel rods, and a box of machinery parts for the Engineer's workshop still aboard. Seven sad families watched the ship leave—oh, well, perhaps we'll have good weather when those refrigerators come north again. . . ." Volume 14, Number 9 (September 1972).

"Some time in March, Pitcairn Island received a request to keep a listening watch each Sunday from late April for the yacht *Fri*. The radio staff established contact with *Fri* and learned that she had had a slow, rough passage, with several breakdowns. Daily reports showed progress to be very slow, but the yacht was sighted on the morning of May 6th, and by 6:30 p.m. the same day she had found an anchorage at Tedside.

"Half of the crew came ashore the following day, and all showed great relief to stretch their legs after their six weeks' voyage. After two nights ashore, the watches were changed; and the remainder of the crew came ashore.

"During the trip to Pitcairn the ship had some of her sails blown out, the engine gave continual trouble, and the steering gear broke at least twice. Needless to say, the crew were hard at work during most of their time here, effecting repairs. Our local engineering staff gave considerable assistance, with welding jobs on the steering gear and anchor windlass. All efforts to cast a new engine bearing were fruitless because of the lack of suitable materials; so, in spite of all the good work that was done while she was here, *Fri* finally sailed with one effective piston in her engine.

"*Fri* was built in 1912 as a 90-foot cargo vessel, to work in the Baltic Sea. She is now owned and sailed by David Moodie, a young American from Vermont who is temporarily domiciled in New Zealand. The remainder of the 13 men (and woman) crew were from New Zealand, U.S.A., France, and Holland.

"Once ashore, the crew were glad to accept the many offers of accommodation which were extended. They proved to be a happy group who were easy to meet and fitted in well with the community during their brief stay. They were, perhaps, disappointed to find that Pitcairners were not fired with a zeal to match their own, but this difference is hardly to be wondered at, considering the different environment from which the visitors have come. At least three of them found local conditions so much to their liking that they expressed the hope that sometime they might return for a longer stay.

"The last of the firewood, fresh water, vegetables, and fruit were loaded on the 13th; and, late in the afternoon, many folk went out to the ship to say farewell to the visitors. At 5:30 p.m., with some local help, the anchor was lifted; and *Fri* left for Mururoa to act as mother ship for any other yachts which join her to protest against French nuclear testing.

"Radio reports received at the end of the month gave her position within 12 miles of Mururoa, in the company of *Spirit of Peace* and another protest yacht. The crew were 'frightened, but determined.'

"The considered opinion of one local gentleman—'They're mad, but brave.'

"What will become of *Fri*? Will the French stop their tests, or will they 'tie a rope around *Fri* and tow her out of the road,' as one person has said? We do not know.

"We wish you well, *Fri* and Ted, Peter Patchouli, Gilbert, Martain, Rau, Emma, David, Naomi, Murray, Allister, Colin and Graeme." Volume 15, Number 5 (May 1973).

"Over the past four years *Sir Percivale* has become a well-known visitor. She has come each year with a job to do, but in most of our minds she is much more than a monitoring vessel. For just over three months she has been in this part of the Pacific; and during that time she visited Pitcairn on five occasions, spending a total of approximately 13 days in the proximity of the island.

"Have you thought of the benefits we gain from her visits? There are the obvious things like the opportunity to trade for goods and sell curios for the cash most of us like to have. There are the extra films we have when the ship is staying overnight. This year there was the trip to Henderson for wood. And what of the less tangible things? Contacts established which may lead to future orders for curios; ideas and information gleaned from the many folk willing to share their knowledge; companionship of visitors to the island and to our homes; and the friendships this engenders. Quite apart from the extra tin of paint or the packet of screws or the pound of butter, we all have much to be thankful for.

"Did you spare a thought for the men who sailed in her when they were spending long periods of time on sea station? Her design makes her an uncomfortable vessel in the best of seas, and a month of unbroken sea duty aboard her probably doesn't arouse envy in any of us.

"No one likes the reason behind her visits to Pitcairn, but we all have to be grateful for the opportunities and experiences she brings us. Now that *Sir Percivale* has left us for another year, life does seem much quieter. For that, too, we say, 'Thank you, *Sir Percy.*" Volume 15, Number 9 (September 1973).

"20th. *Margitta* cruised past the island and then turned and headed straight for the harbour at about 8:30 a.m. . . .

"Four folk from the ship, including the captain's wife, made a hurried trip ashore to get their passports stamped. The frequent sounding of the ship's siren indicated either that the master was an impatient man or that he didn't trust his wife to return to the ship once she got ashore. The distress rocket he eventually fired was sufficient to move things the way he wanted them; the launch returned to the *Margitta* and she left for Panama just before midday." Volume 15, Number 10 (October 1973).

"12th. Royal Yacht *Britannia* (Admiral Trowbridge) arrived at 9 a.m. en route to Rarotonga and New Zealand. Two parties of yachtsmen visited the island during the morning, and Admiral Trowbridge and four officers were invited to lunch ashore with the Adviser and Magistrate. In the afternoon local people were invited aboard the Royal Yacht, where they were entertained with the film 'Jungle Stories' and later given afternoon tea. This informal visit was an enjoyable break for everyone.

"The support vessel *Blue Rover* paid a brief call at the same time, but we did not have the opportunity to visit her in view of

172

the short time available. *Britannia* left the island at 6 p.m."
Volume 15, Number 12 (December 1973).

"For the first time in a long, long memory, January brought forth no ships at all for the Islanders to trade with. We were visited by the yacht *Rainbow*, with a crew of four, on their way to Easter Island; but there were no big ships at all. Day after day the horizon was scanned without success. When one considers that there were times in the past when five ships called on one day, this lapse of shipping was ridiculous. Some believe that the current energy and fuel crisis may be to blame, but these ships that are so necessary to the way of life of the Pitcairn Islanders are becoming less and less frequent. All we can do is hope and pray for a better month in February." Volume 16, Number 1 (January 1974).

"On the 9th, a Saturday, five bells rang; and everyone raced down to the Landing to get into the longboats to go out to a ship that was approaching the Island fast. Off we went; and, as we approached her, the ship duly lowered a rope ladder. Things looked promising. But as we came nearer, we noticed that the rope ladder was lifted up again, even though the ship was stationary. We went alongside and Pervis called out for permission to board. This, however, was curtly refused; and the *Coastal Trader* built up steam and went on her merry way. It was a pleasant ride out in the longboats anyway." Volume 16, Number 2 (February 1974).

"25th. *Ogden Clipper* stayed for just over two hours in good conditions, with a very kind Captain and crew.

" . . . I must relate to you a happening on board the *Ogden Clipper*. I had been up with the Captain in his lounge, with Pervis, our Island Magistrate, when Pervis said he had some bananas for the Captain and asked where he would like them put. The Captain called out to one of the Chinese stewards and told him to go with Pervis and take the bunch below to the cooler. Now our Pervis is a big man—about six-foot-four-inches and around the sixteen-stone mark—and all muscle. Away they went. Also, I don't know if you are aware of the fact that all Pitcairn men wear knives when they go out to ships, for a variety of reasons. . . . Pervis handed the steward this bunch of bananas, and the (steward) proceeded to walk down one of the steep companionways into the bowels of the ship, and Pervis was following with some other fruit. About half way down, Pervis noticed that a piece of rope that was tied around the bunch of bananas had become entangled in one of the rungs of the companionway and, realising that if it should grab, the Chinese steward could have a nasty fall, Pervis whipped out his knife and yelled, 'Hey!' The steward turned around and all he could see was six foot four inches of Pitcairn Islander with a knife in his hand towering over him. With one mighty yell, (he) dropped the bananas and ran for his life. Funny, I never could make out why. What's more, we didn't see him again for the rest of the time we were on board." Volume 17, Number 4 (April 1975).

". . . we had a visit by the 13-metre Ferro-cement yacht *Fairwinds* on the 22nd, November. On board were her owner, Mr. Carl Lipscombe, and his companion, Irene Jans. They had sent a message about ten days previously saying that they would be calling in for water and some supplies before going on to French Polynesia. It was Sabbath morning, about 7:30 when the yacht was sighted, and she was anchored and her weatherbeaten twosome ashore by 10 a.m. The weather was beautifully calm and fine. Light southerly breezes gave a perfect lee in Bounty Bay, and Carl and Irene certainly welcomed the chance to get on good old terra firma again, after eight weeks at sea from Panama to Pitcairn.

"As the weather appeared to be so good and the hospitality of the Islanders the same, the couple decided to stay a few extra days before once more venturing out into the blue Pacific. For the next four days the weather stayed the same, but on Wednesday 26th, the wind started to freshen up and switch around to the northwest. Carl was advised to shift his yacht to a better position in case the wind should come up any stronger; but on looking at the way she was sitting at anchor, he was satisfied that everything was all right. How wrong this was to prove. During the night the wind grew and grew, and with it the sea.

"At 6:30 a.m., Thursday 27th, Carl looked out from where he was staying and couldn't see the masts of the *Fairwinds;* so he rapidly dressed and ran down to investigate. The sight that met his eyes is one I am sure he will never be able to forget. There was the *Fairwinds* on her side, on the rocks on the northeastern side of Bounty Bay being mercilessly pounded by huge wave after huge wave. A long telephone ring was put through, and all able-bodied men and women rushed down to the rocks to see if there was anything they could do, but it was hopeless. It was far too dangerous for anyone to try and board her, and within an hour and a half of Carl's sighting her, she broke up completely, not a hundred yards from where Fletcher Christian burnt and sank the *Bounty.*

"Two hours later, apart from some heavy swells, the sea and wind were relatively calm again. But for poor Carl and Irene, virtually everything was lost. What was salvaged was of little use, and everything they had was tied up in that yacht. Now, they have lost everything. Whoever named it 'The Cruel Sea' was certainly right in this case.

"At the moment Carl and Irene are staying with our Island Magistrate and his wife, but as for the future—they just don't know. Here they are, stuck out in the middle of the Pacific with no way at present of getting away. All we can do at this stage is to hope and pray that something turns up for them that will help them get somewhere so they can start fresh." Volume 17, Numbers 10 and 11 (October-November 1975).

"By Child Reporter Leah. As news got around about the children's party aboard *Sir Geraint* on Sunday, 6 June, it appeared more and more exciting. At last the day arrived. The bell rang at 11 a.m. for men, women and children to go down to the Landing if they wanted to go out to the ship. When the longboats were in the water, people loaded their baskets of fruit, stamps, weaving, and carvings into the boats; and then we were off. It took only a few minutes to get out to the ship; and once there and safely aboard, the children were taken upstairs to the lounge, where they ate and drank until they could eat and drink no more. When lunchtime came soon after, we were still eating and drinking; but we still had to eat our lunch.

"Following lunch, Barney took us to the very bottom of the ship, where the hatches are. There he gave us a ride on the fork-lift, after which he took us up to the bridge, where we saw some children on deck having a swing on a makeshift swing prepared by the officers of the ship for our entertainment. We were also lucky to hear the adults singing Happy Birthday to Rosemary and David.

"Before we left the ship at 5 p.m., we joined the adults of Pitcairn in singing a number of songs, including the Farewell song.

"We came back to the island very tired but happy for having enjoyed such a pleasant day aboard *Sir Geraint*. Farewell, *Sir Geraint*, and thank you for the wonderful time." Volume 18, Number 6 (June 1976).

"STATISTICS. Ships which stopped at Pitcairn as at end of June: 1975—22; 1976—19 and 2 yachts; 1977—15 and 7 yachts (including the brigantine *Eye of the Wind* and *Yankee Trader*). Volume 19, Number 6 (June 1977).

"At a public meeting held in the Public Hall on the 12th, a letter from the Administration regarding the future of scheduled supply vessels to Pitcairn from New Zealand and U.K. was read by Island Secretary Ben to a very attentive, quiet audience.

"The following summary of the main points brought out in the letter will no doubt place overseas friends and relatives in the picture:

". . . Several factors have given rise (to the present scheduled supply-ship situation) which is likely to continue.

". . . conventional freight vessels are rapidly being replaced by container ships. By the end of 1977, for example, it is expected that 80 percent of N.Z.'s exports will leave the country in containers . , . container ships work on a much tighter schedule, and it is uncommon for them to make intermediate calls . . . this therefore affects Pitcairn. Some container ships do not have lifting equipment suitable for unloading small quantities of cargo. . . . Northbound sailings to Europe via Panama have diminished with the reopening of the Suez Canal since all vessels scheduled to call at Mediterranean ports are routed westward from New Zealand.

". . . Southbound sailings have become fewer in number, and there is a growing tendency for those which remain to be routed from Panama to Fiji, thence to Australia and New Zealand . . . this route does not pass close to Pitcairn, and there is little likelihood of such vessels being nominated to supply the island. For this reason the Tonnage Committee is unable to give any commitment on southbound supply vessels in the foreseeable future. There may be the occasional vessel which will provide an opportunity to ship stores from the United Kingdom, but nothing which could really be called a service. . . . The latest advice from the Tonnage Committee indicates that three-monthly northbound sailings can be provided for some time, but the long-term future position is not clear.

". . . Shipping companies are concerned at the increasing costs being incurred by vessels serving Pitcairn.

"Ed. says—Pitcairn is reliant on supply vessels to bring in flour for bread, stores and supplies to maintain and improve existing amenities and machinery, and those extra goodies which perhaps the outside world take for granted. For the records, supply vessels from the U.K. arrived (for 1977): February 27 (*Darro*), May 22 (*Laurentic*), and August 11 (N.Z. *Waitangi*). Supply vessels from N.Z. for 1977 were *Darro* (May 4), *Medic* (November 24) and *Taupo* (December 29), and what of the 1978 year?

"It is obvious that stores and supplies must be ordered in larger bulk than previously to withstand long periods between ships. We must not forget too that we rely on supply vessels to bring mail as well as take mail out." Volume 19, Number 12 (December 1977).

Slipway

After the Pitcairners beat their way back into Bounty Bay through dangerous surf from passing ships, their work is far from done. If the boats have brought cargo, it must be unloaded and transported up to the Edge and on into the village or wherever needed. Then the boats, each weighing between two and three tons, must be hauled out of the water, up the slipway and into the boathouse. For years the task of returning the boats to the boathouse was one of the most difficult jobs on the island. Part of the major improvement project at the Landing in 1976, executed by a team of Royal Engineers and the Pitcairners, included upgrading of the slipway. However, this part of the project could not be completed while the British engineer team was on the island, due to heavy seas at the Landing. Finally, in 1977, the Pitcairners themselves finished the work.

"The arrival of the Dutch cargo vessel *Laarderkerk* on Wednesday 9 March saw the new slipway, which is about two-thirds complete, placed on trial. Only that part of the existing slipway which is submerged by the sea most times remains to be done.

"Basically the new slipway comprises two steel channels laid in concrete running the length of the boathouse and down to the high-water mark, and it is in these two channels that the longboats are made to run down and into the harbour. Timber ribs raised slightly above the concrete and at right angles to the channels were incorporated to protect the boats' woodwork as they run along the channels keeling slightly to one side. In essence, the whole concept was to make things easier when putting the boats to sea.

"How will the new slipway work out? That was the question. Charles, with his handy bottle of oil, went about oiling one of the channels prior to the big event. Then Brian summoned all men to lend a hand . . . this was tension at its best. One . . . two . . . three . . . HAUL!—nothing doing?? One . . . two . . . three . . . HAUL! Away went the boat literally like greased lightning and into the harbour, the friction between the iron runner on the keel of the boat and the steel channel causing a few sparks to fly. The jubilation which spread among the men was tremendous. It certainly was simple, unlike the 'good ole days' of grunting and panting and fuming to get the boats away only to see them stopping in their tracks halfway down the once-wooden slipway.

"The first boat ready, eyes then turned to the second boat,

177

which was in the same channel as the first but higher in the boathouse. After a few coughs and splutters (by Glen and Dennis) the second boat gracefully slid down the slipway and into the sea . . . just like that.

"Although it is still early days, the boats have used the slipway a lot this month; and at each launching one cannot help but be impressed with the New-Look Slipway." Volume 19, Number 3 (March 1977).

"At approximately 6:30 a.m. on July 11, the five strokes on the bell sent the men scurrying down to the Landing like ants to launch the launches as an unexpected ship arrived. . . .

"On reaching the Landing however, the men were stunned, for the lower part of the slipway (submerged by water most of the time) had 'busted up' making it impossible to get the launches back into the boathouse should they be put to sea. Sad to say, the Danish vessel left without anyone having made contact with it.

"However this unfortunate incident saw the men keen to begin work on the lower slipway, and work began in earnest on July 12. Readers will recall that in his final report in May's *Miscellany*, Captain Cowan (of the Royal Engineer team) felt that this work required ideal conditions. In fact, sea and weather conditions plagued the men throughout the works; and in mainly atrocious conditions, the men toiled to ensure that their 'main road' to the outside world would be in tip-top condition should another ship arrive. In brief, work comprised the laying of piles immediately in front of the upper slipway and about 9 feet out into the harbour, an area of about 300 square feet. This meant that the slipway was blocked for two weeks. On the inside of the piles was laid wooden boxing and then the task of laying concrete got underway.

"It appears that the work has been successful from all accounts although there are still the finishing touches to be added. The new lower slipway received a trial run on the 30th of the month, when a ship called; and the launches were launched and hauled back into the boathouse without too much difficulty.

"Other work included the repairing of the private sector of the slipway, which is in very poor condition. At time of going to press (31 July) heavy seas have washed away a lot of the rockfill used to fill in holes before concreting was to take place.

"We hope that August's weather will be more favourable so that this urgent work can be completed." Volume 19, Number 7 (July 1977).

". . . work started on the upper section of the slipway, in front of the private boatsheds, on July 24. The weather once again was against us, with heavy seas and much rain. However, this did not dampen the spirits and enthusiasm of the men, for we were now on the last stage of slipway works.

"The work entailed cementing and laying wooden slippers in the area from the private boatsheds to the water's edge of the main slipway. On the 9th August the concreting and laying of the slippers was finished, and on August 14 cleaning up took most of the day's work. At 1 p.m. slipway works was completed.

"At this stage the slipway seems like a pleasant dream come true and by all accounts is successful. Our 'main road' to the outside world is now opened.

"As a point of interest, since slipway works began in July, a total of 2,302 man-hours was worked." Volume 19, Number 8 (August 1977).

Stamps

Pitcairn's stamps have been popular with philatelists throughout the world since the first definitive issue was released in 1940. Before stamps were printed for issue from the island, until 1926, letters were delivered free worldwide and were franked "Posted on Pitcairn Island: no stamps available." After 1926 the stamps and postal rates of New Zealand were used until the first definitive issue was printed. The Pitcairners carefully guard the integrity of their stamps; and when the infrequent philatelic error does occur, for whatever reason, it is seen as cause for major concern by the islanders. For many years Dr. Arthur A. Delaney, a teacher in New Hyde Park, New York, has been recognized as a leading authority on the stamps of Pitcairn.

"THE POPULARITY OF PITCAIRN'S STAMPS. By Dr. Arthur A. Delaney. Pitcairners are well aware that their postal issues appeal to stamp collectors throughout the world. Tangible evidence of this lies in the fact that the sale of Pitcairn's stamps constitutes the largest single source of island revenue. But, how many Pitcairners have wondered why their stamps have such worldwide appeal?

The writer, who has formed several specialised collections during his twenty-five years of philatelic activity and who has contributed throughout this period to the philatelic press, takes this opportunity to share with his friends on Pitcairn observations of the philatelic scene as it pertains to the island's issues.

"The most obvious factor which underlies the popularity of Pitcairn's stamps is, of course, the appeal of the island's emissions to those who are fascinated by the *Bounty* story. The early history of the island's settlement has been reflected in the

1940 definitives, now rapidly becoming classics in the world of philately. The historical picture presented by these eight stamps has been broadened by the issuance of the 1967 'Discovery' set, the series marking the 150th anniversary of Vice Admiral Bligh's death, and the 'Resettlement' commemoratives of 1961.

"The affection stamp collectors have for the issues of the Pitcairn Islands extends beyond the historical narrative that is related by the island's stamps. It also includes the contemporary. Pitcairn may be only two square miles of volcanic rock located thousands of miles from 'civilization,' but the activities and welfare of its inhabitants are of great concern and interest to the world's philatelists. Fortunately for collectors, much of Pitcairn's contemporary life is also reflected in the island's postal paper. Aspects of today's Pitcairn will be found depicted on the 1957 definitives, issues of the 1964-67 series, and will be featured on the projected 'Handicrafts' (1968) and 'Island Life' (1969) sets.

"The fact that collecting Pitcairn's stamps indirectly aids a pious people whose every way of life seems to be dedicated to their faith has an appeal to Christian philatelists, regardless of denominational affiliation or personal religious persuasion. No collector can look at stamps depicting the pietistical John Adams or the Bounty's Bible without being reminded of God's welcome on remote Pitcairn. But, Pitcairners must be aware of all this. Let us turn our attention, therefore, to some of the more philatelically pragmatic reasons for the popularity of Pitcairn's stamps.

"Stamp collectors have a penchant for completeness. Pitcairn is one of the few 'established' stamp-issuing entities which have been collected with ease and from its first issue to its most recent. Although prices for early Pitcairn issues have been rising, none of the island's postal emissions (with the exception of the 1940 booklet issue) are beyond the average collector's financial means.

"It was mentioned that stamp sales contribute greatly to the island's economy. This is also true of other philatelically respectable countries, such as Liechtenstein and Monaco. The economy of still other nations (not mentioned here) is also bolstered by stamp sales. But there is an ethical difference between the stamp-issuing policies of the Pitcairn Colony and, say, certain African and Mid-Eastern states. Collectors are cognizant of the fact that 'all' Pitcairn stamps serve postal duty, while many issues of the so-called 'emerging nations' are produced solely to separate the collector from his money. These semispurious issues always feature 'popular' subjects and are

180

devoted to themes of 'popular' appeal. They are directed principally to the novice collector, but also seek acceptance by the general, topical and specialist collectors.

"Increasingly, the philatelic fraternity is boycotting such issues. Not only are actual postal considerations of minor importance in determining their issuance, many of these 'stamps' are produced in limited amounts, are issued both perforated and imperforated, are printed in souvenir sheets (also perforated and imperforated), and contain purported 'errors' and untold colour varieties. This practice is philatelic morality at its lowest. Pitcairn has never embarked on such 'philatelic adventures,' and the world's collectors have good reason to believe that its reputation will remain forever untarnished. The few errors and varieties found among Pitcairn's issues are legitimate, all of which have resulted from genuine circumstances. And, it should be noted, all are readily available to the interested collector at reasonable prices that reflect a true market.

"Of great importance in the popularity of Pitcairn's stamps is the fact that they are all supplied through the auspices of the Crown Agents (in London), an efficient and knowledgeable organisation with an excellent reputation in the philatelic world. As some British Colonies have attained full- or semi-statehood status, they have placed their philatelic sales in the hands of various profit-making concerns. The result has been the lessening of once-held fine reputations and the loss of respectability for their issues among collectors. This is particularly true of some of Her Majesty's former colonies in the Caribbean.

"Because of the Crown Agent sponsorship and the high ethics of the island government, Pitcairn has issued stamps of artistic merit, all of which have been executed in good taste. Its issues have been released in reasonable quantities, and the philatelic market has not been inundated with outrageously long sets with high denominations or frequent release of new, often unnecessary, postal paper. A new definitive set every few years and an occasional commemorative seem to be the Pitcairn policy, and it is applauded by the world's collectors.

"One exception to the above observation will be noted by some, but it is not to the discredit of the Pitcairn administration. Pitcairn has participated in every so-called 'omnibus' issue since the 'Peace' stamps of 1946. The Peace Issue, the Silver Wedding stamps (1949), the Coronation stamp (1953) and the Churchill memorials (1966) do pertain to Pitcairn. No collector could argue effectively against Pitcairn honouring, for example, Her Majesty's coronation. An issue such as the 1966 pair which commemorated the World Health Organisation, on the other hand, seems to be out-of-place in a collection devoted to the Pitcairn Islands. The featuring of the large W.H.O. headquarters building on a Pitcairn stamp does strike this collector as being incongruous to the island's milieu! Frankly, most collectors regard many of the 'omnibus' issues as being ugly, and, therefore, incompatible with the beautiful stamps that pertain directly to Pitcairn, her history, geography and people. Since Pitcairn participates in omnibus issues, and since philatelists strive for complete collections, such issues are collected as avidly as are the island's other stamps.

"With but this minor exception, the world's stamp collectors are immensely pleased with the island's stamps and the present stamp-issuing policy. While collectors deplore the unwarranted and frequent issuance of new stamps, the writer knows of no collector of Pitcairn material who would object to a slight increase in the island's modest output of new issues. Indeed, it is difficult to express the anticipation with which the Pitcairn specialist awaits the island's next stamp release." Volume 10, Number 2 (February 1968).

"The news concerning the issuing of three commemorative stamps for Pitcairn towards the end of 1961 or early 1962 will be welcomed by stamp collectors throughout the world. Based on suggestions made by Mr. H. E. Maude, O.B.E., and the advice of the Postmaster General, Fiji, the stamps will commemorate the 100th anniversary of the return of the Pitcairn Islanders from Norfolk Island, 1859-1864, this seminal period witnessing the final settlement of Pitcairn and the beginning of continuous occupation. . . ." Volume 2, Number 2 (February 1960).

"NEW STAMP ISSUE. The Pitcairn Island Post Office is pleased to announce that the new definitive stamps will be on sale on Wednesday, 5th August, 1964.

"There will be twelve stamps, with a total value of 11/10 1/2d, in this set. . . . Each stamp portrays Queen Elizabeth II in the top right-hand corner; across the bottom is printed 'Pitcairn Islands' with a small crown to the left. The main section of the design is of a scene or a bird typifying Pitcairn, as listed below:

1/2 d.	Pitcairn Islands Longboat, under sail.
1 d.	H.M. Armed Vessel *Bounty*
2 d.	Rowing Longboat Home to Bounty Bay
3 d.	Frigate Bird
4 d.	White Bird

182

6 d.	Whale Bird
8 d.	Austin Bird
10 d.	Bosun Birds
1/-	Chicken Bird
1/6	Red Breast
2/6	Ghost Bird
4/-	Wood Pigeon.

Volume 6, Number 5 (April 30, 1964).

"CHURCHILL COMMEMORATIVE STAMPS. These commemorative stamps were released for sale on Pitcairn Island on Monday, 24th January, along with stamps from many other Commonwealth countries. As a set of four stamps (2d., 3d., 6d., and 1/-) these are proving very popular as initial sales are very high. A new stamp issue always means plenty of work for our Post Office staff, as collectors and dealers from all over the world send to Pitcairn for stocks, most of which they desire to be prepared and cancelled as First Day Covers. . . ." Volume 8, Number 1 (January 1966).

"STAMPS HONORING PITCAIRN'S HISTORY. By Arthur A. Delaney. A philatelist once quipped that His Majesty's Armed Vessel *Bounty* should be remembered chiefly as the ship that launched a hundred postage stamps. The Pitcairn Islands have issued just under a hundred postal issues and it is quite obvious that had it not been for the combined efforts of the Bounty's Captain William Bligh, and his Master's Mate, Fletcher Christian, the world today would be minus one stamp-issuing country. Pitcairners, although not renowned for their own stamp collecting activities, are probably even more cognizant than collectors at large of the numbers of stamps that their island has issued, the sale of postage stamps being the largest single source of island revenue ever since the first Pitcairn issue appeared in October 1940. However, how many Pitcairners are aware of the fact that on six separate occasions four other countries have issued a total of twelve stamps relating to Pitcairn's history?

"The first of these non-Pitcairn issues was put out by the Kingdom of Tonga on July 1st, 1953. Reproduced on this 5/- definitive stamp was a scene identified simply as 'The Mutiny of the Bounty.' This was a reproduction of an old print by R. Dodd, published in London in 1790. It depicts Christian and his fellow mutineers casting Bligh adrift and is reproduced in part on the 1d. and 2/6 stamps of Pitcairn's 1940 definitive series. The 8c. value of the recent Pitcairn set commemorating the 150th anniversary of Admiral Bligh's death reproduces the entire print.

Chronologically, the scene depicted on the purple and gold Tonga issue must have occurred an hour or so after Bligh and his loyal men had set out on the long open-boat voyage to Dutch Timor. The right-hand side of the stamp shows the *Bounty*, while the famous ship's launch is seen at the lower left-hand corner. In the background, set against a sunset, are the outlines of Tofua and Kao, two islands in Tonga's Ha'apai group. The sunset scene of course, is an inaccuracy; Bligh was cast adrift after dawn. Tofua and Kao are pictured on the stamp because Bligh touched there in April-May, 1789.

"Most Pitcairners will remember the three-value set which their island issued on 15 November 1961 to commemorate the return of the islanders from Norfolk. The 3d. pictured Simon Young and Pitcairn, while the 6d. reproduced maps of the two islands, and the 1/- value depicted the migrant schooner *Mary Ann*. Five years prior to this set being issued, Norfolk had celebrated the centenary of the landing of the Pitcairners on that island in June 1856. The most severe drought in Pitcairn history, in which the islanders suffered from both famine and disease to the extent that 'in one week there were not ten persons capable of obtaining help for their own wants,' forced a long-contemplated move. In 1856, the entire population was taken to Norfolk in the chartered transport *Morayshire*. The two stamps which Norfolk issued to mark the centenary of this historic event, 3d. and 2/- values, carry a common design which depicts the orginal Norfolk Seal as well as the landing of the first Pitcairn settlers.

"The purpose of the *Bounty's* voyage is often obscured by the mutiny and the subsequent settlement of Pitcairn. It will be recalled simply that Captain Bligh was commissioned by his King to transport breadfruit trees from Otaheite (Tahiti) to the newly established Botanic Gardens on St. Vincent. The breadfruit was to be cultivated in order that inexpensive nourishment be provided for the slave labourers on the British plantations in the West Indies. The mutiny, of course, prevented Bligh from carrying out his assignment. Forgotten by many is the fact that Bligh later accomplished his mission in 1793, successfully transporting 300 breadfruit plants from Tahiti to Kingstown in *H.M.S. Providence*. On 23 March 1965 St. Vincent issued a set of four stamps commemorating the 200th anniversary of the Botanic Gardens. The 1c. value pictures tropical fruit, and the 25c. and 40c. issues present various views of the Gardens, while the 4c. directly ties the series to Pitcairn history by depicting a breadfruit and Bligh's ship, the *Providence*. Considering all the difficulties Bligh had in providing the British Caribbean with breadfruit, it is ironic that the slaves found this food unpalatable!

"Norfolk Island is the only country which has on three occasions issued Pitcairn-related stamps. The second was on 16 October 1967, when Norfolk placed on sale its annual Christmas stamp. Because so many inhabitants of Norfolk share a common ancestry and faith with those on Pitcairn, the 5-cent 1967 annual presented as its subject the John Adams prayer. Adams, of course, was the mutineer from the *Bounty* who survived longest on Pitcairn. After the turbulent founding of the Pitcairn colony, he became the leader of the community, teaching his people from a Bible taken from the *Bounty*. (On two occasions, Adams and the *Bounty's* Bible were depicted on Pitcairn issues.) The Adams Prayer is reproduced in full on a scroll in the stamp design along with a candle to suggest illumination. The stamp, printed in three-colour photogravure by Harrison and Sons Limited of London, was designed by B. G. W. McCoy. The writer wonders if the stamp's designer is a descendant of 'The Real McCoy'—William McCoy of *Bounty* fame.

"In December 1967 Pitcairn released a three-value set to mark the 150th anniversary of Captain (later Vice Admiral) Bligh's death. Concurrently, Fiji also issued a three-value set. Designed by Victor Whiteley, the 4d. value shows a bust-like portrait of the Admiral with *H.M.S. Providence*, in which he sailed near Fiji in 1792. An eighteenth-century chart of *Feejee* provides an interesting background. The one-shilling stamp shows the *Bounty's* longboat being pursued by a double canoe in what is now called 'Bligh Water.' The Admiral's tomb in St. Mary's churchyard, next to Lambeth Palace in London, is depicted on the 2/6 stamp (and also on the 20c. value of the Pitcairn series). The Fiji stamp includes the Admiral's hat, sword, and Union Jack flag in the foreground.

"A series of stamps featuring ships associated with the history of Norfolk Island was begun in 1967 and completed in June 1968. On 18 March 1968 Norfolk's 20c. value was released. This stamp pictures the schooner *Pitcairn*, a ship sponsored by the Seventh-day Adventist Church and which maintained for a decade a regular sailing schedule between San Francisco, Pitcairn, and Norfolk Island. The vessel carried island mail from its maiden voyage on 25 November 1890 until its services were discontinued in 1900. When one considers the long history of little Pitcairn and the lands and people influenced by it, one can be assured that this last Norfolk stamp will not be the last to relate to the 'Pitcairn story.'

"There is an ever-growing number of philatelists who specialise in Pitcairn Island stamps. Imbued with the collector's penchant for completeness, these specialists are now including the non-Pitcairn issues which relate to the island's history. These stamps, still few in number, are easily acquired and form an integral part of any stamp collection devoted to Pitcairn and its fascinating history." Volume 10, Number 8 (August 1968).

"BURNING STAMPS ON PITCAIRN. By Dr. Arthur A. Delaney, New York. The reasons for the philatelist's high regard for Pitcairn's postal paper are many. Pitcairn's stamps are artistically created; new issues appear infrequently; sets are neither excessively long nor are they composed of unusually high denominations; and, fabricated 'errors' and souvenir sheets produced solely to separate the collector from his money are unknown to Pitcairn philately. Of no mean importance is the fact that all Pitcairn stamps serve postal duty and all are on sale for a specific period.

"Collectors have always had the assurance that adequate time is available for the purchase of a Pitcairn issue, but they also know that when the period of issue expires, stamps are withdrawn from sale, the remaining stock being destroyed by fire. The consigning of Pitcairn's stamps to the flames testifies to the Pitcairn government's desire to fulfill its obligation to the philatelic fraternity by not keeping an obsolete issue in stock for the purpose of making extra sales.

"A number of reputable stamp-issuing governments provide detailed information about the destruction of expired postal issues and some even supply pictorial evidence of the process. From time to time, these accounts and their accompanying photographs have appeared in the philatelic press.

"To the writer's knowledge, no details or pictures of the destruction of Pitcairn's stamps have ever appeared in an American philatelic periodical. Perhaps the Pitcairn government did not believe it was necessary to supply such information, but more probably it is that Pitcairn is too small a country to maintain an expensive public relations department. Thus, the following is a brief account of the burning of expired Pitcairn stamps as told to the writer by one of the participants, Bert Reeves (ex-education officer/government adviser and auditor and editor of *Miscellany*.—Editor.)

"As in postal establishments the world over, every stamp in Pitcairn's tiny post office must be accounted for—and although it is reputed to be the smallest post office in the South Pacific, it has lots of stamps! At the end of each month, Oscar Clark, Pitcairn's present postmaster, counts the stamps on hand. The number is then checked by the auditor.

"When a particular issue is to be withdrawn, a similar process takes place. Oscar counts the number of stamps to be destroyed, and the auditor verifies the count. The doomed adhesives are then placed in the post office safe, where they remain for one month.

"After the month has passed, the Day of Burning occurs. The stamps are removed from the safe by the Postmaster and Auditor. They are then recounted by the postmaster, auditor, Island secretary and Chief Magistrate, presently Ben Christian and Pervis Young.

"As the reader might readily surmise, both gentlemen are descendants of the *Bounty* mutineers. Secretary Christian's ancestor is Master's-Mate Fletcher Christian and Magistrate Young is a descendant of Edward Young, one of the *Bounty's* midshipmen. It is now time for the burning to take place.

"The stamps are placed in sight of all and where supposedly they cannot be purloined. No case of filching prior to burning has ever been discovered on Pitcairn. A forty-four-gallon oil drum is rolled out in front of the post office, and a fire is kindled with gasoline and paper. The four participants gather around the fire, crumple sheets of stamps so as to ignite them easily, and then toss beautiful Pitcairn postage to its fiery fate.

"As soon as the burning is completed, auditor, postmaster, magistrate and secretary comb through the ashes to make sure they are in fact ashes and not a mixture of cinder and usable postage. As an added precaution, the ash is sifted further. Presumably, it is then mixed with the already highly fertile Pitcairn soil.

"The burners then move into the post office where they attest to the fact that the auditor has indeed complied with regulations and that postage marked for destruction has been burned.

"Four copies of this certificate are signed by the auditor, postmaster, secretary, and magistrate. A copy is retained in the post office; the island secretary keeps a copy, and one is placed in the adviser's file.

"The fourth is sent to Suva, Fiji, from where Pitcairn's postal affairs are administered. Relatively few collectors are aware that the Governor of Fiji is also the Governor of Pitcairn and that the Crown Commissioner for Pitcairn maintains his office not on Pitcairn but in distant Suva.

"The task of disposing of withdrawn Pitcairn stamps is one which is performed meticulously. It is a serious obligation on the

187

Island and has been carried out over the years without error." Volume 11, Number 7 (July 1969).

One of the few serious philatelic errors relating to Pitcairn's stamps occurred in 1971 in connection with an overprint of a current island stamp which was to mark the visit of Prince Philip to Pitcairn. The Pitcairners were at first told that only 1,000 of the overprinted stamp would be placed on sale; then, to their great embarrassment, they learned that more than 40,000 had actually been overprinted and offered for sale, although only 1,000 were made available on Pitcairn. *Miscellany* . . . duly recorded the philatelic mistake.

"STAMP NEWS. To commemorate the visit of His Royal Highness Duke of Edinburgh to Pitcairn on 22/2/71 a special stamp was issued, being an overprint of the current 10-cent definitive issue. Our thanks are due to Crown Agents, London, for these souvenirs of the visit as they had the forethought to prepare the stamps and forward them to us by the Royal Yacht *Britannia*.

"Unfortunately for stamp enthusiasts, only 1000 stamps were issued, all being sent to Pitcairn Island.

"Please note, however, that it is impossible to obtain any of these stamps from the Post Office, as all stamps were sold out on the day of issue. . . ." Volume 13, Number 2 (February 1971).

"STAMP NEWS. In the February issue we published news of a special issue which was released to commemorate the visit to Pitcairn by HRH Duke of Edinburgh on 22/2/71. It was stated that 'only 1000 stamps were issued, all being sent to Pitcairn Island.' At the time of writing, this statement was believed to be correct. However, very recently it has become apparent that this statement in fact was incorrect and must be corrected.

"In point of fact only 1000 stamps were received here, and all were sold on first day of issue. Of these 1000 stamps, 300 were sent to 3 regular, large stamp-dealer customers (on the recommendation of the Administration); 800 of these 1000 stamps were cancelled as First Day Covers.

"We now find 40,400 stamps were issued. All of these were sold by the printers, and we have been informed that we will be unable to purchase any more of this issue. Local stamp dealers were very disappointed to hear this news, as it means that for the first time in more than 20 years they will be unable to fulfill standing orders for their regular customers." Volume 13, Number 4 (April 1971).

"The 4th of April saw the first day of issue of the South Pacific Commission 25th Anniversary stamps. Orders were slow to come in initially, but on the 4th the Post Office staff was busily employed attending to requests for stamps. Extra help was eventually needed, and several local ladies were employed on a part-time basis to cope with the demand." Volume 14, Number 4 (April 1972).

"STAMP DESTRUCTION. Having been withdrawn from the Post Office for the required time, the unsold stamps of the South Pacific Commission Commemorative Special Issue were destroyed by fire on the 25th of August. After a final count made by the Island Magistrate, Island Secretary, and Government Adviser, the residual stamps were consigned to a fiercely burning drum. At the conclusion of the burning the ashes were ceremoniously stirred and examined and destruction was judged to be complete.

"The Destruction Certificate showed that $3,857.70 worth of stamps had been sold during the three months of sale." Volume 14, Number 8 (August 1972).

"Post Office staff had a busy time with a First Day of Issue of the Royal Silver Wedding Anniversary stamps on November 20th. Oscar reports that all 20-cent stamps were sold out; and only a small number of 4-cent stamps remain—this from an original supply of 15,000 of 20-cent stamps and 20,000 of 4-cent stamps.

"Unfortunately, some orders for First-Day Covers were received too late; and these could not be fulfilled. Some other orders were received after all of the 20-cent stamps had been sold, but the Administration has been notified of this, and there may yet be a chance that these orders can be serviced.

"Oscar reports that 3750 First-Day Covers were cancelled on official Silver Wedding Envelopes, and 1174 other FDC's were serviced on the first day of issue. . . ." Volume 14, Number 11 (November 1972).

"STAMP NEWS. Oscar reports a new record created by the special Royal Silver Wedding issue—the whole issue has been sold out, and none remain for sale or destruction.

"The new 50-cent definitive, first issued on January 2nd, has netted sales of over 4000 so far.

"SPECIAL ISSUE. Flowers [Stamp issue] to be released in March or April: 4 cents (rose apple); 8 cents (mountain apple); 15 cents (rata); 20 cents (dorcas flower); 35 cents (guava)." Volume 15, Number 1 (January 1973).

"On the 19th of March, what remained of the Royal Wedding Issue of stamps were burnt in the Square, under the supervision of the Island Magistrate, the Island Secretary, and the

Government Adviser. Following is a report by one of the schoolchildren, Meralda Warren: 'On Tuesday, 19th March, at 8:30 in the morning, the schoolchildren went down to the Post Office to watch Pervis, Ben, and Mr. Shea burn the stamps. The primers were taken down by Mr. Shea in the car, and the senior girls and Michael with with Mrs. Shea and Antony.

" 'Some of the stamps were blazing in a drum, while Pervis, Ben, Mr. Shea, and Mrs. Dever where throwing more stamps on the fire. As we gathered around, we were given some of the stamps to throw on the fire. Mento kept the fire going by throwing diesel onto it, and he stirred the fire with a pipe. The fire and the sun were extremely hot.

" 'In a matter of minutes every stamp was reduced to ashes. The primers walked back to school and the seniors rode back in the Mini-moke.' " Volume 16, Number 3 (March 1974).

"On the 22nd of July, 1975, the special issue of stamps named 'Mailboats' will go on sale. These special issues only last for three months, and demand is sure to be high for this issue.

"There are four denominations in the issue and a souvenir sheet containing all four stamps. The stamps are (in New Zealand Currency):

4-cent—which depicts the *Seringapatam*, which carried the first-ever letter from Pitcairn, dated 17th March 1830.

10-cent—which depicts the Missionary Schooner *Pitcairn*, which was built by the Seventh-day Adventist Society and carried mail for 10 years between Pitcairn and San Francisco.

18-cent—which depicts the *H.M.S. Athenic*, which served in the New Zealand service for 27 years and was a regular caller at Pitcairn.

50-cent—which depicts the *S.S. Gothic*, which also served as the Queen's Royal Yacht during Her Commonwealth Tour of 1954. She and her sister ship the *Ceramic* were regular callers at Pitcairn until 1969." Volume 17, Number 6 (June 1975).

"A LOOK AT PITCAIRN WITH A SET OF POSTAGE STAMPS. By Pastor J. J. Dever. I'm one of the fortunate ones, appointed with my wife to Pitcairn for two years. Perhaps we can help you to get a better look at Pitcairn through the pictures on its present definitive set of stamps.

"The one-cent stamp, as you could readily recognize, pictures Pitcairn just as you see it when hove-to on the North side of the Island, or 'Down Isaac' as the Islanders say. Isaac is the name of the rocky ledge right in the middle of the rocky coast. . . .

"The Chronometer on the 2-cent stamp, though not now on Pitcairn, undoubtedly timed the arrival of the *Bounty*.

190

"The 3-cent stamp shows the old *Bounty* anchor, submerged in the sea off Bounty Bay from 1790 until 1957, when it was recovered and mounted in the Square at Adamstown, directly behind Isaacs, with Taro Ground behind.

"The history of Pitcairn is tied in closely with the H.M.S. *Bounty*, a British naval vessel, and the 4-cent stamp shows details of the vessel. A look at this stamp under a magnifying glass is most rewarding.

"History books tell of the venture in 1787, when Captain Bligh, with Fletcher Christian serving as his mate, were commissioned to gather breadfruit plants in Tahiti and transport them to the West Indies. The 5-cent stamp accurately represents the supply of pots, the potted plants, and the size of the fruit. The trees grow to 50 feet, and the fruit [one] will fill a hat. It grows plentifully on Pitcairn and is eagerly sought for its fruit in season. Delicious when cooked.

"To come ashore into tiny Bounty Bay, as seen in the 6-cent stamp from the vantage of Little Edge high above the Landing, is always a thrill and a challenge.

"The only way of getting mail or cargo to or from visiting ships is per the longboats, pictured breasting the waves in the 8-cent stamp. The sea literally changes its moods from day to day. It seems to delight itself in rousing when ships come. Days of beautifully calm and heavenly blue seas go by with many an expressed wish for a ship 'to come while the sea is good.'

"When a ship is approaching today, it generally radios in while still a day or two away, to give an estimated time of its arrival and an indication whether it will stay and for how long. But for 130 years a regular watch was kept on Ship Landing Point, perched precariously above Bounty Bay, as seen in the 10-cent stamp. The ship approaching from Panama way looks as though, typically, it will pass us by. Opportunities to post letters these days are few. Hence the very real value of Pitcairn postmarked stamps

"Away to the northwestern end of Pitcairn, just under Big Ridge, is Christian's Cave. Look at the 15-cent stamp and imagine that you took the picture—a wonderful panoramic shot of Adamstown and, a mile away, Ship Landing Point. Most of the Pitcairners' homes are 'down there,' and from our mission home right in the middle of the picture we look daily up to Christian's cave, as indeed most of the homes do, and we wonder what he thought in his hideaway in 1790.

"The 20-cent stamp shows the oldest building on Pitcairn. Built by Thursday October Christian, it still reminds us of the hard work of the first local-born generation. An iron roof protects this historic structure, while the originally placed heavy and rugged stones still support the massive bottom plates. Nothing ever came easy on Pitcairn. Local inhabitants still work hard for what they can wrest from the land or the sea. Thursday's descendants and other sons and daughters of the mutineers to the fifth and sixth generation still live nearby. Christians, Youngs, Browns, Warrens, and Clarks make up the population today. The first two families are originals, the others came long ago and married into earlier families.

"Perhaps to the local invention of the Pitcairn wheelbarrow, and the design and construction of the locally made longboats, the next 'biggest thing' to be set up on Pitcairn was the Flying Fox, which carries cargo from the Landing in the Bay to the Edge, some 300 or more feet above. Fletcher Christian and his cohorts, assisted by their Tahitian womenfolk, had to manhandle every piece of personal belongings or equipment they salvaged from the *Bounty*, up the Hill of Difficulty, as it is still known today, but without any sort of road whatsoever. Even today it still lives up to its name, especially when wet and consequently slippery. Looking at the 25-cent stamp, you need to imagine yourself unloading the 'tray' of drums or packages and viewing the Bay away down below.

"The 30-cent stamp pictures the Radio Station up on Taro Ground, 900 feet above sea level. In 1921 a visual communications lamp first 'talked' to passing ships. Today Pitcairn regularly broadcasts meteorological information, as well as private and Government cables. The radio masts on this stamp have perhaps the most uninterrupted view of the sea all around the compass of any similar masts anywhere in the world.

"The 40-cent stamp gives a reason for the Pastor being here. The Bounty Bible used by converted mutineer Alexander Smith changed his life and the lives of the nine women and 20 children left in his care when the rest of the original sailors from the *Bounty* had died or met their fate at the hands of their erstwhile mates. It inspired Smith to change his name to John Adams. Though safely encased beside the pulpit of the Seventh-day Adventist Church on the island, its messages are being even more safely encased still in Pitcairners' hearts. The Pastor's wife serves as the Island's Medical Officer.

"Pitcairn Island has its own Coat of Arms, represented on the 50-cent stamp. In the five colours of Heraldry—blue, green, red, black, and purple, and two metals—gold and silver. The original design was suggested by Pitcairners and the Pastor of the day,

192

Pastor Walter G. Ferris, finally prepared by the Royal College of Arms in London, and accepted by the Queen. A shield at the base has the *Bounty* anchor in gold and above it the Bounty Bible in silver in the honour point. Above it is a helmet supporting the unique Pitcairn wheelbarrow (wheel well to the front, runners at the rear sides, and hook-shaped handles to allow for half-wheeling, half-skidding down the steep tracks from gardens and forest), possibly the major invention to spring from Pitcairner genius. A sprig of Miro, together with leaves and a bud, reminds of the only industry on the Island—the carving of curios from this exotic wood. The triangular border symbolises Pitcairn, rising from a green sea into a blue sky. Most of the Miro wood has had to be brought from Henderson Island. . . .

"In 1975 a one-dollar stamp, bearing a large portrait of Her Majesty Queen Elizabeth of England, and of Pitcairn, will be added to the set.

"Public revenue on Pitcairn comes almost exclusively from the sale of postage stamps. Much of the private income of the Pitcairners also comes from retailing stamps—mint or cancelled, definitives or first-day releases of special issues. Remoteness, the growing infrequency of ships, and the ever-present dangers of the sea which accompany every stamp that leaves Bounty Bay gives Pitcairn stamp a lasting value. . . ." Volume 17, Number 12 (December 1975).

"During the early part of March, the remaining stamps of the 'Insects' special issue went up in the proverbial cloud of smoke. The Destruction Certificate showed that the sales for this issue amounted to $5,991.40. . . ." Volume 18, Number 3 (March 1976).

"Postmaster Oscar Reports. With the sun casting its evening shadows over Adamstown on Sunday, September 11, there was sadness as we silently said good-bye to Pitcairn's eight-year-old Fourth Definitive stamps forever. As Postmaster, I had become attached to the said stamps, selling many of them over the Post Office counter to literally thousands of people, 'Outsiders' as well as locals. And to think that this day marked the end for such stamps.

"However, Monday, September 12 dawned bright and beautiful, welcoming our new Fifth Definitive issue. First-day sales on Pitcairn were hectic, as locals took advantage of ensuring they had First-Day Covers with the new stamps, in anticipation of overseas orders, sales aboard passing ships, and so forth. If I may, I would like to convey my special thanks to the five 'busy bees' who assisted the Postal staff in the preparation of 3040 covers.

193

"The general consensus of opinion among the local folk regarding their new definitives is that they look attractive and are colourful. As with the previous definitives, further aspects of Pitcairn life unfold, revealing to recipients of such stamps the romantic aura which surrounds our tiny and isolated island.

"But let us return once more to follow the inevitable and undignified destruction of surplus stamps of the Fourth Definitive issue. On Thursday, September 15, Island Magistrate Ivan and Island Secretary Ben spent at least five hours counting, recounting, and yet recounting surplus stocks of stamps to be destroyed by fire. It certainly was a long day, so much so that Dobrey and Irma (respective wives of Ivan and Ben) were concerned to such an extent that they turned up at the Square to see that their husbands were all right. At last, figures tallied with Auditor Tom Whiu; and at 2 p.m. same day surplus stamps of the Fourth Definitive issue amounting to $16,639.63 were set ablaze in the fiery furnace. Yes, a sad moment it was to watch the stamps 'go up in smoke.' A touch of hilarity, however, brightened our faces, when unofficial Mayor Mento decided to throw his cap into the fire along with the burning stamps. When Ivan, Ben, and Tom were satisfied that all stamps were destroyed, the Destruction Certificate was duly signed, signifying that all was carried out correctly. Volume 19, Number 9 (September 1977).

Sugar Cane

"July 4-6—Grinding sugar cane and boiling molasses went on all day and much of the night too, as families combined to share the task of cutting, carting, and grinding the sugar cane to extract the juice, which was then boiled into molasses. The antiquated mill which has been used for many years should by now have seen its last season, as the Council has ordered a new unit, and this will be driven by the power take-off on the tractor, therefore the combined pushing on the crossbars by a number of people should no longer be required. . . ." Volume 8, Number 7 (July 1966).

"SUGAR CANE TIME AGAIN. First of all the cane is cut and trimmed at the gardens and is then transported to the sugar mill, where it is to be pressed. This mill is a very old one and works on a simple principle of two heavy rollers squeezing the juice out of the cane. The cane is fed in by hand; and the rollers are turned by manpower, using long poles pushed by members of the community—and this is a real community effort.

"The sugar-cane juice is collected in large tubs and then carried up to the fire house, where a blazing fire is set under a

194

shallow tray into which the juice is poured. Periodically, while the juice is boiling, the liquid is skimmed; and, when the time is judged right, the rich molasses is poured into containers ready to be taken home. There is nothing sweeter than to sample fresh molasses on fresh pancakes—beautiful. This is just another example of what can be accomplished in a small community when everyone joins in to help." Volume 17, Number 5 (May 1975).

Tractor

"FROM MANPOWER TO HORSEPOWER. By Brian Webb. On Sunday, 10th January 1965, the throb of a diesel tractor engine shattered the silence of a sunny Pitcairn morning, and with it began a new era for those who live on this South Pacific Island paradise. The Bristol crawler and a Massey Ferguson wheeled tractor are the first motorized vehicles to be owned and used by the islanders. This major step forward is aimed at making the way of life easier. Other equipment, including a bulldozer blade, ripper, winch, and bucket on the crawler, and a hole-borer on the wheel tractor, will help also.

"With the development of new roads servicing the town and giving access to the high-plateau agricultural lands and the radio station, a lot of the drudgery will be taken out of transporting fuel, wood, vegetables, fruit, ship's cargo, etc. No longer will a large team of men have to pole heavy equipment from the landing up hundreds of feet to either the Edge or Taro Ground. Many back-breaking and weary man-hours will be saved on other work, such as clearing and preparing gardens, where possible, and the cutting of firewood into suitable lengths for the fires. All this will mean more time for other more productive work, an example being the better care of pineapples and citrus fruits by proper pruning and cultivation.

"The establishment of this new equipment is almost completed, and soon your own island people will be left to use it. At first day they will lack experience and therefore may make mistakes and be slow, but given a chance their efficiency will increase.

"With these machines and the advantages they possess, there comes an element of danger. Danger which only exists if the operators and those nearby are careless, foolish, ignorant, or negligent. The drivers have been taught about the dangers that exist and how to avoid them. They have a multitude of things to concentrate on when using the tractors and must not be distracted from their job. If you, the people of Pitcairn, wish to avoid the possibility of accidents with this useful equipment, please do not try to attract the driver's attention until he has stopped, unless of course he is in a dangerous position of which he is not aware.

"Children are always curious and attracted to tractors, and this immediately places them in danger if they get close to the machines. Many children have been killed on farms in New Zealand by tractors because they wandered close to such hazards. As a driver is concentrating on manoeuvring his machine, plus the fact that the child is small and can be easily hidden from view, nasty accidents have occurred. A child has not the strength of an adult to look after himself and should never be allowed to ride on tractors or associated equipment except on a transport tray or trailer, and then only when they are seated.

"Treat this new equipment with respect, don't fool with it, and it will be of immense value in making life easier. Remember that tractors are not toys." Volume 7, Number 2 (February 1965).

Visit of Bligh

"The *Port Nelson* brought another surprise visitor, but in this case he was only ashore on Pitcairn for a couple of hours. A Mr. Maurice Bligh—descendant of Captain Bligh of *Bounty* fame, no less, was a passenger en route to U.K. and was able to come ashore and have a quick trip around the island.

"Maurice Bligh, age about 23 years, a publisher in the U.K., had previously hoped to be able to visit Pitcairn Island for a few weeks to gather material for a book he is writing. However, although this was not in the end possible, he did appreciate the opportunity for a quick tour of the island in Pastor's Mini-moke. As it is extremely rare for passengers of passing ships to be able to come ashore, he was fortunate indeed." Volume 13, Number 11 (November 1971).

Weddings

The earliest marriages on Pitcairn were marked by a ceremony derived from the liturgy of the Anglican Church; and all had to meet the approval of John Adams, who opposed early marriage because he felt that motherhood would remove the bride from productive labor in the fields. The age requirements were 18 for women and 20 for men. Intermarriage with close relatives has been the rule; but, contrary to widely held views that such practice would weaken the race, the population has remained tough, even vigorous. No solid evidence of harmful effect from this practice has been discovered. Today, with the island population at such a low figure, marriages are infrequent and

196

are often occasions for island-wide participation.

"Tom and Betty (Christian) were married in the Church on the afternoon of Wednesday, 18th May. The day dawned wet and miserable, but by midmorning the sun was doing its best to break through the cloud, and by wedding time it was gloriously fine, though a little muddy. Following the church service, photographs of the day's important people were taken outside the church; and then, to obtain better light and an alternative setting, the bridal party and parents went down to the mission lawn for further photographs to be taken. With plenty of cameras around, it is to be hoped that some good shots were obtained in spite of the fact that we know of some 'flashes' that did not light up and one film that snapped. . . .

"Whilst the formal photography was being completed, many other women were busy putting the final touches to the magnificent array of food prepared for all in the hall. With plenty of cakes, jellies, fruit, and ice cream etc., it is a wonder where it all went. After all had consumed more than enough, the surplus provided a supper for all those who attended pictures that evening. We also believe that the bridal couple collected enough rice from their room later on to do another meal!

"Readers will recall that during the Editor's leave last year, Betty kept *Miscellany* moving by providing you with two interesting issues, and now *Miscellany* wishes Mr. and Mrs. Newlywed Christian many many years of married bliss. (Note: When Miss Betty Christian marries Mr. Thomas Christian, the bride doesn't even get a change of name; but we did hear in the Post Office a few days ago that Betty was at least able to alter her 'sender' name stamps from singular to plural—we mean a 'Miss' to a 'Mrs.')" Volume 8, Number 5 (May 1966).

"Tuesday, 7th June: Reynold and Nola were married in the Pastor's residence at 11 a.m. Muddy conditions outside in no way distracted from the tasteful way Mrs. Webster had arranged her front room for this occasion. The short service was followed by the usual round of photographs and then concluded with welcome light refreshments. In the evening all were invited to eat at Gina's house. Despite inclement weather a thoroughly enjoyable time was had by all. The editorial staff of *Miscellany* wish Mr. and Mrs. Newlywed Warren a very happy future." Volume 8, Number 6 (June 1966).

"Mr. and Mrs. Lindsay: John and Pauline were married on 28th September by the retiring Island Magistrate, Mr. John Christian, M.B.E., as one of his last official duties. Conditions were rather wet and muddy, but cleared overhead to welcome the bride's

197

arrival. That evening all were invited to tea at Wallace's house, where a very enjoyable time was had by all those who turned up." Volume 8, Number 8 (September 1966).

"PITCAIRN WEDDING. Dale Evans was the 'Quiet Man' of the American Geodetic Team and made many good friends on the island. However, his friendship with Melva went a little further than with the rest of us. His announcement of his engagement to Melva and of their plans for the wedding was unexpected, but greeted with delight by all.

"So it was that early Christmas Day found most residents donning their best clothes to attend the wedding at the church, scheduled to start at 10 a.m. Dale stayed in Vula's house on Christmas Eve, where last-minute organisation was planned. Naz seemed to collect most of the chores and finished up as photographer, chauffeur, and sound technician—all of which he handled well. Jack was best man and carried out his various duties with the air of one who has had plenty of experience.

"The day dawned fair and warm, and on entering the church one was struck by the beauty of the flower arrangements and general attractive appearance of the altar and surrounding area. Soon everyone was in place (the bride, looking radiant, only one minute late), and Pastor Ferris conducted the short but beautiful wedding service. The best man had the ring, Anderson gave the bride away, and so the happy couple were wed.

"While the bridal party, consisting of bride and groom, best man, and bridesmaid (Carol), were being photographed, everyone moved to the Court House, where a sumptuous feast had been spread. After the usual toasts the newlyweds drove off in style in Pastor's Mini moke.

"While they plan to eventually make their home in the States, Dave's job will see them travelling about for a few years yet, and they next expect to be living in the Azores.

"Wherever they are, may they be assured that we wish them every good fortune and happiness and that we look forward to hearing from them wherever they may be." Volume 9, Number 12 (December 1967).

"From the time of the posting of 'marriage papers' on the notice board outside the Island Secretary's office on 26th January, there was growing excitement as the time approached for the wedding of Olive Brown, eldest daughter of Len and Thelma, and Steve Christian, second son of Ivan and Dobrey.

"At 3:30 p.m. on Wednesday, February 16th, all those who were able gathered in the church to attend the first wedding to be held on the Island in five years.

"Many worked hard to make this a memorable occasion; and the church, beautifully decorated with flowers and ferns, made an attractive setting for the ceremony, which was conducted by Pastor Webster. Irma acted as organist.

"The bride, who was given away by her father, wore a floor-length white satin gown, while the matron of honour, Betty Christian, wore a long nylon voile dress in soft gold tonings.

"Oscar Clark acted as best man.

"After the church service the guests enjoyed the afternoon tea in the Hall. This was a credit to all those who helped to prepare it and was a meal in itself, with such delicacies as roast bananas, juicy corn cobs, bread sticks and rolls, toasted sandwiches, cakes by the dozen, and ice-cream, jellies, and fruit. Few would be the homes where a meal was cooked that evening.

"The reception was climaxed by the bride and groom cutting the wedding cake, which had been made and iced by Mrs. Webster.

"This was a solemn yet joyful occasion, and we all wish Olive and Steve a very happy future together." Volume 14, Number 2 (February 1972).

"THAT BUSY DAY. After the frantic bustle of three ships on one day there was still time and energy to celebrate the wedding of Brenda and Mike.

"On the 3rd of August, the marriage of Michael Randall and Brenda Christian was celebrated in the Pitcairn Island Church, Pastor Webster officiating.

"The bride wore a floor-length dress of white silk crepe. The bridesmaids, Carol Christian and Julie Christian, wore dresses of pale-blue brocade, and junior bridesmaid Janet Young and flower girl Anne Young wore dresses of lemon lace. Best man was Jim Collier, and groomsman was Steve Christian.

"Following the wedding, a reception was held in the Courthouse. A fine breakfast was provided by Dobrey and Ivan, the bride's parents. Jim read out cables of congratulation and enlivened the proceedings generally.

"The future home of Mr. and Mrs. Randall is likely to be Brecon, Wales, where Mike hails from.

"The fortuitous arrival of the Sir Percivale enabled five of Mike's monitoring associates to attend the wedding, and this no doubt afforded him pleasure." Volume 14, Number 8 (August 1972).

"WEDDING BELLS ARE RINGING IN THE CHAPEL. The wedding of Jay Warren and Carol (nee Christian) took place on Thursday, May 20, at 2 p.m., with Pastor Newman officiating.

The bride, escorted up the aisle by her father Charles, wore a long white crystalline frock under a guipure lace jacket with Bishop sleeves and full-length tulle veil and embroidered border. Meralda Warren, sister of the groom, was bridesmaid, and wore a long pale-pink frock under a deep-pink lace coat. Dressmaker for this occasion was Mrs. Peri Whiu. Oscar Clark was best man.

"The church and Public Hall were beautifully decorated with flowers and greenery, and the bridal couple wish me to convey their thanks to everyone concerned for the splendid job in this respect.

"Following the wedding ceremony, and after numerous photographs were taken to record this event, the bridal party led the way into the Public Hall, where the wedding reception was held. A two-tier wedding cake, made and decorated by Mrs. Newman, adorned the refreshment table.

"To Jay and Carol we offer our warmest congratulations." Volume 18, Number 5 (May 1976).

"IT FINALLY HAPPENED. After a few months of waiting, the marriage of Brian Young and Kari Boye was celebrated in the Pitcairn Island Church, on the 17th of May, with Pastor Ferguson officiating.

"Betty Christian was matron of honour. Anna Young and Jackie Christian were flower girls, and Dennis Christian was best man.

"Following the Wedding, a reception was held in the Court House. All sorts of fine delicacies were provided.

"The future home of Mr. and Mrs. Young is on the island, where their new home is already started. But maybe someday they'll visit Norway, where the bride hails from. (Yvonne Brown—roving reporter). Volume 20, Number 5 (May 1978).

Waterspout

"In a gray, lowering sky on the 26th, a huge waterspout was seen off the island, directly out from the school. We watched it anxiously for some time as it approached closer and were very relieved to see that it would pass clear of Matt's Rock. The sea, otherwise calm, was very disturbed at the base of the spout, and soon Pitcairn was being drenched by torrential rain. So heavy was the downpour that five waterfalls were soon cascading down the rock face above Christian's Cave." Volume 10, Number 1 (January 1968).

Whales

"Whales have been sighted on several occasions over the last few weeks. The men have been out fishing quite a bit this month, but no one seems to have tried to catch one of these big chaps. It would be fantastic, wouldn't it, Floyd?" Volume 4, Number 6 (June 1962).

"A WHALE OF A TALE. Or should that read, 'A Tail of a Whale'? I guess that by now most readers know that Pitcairners love their fish and their fishing. Well, during this month, Steve Christian, Brian Young, and Kari Boye were out fishing in one of the small canoes. Brian was in the water, speargun in hand, when the other two noticed a whale surface about 20 feet from where Brian had gone down. Brian, of course, was quite oblivious of the fact that he had nature's largest mammal as his closest companion, until he surfaced for air and was quickly notified of the visitor to our Territorial Waters. Kari was thrilled and let fly with a whole reel of film. But her feeling of thrill was short lived as Steve decided to go in and have a closer look. He used the excuse that Kari could get better shots from a closer range—actually he wanted to get into the water himself and have a close look which he did. I've heard through the proverbial grapevine that Kari's suntan, which we have all come to envy so much, suddenly turned to a much paler shade. Evidently, though, it was quite a friendly whale; and Steve went right alongside it and had a good look without any bother. This visitor to our shores stayed about a week—then away to whatever place whales go when they go away." Volume 17, Number 9 (September 1975).

"MAN OF THE MONTH. Meet Kay Brown (affectionately known to all on Pitcairn as Nig), Trainee Engineer and Trainee Radio Operator. He gets special mention this month because: He went fishing and came across what he thought was a sandbank sticking up out of 200-foot-deep water. While resting on the sandbank, it started moving; and to his amazement it turned out to be a whale wallowing in the sun." Volume 19, Number 10 (October 1977).

Wind Power

"By Tom Christian. Can 'wind-generated power' supply the needs of Pitcairn? If so, what advantage would there be?

"As a little boy growing up, I can barely remember the windmill installed by two Americans and left in the care of Andrew Young, to power a 'Ham' radio station to contact ships approaching the Island. This was back in 1938, and today Pitcairn's Cooperative Store stands where the wind tower stood, close to the centre of Adamstown. Since then, as far as I know, there have only been three other 'Wind Plants' on Pitcairn.

"When I took over the radio station at Taro Ground in 1955, the main source of power there was a 32-volt, four-bladed-propeller wind plant, keeping two 24-volt battery banks charged, which in turn powered the Official Radio Station. This plant, which is still standing today, but is awaiting placement parts, is no longer the Radio Station's main energy source, but has served extremely well for many years. I was so impressed with its performance that in 1958 I wrote to the suppliers in Australia asking for a price quotation and information on a plant which I could someday be able to buy.

"Since then 16 years have gone, and all along wind power has been in my mind. Why? Because most of the time there is an 11 to 15-knot breeze blowing, and should we not try to harness this readily available energy source rather than struggle through sometimes dangerous, rough seas to land fuel oil on Pitcairn? Secondly, our present diesel supply (56 Kw, 3-Phase, 230 Volts) supplies power only on an average of five hours in 24, and due to high fuel consumption it would be considered uneconomic to run much more than this. In addition to fuel costs, there is the 'wear and tear' on the Plant itself, and already 'wear and tear' is showing on this plant installed in 1968.

"Early in 1973 I again set out to gather all possible information on current wind generators; and, after many informative discussions with 'Ham Radio' friends around the world, some kind American 'Hams' decided to try and help toward a 'Wind Project.' Others joined in; and through our friends at the 'Voice of Prophecy' in Glendale, California, more publicity was given. The energy crisis helped promotion; and kind contributors—mostly Seventh-day Adventists across the country—gave donations which amounted to enough to make a definite purchase, for which we are grateful.

"By radio we started shopping, and it didn't take long to determine that there are only two current manufacturers of suitable wind plants in the world—Australia and Switzerland. Information soon came by radio and mail, and it was no problem to discuss the Swiss machines directly with a radio friend in Switzerland, and the Australian machines with radio friends in Australia. Because of many factors involved, we decided to make a purchase from Australia, even though the Swiss made the larger machines—five to six Kw.

"In June the Australians made a reasonable offer, if we bought two plants together. And so the deal was finally made for the wind plants and batteries. Arranging shipping delivery directly from Australia proved impossible; so the equipment—a total of 72 packages (4200 kilos)—was shipped to Auckland, where it awaited available shipping. In September the supply tanker

R.F.A. Brown Ranger arrived with Island supplies—our wind equipment being among them. After landing and checking everything, to our dismay we found that two cases, containing the propellers and a bundle of steel, were missing. The ship was thoroughly checked, and the Officers confirmed that nothing else was aboard for us.

"After weeks of searching in Auckland, the Agents, pressured by radio friends, located the missing propellers; but the steel, 10 feet in length, could not be found. Radio friends in Sydney then took over and talked the firm into shipping replacement steel now, to claim on insurance later. So just a few days ago Pitcairn's old friend, Nelson Dyett, picked up the replacement steel (200 kilos), which Air New Zealand flew from Sydney to Christchurch and then to Wellington, and had it put aboard the German freighter *Badenstein* to add to the two missing cases previously loaded in Auckland. The Captain kindly offered to deliver them, and he expects to leave New Zealand about December 17th. It will be 1975 before we install the plant and have it operational, and several months . . . before we know if it is a 'good thing.'

"A suitable windy location is essential, where trees, and particularly coconut palms, don't cause turbulence. We plan to install one at 'Eme Blow,' approximately 200 feet above sea level and 350 feet from my location. This will be used primarily to charge batteries and eventually to keep Radio Station VR6TC on the air in the event of diesel power failure and to operate other equipment once I can afford a suitable DC/AC inverter.

"The other plant may be installed near the cemetery, depending upon the performance of the first, and will be used to operate something beneficial to this community. Apart from getting materials and concreting foundations and assembling the tower itself, we are faced with a financial problem. The plants supply 110 volts DC, which has limited use other than lighting, and with only two kilowatts of power (unless a strong wind is blowing and batteries are fully charged)—the equivalent of twenty 100 watt lamps—it is rather difficult to know exactly what to do.

"We need a two- to three-Kw. Inverter that would supply 230 Volts, 50 Hertz AC, so we could run, perhaps, a freezer unit for the community, or supply power to the church for perhaps an organ or such, or else whatever is reasonable. However, world quotes on DC/AC Inverters are close to a dollar (U.S.) per watt, or $2000-$3000 for a 2- to 3-Kw. unit. We should have close to $1000 U.S. to start towards this but cannot be sure until all costs involved in shipping the missing items are on hand.

"Will wind power be free? Costs are tremendous. In U.S. dollars, shipping from Sydney to Auckland alone was $660. The wind plants' Australian price, prior to the Australian devaluation, was $2450, plus $630 for a 40-foot tower, plus $1650 for a 270-Amp/Hour, 110-volt battery bank, which should give ten years' service if looked after.

"What then is the advantage? I am uncertain yet, but if we can prove that wind power is a practical proposition for Pitcairn we someday can perhaps cut fuel costs by at least 75 percent by using an energy that is readily available and which will never be depleted. Apart from painting to prevent rust and corrosion, and looking after the batteries, all the maintenance that is required, according to the manufacturers, is changing one quart of gear oil every five years. The plants have automatic three-blade, variable-pitch, 12-foot-diameter propellers, designed to charge in 8-30 MPH winds and to withstand 80 MPH winds, which are very rare on Pitcairn.

"Back to our opening question. If the editor gives us space, I will again comment on the performance after several months' use.

"Our second question. Power 24 hours a day to supply lighting, refrigerators, deep freezers etc. Stove ranges consume too much power for current plants; so, housewives, wait a little longer.

"Worldwide experiments are well underway, and NASA is expecting to put a 100-Kw, 125-foot-diameter windmill in operation in Ohio, U.S.A., by July 1975. Maybe we will have the solution within a few years.

"But until then—do you know that most diesel plants require an overhaul every 1000 hours of use, which is only 42 days of continuous use? Don't you think then, that changing a quart of lube every five years compares more than favourably?" Volume 16, Number 15 (November 1974).

Women

"A WOMEN'S DAY ON PITCAIRN. By Roy Clark. Actually there are no schedules nor days of rigid rule in a woman's life on the island. Of course there are the chores, such as preparing meals, baking, cleaning, washing, ironing, the care of the children, and a hundred and one other tasks, as well as the weaving of baskets; but these all are subservient to capricious whims and inclinations.

"Mostly, time has no reckoning in a woman's life other than of necessity for going to the passenger ships, doing what is required of them by law, and attending religious services. As a whole, island life is not run by clocks, for time is rarely considered, and when it is so, is of secondary importance only.

"The island women are industrious and hard-working, and we wonder at times if their day is not more strenuous than that of the men. More often than not the women can be seen with machetes, hoe, and adz, clearing new land for planting, and in the gardens working equally with the men. It is also quite customary to see women with heavy, cumbersome wheelbarrows, negotiating steep pathways and then pushing them home again with heavy loads of firewood.

"Their day commences at daylight and ends late at night, mostly between the hours of 10 and 11. They are never idle, except at times when visiting neighbors for an exchange of views on island gossip or gathering in 'the Square' on special occasions such as mail days or to watch the sharing of goods and provisions obtained from passing ships.

"This is one aspect of a woman's day on Pitcairn. The other side is entirely different and proves the biblical phrase, 'Sufficient unto the day is the evil thereof,' for when whim and desire overcome the call of duty the women surely do 'let things go,' and when fed up with domestic cares all housework goes by the board. The children return home from school to find their mothers have gone fishing or perhaps into the bush for guavas or Job's tears.

"In the twilight they come home and find perhaps a meal cooked by their husbands or some leftovers from breakfast warmed ready for them.

"Thus ends a woman's day on Pitcairn when the routine of the house becomes irksome and wearying." Volume 5, Number 3 (March 1963).

"THE WOMEN PROVE THEIR WORTH. From its earliest days of settlement women have played a very important part in the life of Pitcairn. This was recognised 140 years ago, when, in 1838, male and female Islanders over the age of 18 years were given a vote in selecting an Island Magistrate and Council. This was some 91 years before women in Britain were given the vote.

"On Monday the 13th of March, the women of the Island were again to prove their worth and their adaptability, in helping take a longboat out to a visiting ship. Because most of the able-bodied men were away at Oeno, the Island had only a skeleton population of women and old-age pensioners. When the Oeno party heard of the visiting ship, they would have returned; but a strong headwind and big seas prevented them.

"So when the bell tolled out its rhythmic five chimes, a very mixed crew filtered down to the Landing. But Pitcairners are not the sort of people to let a visiting ship pass without making every attempt to reach it; even though the crew was rather nondescript, the sea choppy, and the longboat engine unreliable. (This was the boat which had broken down the last three times out, but then there had been a second boat to assist.) The women spread themselves on either side of the longboat, and after several heaves the women soon had the longboat down the slipway and into the water. We clambered aboard; and, with Olive and Yvonne as engineers and Brian as coxswain, we were on our way. As usual, moderate seas made some of our intrepid sailors seasick. Because the girls had been so efficient we were about an hour early for the approaching ship, which was well out of the water and rolling heavily. Andrew Young, who does not normally come out to ships now, stayed with the boat, while the rest of us spent a couple of hours on board.

"And then began the long trip back to the Island, for we had drifted five to six miles out in the fresh wind. This took over an hour in the pitch black, as we only travelled at half speed in an attempt to reduce the spray which was drenching us. Finally the Landing loomed up out of the darkness, a welcome sight to us all. With Olive acting as winchman, the boat slid up the slipway more smoothly than I have ever seen it go with its normal crew.

"I think there is a lesson in this story: that the elderly folk and the women on the island are a potentially powerful force. The elderly for the wisdom they have gained over the years. Yet we do not have one pensioner on the Council. (There are 15 pensioners on the Island.)

"The women have talents which are often largely unexploited. Is there any reason, with our manpower shortage on the Island, why we should not have women as engineers, electricians, tractor drivers, or even as Island Secretary or Island Magistrate in the future?

"Even our 1971 laws reflect a bias against women which would be found in very few other countries. For example: Local Government Law P. VI. D-2 states that 'No woman shall visit any ship other than a passenger ship, without the general or special permission of Council.'

"With a change in attitudes and a change in the Laws I am sure we will see the women on the Island taking a more active part in the running of the Island in the future.—Editor." Volume 20, Number 3 (March 1978).